T0360658

THE TIME-DISCRETE METHOD OF LINES FOR OPTIONS AND BONDS

A PDE Approach

THE TIME-DISCRETE METHOD OF LINES FOR OPTIONS AND BONDS

A PDE Approach

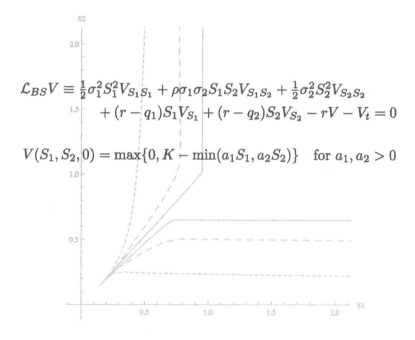

$$\mathcal{L}_{BS}V \equiv \tfrac{1}{2}\sigma_1^2 S_1^2 V_{S_1 S_1} + \rho\sigma_1\sigma_2 S_1 S_2 V_{S_1 S_2} + \tfrac{1}{2}\sigma_2^2 S_2^2 V_{S_2 S_2}$$
$$+ (r - q_1)S_1 V_{S_1} + (r - q_2)S_2 V_{S_2} - rV - V_t = 0$$

$$V(S_1, S_2, 0) = \max\{0, K - \min(a_1 S_1, a_2 S_2)\} \quad \text{for } a_1, a_2 > 0$$

Gunter H. Meyer

Georgia Institute of Technology, USA

 **World Scientific**

NEW JERSEY · LONDON · SINGAPORE · BEIJING · SHANGHAI · HONG KONG · TAIPEI · CHENNAI

Published by

World Scientific Publishing Co. Pte. Ltd.

5 Toh Tuck Link, Singapore 596224

USA office: 27 Warren Street, Suite 401-402, Hackensack, NJ 07601

UK office: 57 Shelton Street, Covent Garden, London WC2H 9HE

Library of Congress Cataloging-in-Publication Data
Meyer, Gunter H.
   The time-discrete method of lines for options and bonds : A PDE approach / Gunter H. Meyer, Georgia Institute of Technology, USA.
      pages cm
   Includes bibliographical references.
   ISBN 978-9814619677 (hard cover : alk. paper)
   1. Derivative securities--Mathematical models. 2. Options (Finance)--Mathematical models. 3. Bonds--Mathematical models. 4. Discrete-time systems. 5. Differential equations, Partial. I. Title.
   HG6024.A3M49 2015
   332.64'5701183--dc23

                                                               2014029166

British Library Cataloguing-in-Publication Data
A catalogue record for this book is available from the British Library.

In-house Editor: Qi Xiao

Printed in Singapore

Preface

In these notes we discuss some of the issues which arise when the partial differential equations (pdes) modeling option and bond prices are to be solved numerically. A great variety of numerical methods for this task can be found in textbooks and the research literature, and all are effective for pricing Black Scholes options on a single asset and bonds based on a one-factor interest rate model, particularly when prices far enough away from expiration are to be found.

However, there are financial applications where pde methods have to cope with uncertainty in the problem description, with rapidly changing solutions and their derivatives, with nonlinearities, non-local effects, vanishing diffusion in the presence of strong convection, and the "curse of dimensionality" due to multiple assets and factors in the financial model. All these complications are inherent in the pde formulation and must be overcome by whatever numerical method is chosen to price options and bonds accurately and efficiently.

The focus of these notes is on identifying and discussing these complications, to remove uncertainty in the pde model due to incomplete or inconsistent boundary data, and to illustrate through extensive simulations the computational problems which the pde model presents for its numerical solution. We concentrate on pricing models which have been presented in the literature, and for which results have been obtained with various numerical methods for specific applications. Here we shall search out problem settings where the complications in the pde formulation can be expected to degrade the numerical results.

We do not discuss different numerical methods for the pdes of finance and their effectiveness in solving practical problems. All simulations will be carried out with the time-discrete method of lines. We view it as a flexible tool for solving low-dimensional time dependent pricing problems in finance. It is based on a solution method which for simple American puts and calls is algorithmically equivalent to the Brennan-Schwartz method. For multi-dimensional problems it is combined with a locally one-dimensional line Gauss Seidel iteration. The method is introduced in detail in these notes. We think that it performs well enough that we offer the results of our simulations as benchmark data for a variety of challenging financial applications to which competing numerical methods could be applied.

The notes are intended for readers already engaged in, or contemplating, solving numerically partial differential equations for options and bonds. The notes are written by a mathematician, but not for mathematicians. They are "applied" and intended to be accessible for graduates of programs in quantitative and computational finance and practicing quants who have learned about numerical methods for the Black Scholes equation, the bond equation, and their generalisations. But we also assume that the readers have not had a particular exposure to, or interest in, the theory of partial differential equations and the mathematical analysis of numerical method for solving them. There are many sources in the textbook and research literature on both aspects, a notable example being the rigorous textbook/monograph of Achdou and Pironneau [1]. But such sources would appeal more to specialists than to the readership we hope to reach.

These notes are not a text for a course on numerical methods for the pdes of finance, nor are they intended to answer real questions in finance. The pde models discussed at length below are drawn from various published sources and readers are referred to the cited literature for their derivation and discussion. On occasion the models will be modified because finance suggests it or mathematics demands it. They will be solved numerically with assumed data, frequently chosen to accentuate the severity of the application and the behavior of the solution. Financial implications of our results will mostly be ignored. Although not a textbook, this book could serve as a reference for an advanced applied course on pdes in finance because it discusses a number of topics germain to all numerical methods in this field regardless of whether the method of lines is ever mentioned.

Both the pde problem specification and its numerical solution will be of interest. We shall assume that given a financial model for the evolution of an asset price, a volatility, an interest rate, etc., the pricing pde can be derived under specific assumptions reflecting or approximating the market reality. The validity of the pde, usually a time dependent diffusion equation, is not considered in doubt.

However, the pde does not constitute the whole model. The pde is only solvable if the problem for it is (in the language of mathematics) "well posed", meaning that it has a solution, that the solution is unique, and that the solution varies continuously with the data of the problem. If the pde is to be solved numerically, then in general it must be restricted to a finite computational domain. In order to be well posed an initial condition and the behavior on the boundary of the computational domain must be given. The initial condition is usually the pay-off of the option or the value of the bond at expiration, both of which are unambiguous and consistent with the pricing problem being well posed. For options the pay-off tends to introduce singularities into the solution or its derivatives which can make pricing of even simple options like puts and calls near maturity a challenging numerical problem.

In contrast to the certainty about initial conditions, the proper choice of boundary conditions can be complicated. The structure of the pdes arising in finance can exert a dominant influence on what boundary conditions can be given, and where, to retain a well-posed problem. This is often not a question of finance but relates to a fairly recent and still incomplete mathematical analysis of admissible boundary conditions for so-called degenerate evolution equations. While the mathematical theory is likely to be too abstract for the intended readership of these notes, we hope that sufficient operational information has been extracted from it to give guidance for choosing admissible boundary conditions. The most difficult case arises when for lack of better information a modification of the pde itself is used to set a boundary condition on a computational boundary. This aspect of the pde model is independent of the numerical method chosen for its solution. However, mathematically admissible boundary conditions are usually not unique. Some preserve the structure of the boundary value problem required for the intended numerical method but are inconsistent financially, while other admissible boundary conditions may be harder to incorporate into a numerical method but may yield solutions which are less driven by where we place the computational boundary. Simulation seems the only choice to check how uncertain boundary data will affect the solution.

The book has seven chapters. Section 1.1 of the first chapter reflects the view that once a well-posed mathematical model is accepted, then the solution is unambiguously determined and its mathematical properties must be acceptable on financial grounds. The examples of this section are based on elementary mathematical manipulations of the Black Scholes equation and its extensions and formally prove results which often are obvious from arbitrage arguments. Section 1.2 concentrates on a discussion of admissible boundary conditions for degenerate pricing equations in finance. It introduces the Fichera function as a tool to determine where on the boundary of its domain of definition the pricing equation has to hold, and where unrelated conditions can be imposed. We illustrate the application of the Fichera function for a number of option problems including cases where boundary conditions at infinity have to be set. We then consider the problem of conditions on the boundary of a finite computational domain where financial arguments often do not provide boundary conditions. We show that reduced versions of the pde can provide acceptable tangential boundary conditions known as Venttsel boundary conditions.

Chapter 2 introduces the method of lines for a scalar diffusion equation with one or two free boundaries. It will then be combined with a line Gauss-Seidel iteration to yield a locally one-dimensional front tracking method for time-discretized multi-dimensional diffusion problems subject to fixed and free boundary conditions.

Chapter 3 discusses in detail the numerical solution of the one- dimensional problems with the so-called Riccati transformation. It is closely related to the Thomas algorithm for the tri-diagonal matrix equation approximating linear second order two-point boundary value problems and is equally efficient.

The next four chapters consist of numerical simulations of options and bonds. The numerical method chosen for the simulations is always the method of lines of the preceding two chapters, but the numerical method intrudes little on the discussion of the pde model and the quality of its solutions.

Chapters 4 and 5 deal with European and American options priced with the Black Scholes equation. Comparisons with analytic solutions, where available, give the sense that such options can be computed to a high degree of accuracy even near expiration.

Chapter 6 concentrates on fixed income problems based on general one-factor interest rate models, including those admitting negative interest rates.

The experience gained with scalar diffusion problems is brought to bear in Chapter 7 on options for two assets, including American max and min options. It is shown that on occasion front tracking algorithms for American options can benefit by working in polar coordinates when the early exercise boundary on discrete rays is a well defined function of the polar angle.

The last example of an American call with stochastic volatility and interest rate suggests that the application of a locally one-dimensional front tracking method remains feasible in principle but presents hardware and programming challenges not easily met by the linear Fortran programs and the desktop computer used for our simulations.

Throughout these notes we give, besides graphs, a lot of tabulated data obtained with the method of lines for a variety of financial problems. Such data may prove useful as benchmark results for the implementation of the method of lines or other numerical methods for related problems. As already stated, the financial parameters are only assumed, but our numerical simulations appear to be robust over large parameter ranges for all the models discussed here. This may help when the method of lines is applied as a general forward solver in a model calibration.

Finally, we will admit that the choice of financial models treated here is more a reflection on past exposure, experience and taste than an orderly progression from simple to complicated models, or from elementary to relevant models. Our judgment of what questions are relevant in finance is informed by the texts of Hull [38] and Wilmott [64], while the more mathematical thoughts were inspired by the texts of Kwok [46] and Zhu, Wu and Chern [67], which we value for their breadth and mathematical precision. So far, the method of lines has proved to be a flexible and effective numerical method for pricing options and bonds, and as demonstrated in a concurrent monograph of Chiarella et al. [17], it can hold its own against some competing numerical methods for pdes in finance. MOL cannot work for all problems, but we do not hide its failures.

G. H. Meyer

Contents

Acknowledgment

I am grateful to the School of Mathematics of the Georgia Institute of Technology for remaining my scientific home in the years since my retirement. Interaction with colleagues, teaching the occasional course, and having access to the resources of the School and the Institute have made this time an unbroken, and unexpected, sabbatical.

The most important resource has been the cooperation of Ms. Annette Rohrs of the School in producing this book. In spite of a varied and steadily expanding workload, she has once again managed to turn scribbled and ever changing notes into a camera-ready book. Without her help I would not have started this project and could not have finished it. Thank you again, Annette.

Chapter 1

Comments on the Pricing Equations in Finance

The two dominant pricing equations of these notes are the Black Scholes equation for the price $V(S, t)$ of an option

$$\mathcal{L}_{BS}V \equiv \frac{1}{2}\sigma^2 S^2 V_{SS} + (r - q)SV_S - rV - V_t = 0 \qquad (1.1)$$

for $0 < S < \infty$ and $t \in (0, T]$, and the bond equation for the price $B(r, t)$ of a discount bond

$$\mathcal{L}_B B \equiv \frac{1}{2}w^2 B_{rr} + (u - \lambda w)B_r - rB - B_t = 0 \qquad (1.2)$$

for, usually, $0 < r < \infty$ and $t \in (0, T]$, where $t = T - \tau$ for calendar time τ denotes the time to expiry. Both equations are augmented by the values $V(S, 0)$ and $B(r, 0)$ at expiration $t = 0$ and by boundary conditions on V and B which are determined by the specific application. The aim is to find "a solution" of the pricing equation which also satisfies the given side conditions.

These equations, and their multi-factor generalizations, are special forms of a so-called evolution equation

$$\mathcal{L}u \equiv \sum_{i,j=1}^m a_{ij}(x, t)u_{x_i x_j} + \sum_{i=1}^m b_i(x, t)u_{x_i} + c(x, t)u \qquad (1.3)$$

$$+ d(x, t)u_t = f(x, t)$$

where $A = (a_{ij}(x, t))$ is a symmetric matrix, $d(x, t) \neq 0$, and where $(x, t) = (x_1, \ldots, x_m, t)$ denotes the $m+1$ independent variables. Typically x belongs to an open bounded or unbounded set $D(t)$ in R_m with boundary $\partial D(t)$, and t belongs to an interval $(0, T]$. We remark that time dependent domains $D(t)$ are common in the free boundary formulation of American options.

If the matrix A in (1.3) is positive definite then the equation is known as a parabolic or, somewhat imprecisely, a diffusion equation. In finance the

1

matrix is often non-negative definite which complicates its analysis. For simplicity we shall call (1.3) a diffusion equation even if A is only semidefinite.

The most famous example of a diffusion equation is the simple heat equation for conductive heat transfer

$$\mathcal{L}u \equiv u_{xx} - u_t = 0$$

which often can be solved analytically. It is well known that the Black Scholes equation (1.1) for constant parameters can be transformed to the heat equation through a change of variable, and that the corresponding Green's function solutions are the Black Scholes formulas for various European options (see [33] and Example 1.1). When analytic solutions are not available one usually resorts to numerical solutions.

The partial differential equations of finance are mathematical models which are derived in many textbooks under specific market assumptions and simplifications which do not necessarily reflect the market reality (see, e.g. [64]). But once the model equations and their initial and boundary conditions are accepted, one also has to accept the qualitative and quantitative behavior of their solutions which is entirely determined by the structure of the mathematical problem and not the application. One cannot assume a priori that the mathematical solution will show all the properties which are obvious for financial reasons. Instead, one has to prove that the mathematical solutions are consistent with financial arguments. If not, the model would have to be changed.

1.1   Solutions and their properties

The user of the partial differential equations of finance tends to assume that the mathematical problem has a solution. The user also tends to have a strong intuitive sense of whether an approximate or numerical solution is "correct". To a mathematician the problem is not quite so simple because the meaning of solution is ambiguous. A problem may not have a solution in one sense but may well have a unique solution if the class of admissible functions is broadened by allowing certain types of discontinuities. Moreover, an approximate solution may well solve a closely related problem while the actual formulation does not have any solution.

There is a comprehensive mathematical theory on the existence, uniqueness and properties of solutions of parabolic problems (see, e.g. [28], [47],

[48], and research on its extensions continues unabated. Here, to characterize solutions of differential equations without going into technical detail, the following few (very loose) definitions are convenient:

Definition. A function u is smooth if it has as many continuous derivatives as are needed for the operations to which it is subjected.

Definition. A classical solution of (1.3) subject to an initial condition at $t = 0$ and to boundary conditions on $\partial D(t)$ is a function which is continuous on the closed set $\overline{D(t)} \times [0, T]$, smooth on $D(t) \times (0, T]$, and which satisfies point for point the equation and the initial and boundary conditions.

Definition. A weak solution is a function which satisfies the equation (1.3) and the side conditions in an "integral sense" (see, e.g. Section 1.2.1).

For example, the Black Scholes formula for a European put is a classical solution of the Black Scholes equation (1.1) and the pay-off and boundary conditions

$$V(S, 0) = \max\{0, K - S\}$$
$$V(0, t) = Ke^{-rt}, \quad \lim_{S \to \infty} V(S, t) = 0$$

while the Black Scholes formula for a European digital call with initial condition

$$V(S, 0) = \begin{cases} 0 & S < K \\ 1 & S \geq K \end{cases}$$

is not a classical solution because $V(S, 0)$ is discontinuous at the strike price K. Similarly, the solution for an up (or down) and out barrier option generally has a discontinuity at expiration at the barrier and is therefore only a weak solution. We mention that classical solutions are always weak solutions.

Many of the conceptual problems due to discontinuous initial/boundary conditions can be circumvented if we think of approximating the data by continuous functions. For example, the digital call $V(S, t)$ may be defined as

$$V(S, t) = \lim_{\epsilon \to 0} V_\epsilon(S, t)$$

where

$$V_\epsilon(S, 0) = \begin{cases} 0 & S < K - \epsilon \\ (S - (K - \epsilon))/(2\epsilon) & K - \epsilon \leq S \leq K + \epsilon. \\ 1 & S > K + \epsilon \end{cases}$$

The existence theory for diffusion equations implies that $V_\epsilon(S,t)$ is a classical solution of the approximating problem, and theoretical a priori estimates can be invoked to show that $V_\epsilon(S,t)$ converges to $V(S,t)$ in a mean square sense. As we shall see in subsequent sections, discontinuous solutions tend to be difficult to compute accurately.

The existence theory for solutions of parabolic problems can be exceedingly abstract and technical, but a priori information on the properties of smooth solutions can often be obtained quite simply with the so-called maximum principle for parabolic equations (see, e.g. [28]). In its simplest form it is little more than the second derivative test of elementary calculus.

A maximum principle: Consider the Black Scholes equation (1.1) with $r > 0$: Let $V(S,t)$ be a smooth function which satisfies

$$\mathcal{L}_{BS} V(S,t) \leq 0 \quad \text{for } S \in (0,\infty) \text{ and } t \in (0,T].$$

Then V cannot have a negative relative minimum in $(0,\infty) \times (0,T]$.

To prove this assertion we note that if V had a negative relative minimum at some point (S^*, t^*) then necessarily

$$rV(S^*, t^*) < 0$$
$$V_S(S^*, t^*) = 0$$
$$V_t(S^*, t^*) \leq 0$$
$$V_{SS}(S^*, t^*) \geq 0.$$

These inequalities would imply that

$$\mathcal{L}_{BS} V(S^*, t^*) > 0$$

which contradicts the assumption $\mathcal{L}_{BS} V \leq 0$. Hence there cannot be a negative relative minimum.

If $\mathcal{L}_{BS} V \geq 0$ then an analogous argument rules out the existence of an interior positive relative maximum of $V(S,t)$.

It is a consequence of the maximum principle that if

$$\mathcal{L}_{BS} V(S,t) = 0, \quad S_0(t) < S < S_1(t), \quad t \in (0,T]$$

then V can attain a negative absolute minimum only either at $t = 0$ or on the lateral boundaries $S_0(t)$, $S_1(t)$, $t \in (0,T]$. Similarly, a positive absolute maximum can be attained only on the boundary.

Equivalent properties can be deduced for the solution of the bond equation for $r > 0$. Moreover, the maximum principle can be shown to hold for the multidimensional equation (1.3). For example, if $A(x,t)$ is positive semi-definite, if $c(x,t) \leq c_0 < 0$, and if $d(x,t) \leq 0$ then the solution u of

(1.3) cannot have an interior positive relative maximum or negative relative minimum at any point (x,t) for $x \in D(t)$ and $t \in (0,T]$, where $D(t)$ is an open set in R_m.

We shall now use the tools for partial differential equations to prove that the Black Scholes option price has properties which are expected on financial grounds.

Example 1.1. Positivity of option prices and the Black Scholes formulas.

If $V(S,t)$ is a smooth bounded solution of (1.1) defined on $[0,\infty)$ then it follows from Example 1.12 on p. 34 that

$$V(0,t) = V(0,0)e^{-rt}$$

is the only admissible boundary condition for (1.1) at $S = 0$. Moreover, if either

$$\lim_{S\to\infty} V(S,0) = A \text{ or } \lim_{S\to\infty} V_S(S,0) = B$$

then we see from Example 1.17 on p. 42 that

$$\lim_{S\to\infty} V(S,t) = Ae^{-rt} \text{ or } \lim_{S\to\infty} V_S(S,0) = Be^{-qt}$$

are the correct asymptotic boundary conditions. If the pay-off $V(S,0)$ is non-negative or $B > 0$, and if the asymptotic condition is imposed at a barrier $X \gg 0$, then the maximum principle and the boundary conditions rule out negative values for $V(S,t)$ on $[0,X] \times [0,T]$ for all $X > 0$.

If no asymptotic limits are known but $V(S,0) \geq 0$ for all S, and if the financial parameters in Equation (1.1) are constant, then we can deduce the positivity of V from its Green's function representation. Indeed, it is known from PDE theory [10] that the initial value problem for the heat equation

$$\mathcal{L}u \equiv u_{xx} - u_t = 0, \quad -\infty < x < \infty, \quad t > 0$$

$$u(x,0) = f(x)$$

has a solution of the form

$$u(x,t) = \int_{-\infty}^{\infty} G(x-y,t)f(y)dy \tag{1.4}$$

with

$$G(x,t) = \frac{1}{\sqrt{4\pi t}} e^{-x^2/4t}$$

provided f is such that the integral exists and can be differentiated with respect to x and t. If f is continuous and satisfies the growth condition

$$|f(x)| \leq Me^{Ax^2} \quad \text{for constants } A, M > 0,$$

then (1.4) is a classical solution for $t \in [0, 1/4A)$. Moreover, it is the only solution which satisfies a growth condition like

$$|u(x,t)| \leq M'e^{A'x^2} \quad \text{for constants } M', A'.$$

All other solutions grow faster at infinity and are not relevant for options and bonds. Note that if $f(y) \equiv 1$ then $u(x,t) \equiv 1$ is the only bounded solution which implies that for all x and for $t > 0$

$$\int_{-\infty}^{\infty} G(x-y,t)dy = 1.$$

If f is only piecewise continuous with finitely many bounded jumps then (1.4) still solves the heat equation but

$$u(x,t) \to f(x_0) \text{ as } (x,t) \to (x_0, 0)$$

only if x_0 is a point of continuity of f.

Note that if f_ϵ is a continuous mean square approximation of f such that

$$\int_{-\infty}^{\infty} (f_\epsilon(y) - f(y))^2 dy \leq \epsilon$$

then

$$u_\epsilon(x,t) = \int_{-\infty}^{\infty} G(x-y,t)f_\epsilon(y)dy$$

is a classical solution which converges pointwise to $f_\epsilon(y)$ as $t \to 0$. It follows from Schwarz's inequality that

$$[u(x,t) - u_\epsilon(x,t)]^2 = \left[\int_{-\infty}^{\infty} G(x-y,t)(f(y) - f_\epsilon(y))dy\right]^2$$

$$\leq \int_{-\infty}^{\infty} G(x-y,t)dy \int_{-\infty}^{\infty} G(x-y,t)(f(y) - f_\epsilon(y))^2 dy$$

$$= \int_{-\infty}^{\infty} G(x-y,t)(f(y) - f_\epsilon(y)^2)dy$$

because $G > 0$ and $\int_{-\infty}^{\infty} G(x-y,t)dy = 1$. Integrating both sides with respect to x leads to

$$\int_{-\infty}^{\infty} [u(x,t) - u_\epsilon(x,t)]^2 dx \leq \int_{-\infty}^{\infty} \int_{-\infty}^{\infty} G(x-y,t)(f(y) - f_\epsilon(y)^2)dx\,dy$$

$$= \int_{-\infty}^{\infty} (f(y) - f_\epsilon(y))^2 dy.$$

Hence the initial mean square approximation error does not increase with time which motivates (but does not justify) the smoothing of discontinuous option pay-offs.

The Black Scholes equation for constant parameters can be transformed into the heat equation as described in detail in many texts (see, e.g. [67, p. 107], [64, p. 92], [46, p. 51]). It leads to the following representation of the solution V of (1.1)

$$V(S,t) = e^{-rt}u(z,\tau)$$

where

$$u(z,\tau) = \int_{-\infty}^{\infty} G(z-y,\tau)V(e^y,0)dy \qquad (1.5)$$

and

$$z = \ln S + (r - q - \sigma^2/2)t$$

$$\tau = \sigma^2 t/2.$$

It follows from (1.5) by inspection that for any pay-off $V(S,0) \geq 0$ the corresponding Black Scholes option price is non-negative.

We note that for any $A > 0$ and any $\alpha \in (-\infty, \infty)$ the inequality

$$|\alpha y| \leq Ay^2 \text{ holds for } |y| \geq |y_0| = \frac{|\alpha|}{A}$$

so that

$$e^{\alpha y} \leq e^{|\alpha y|} \leq e^{|\alpha y_0|}e^{Ay^2} \quad \text{for all } y.$$

Therefore, if (1.1) models a power option with pay-off

$$V(S,0) = \max\{0, Q(S)\}$$

where

$$Q(S) = Q_0 + \sum_{i=1}^{N} Q_i S^{\alpha_i} \quad \alpha_i \in (-\infty, \infty)$$

then (1.5) defines a bounded solution for $t \in [0, \infty)$.

For piecewise continuous linear pay-offs the integral (1.5) can evaluated analytically in terms of error functions. Since error functions are nowadays intrinsic functions in program libraries, we have de facto an analytic solution for many European option pricing problems [33].

The best known pricing formulas describe the plain European put and call

$$p(S,t) = Ke^{-rt}N(-d_2) - Se^{-qt}N(-d_1)$$

$$c(S,t) = Se^{-qt}N(d_1) - Ke^{-rt}N(d_2)$$

where

$$d_1 = \frac{\ln(S/K) + (r - q + \sigma^2/2)t}{\sigma\sqrt{t}}$$

$$d_2 = d_1 - \sigma\sqrt{t}$$

$$N(x) = \frac{1}{\sqrt{2\pi}} \int_{-\infty}^{x} e^{-s^2/2} ds.$$

They yield the boundary values

$$p(0,t) = Ke^{-rt}, \quad \lim_{S\to\infty} p(S,t) = 0$$

$$c(0,t) = 0, \quad \lim_{S\to\infty} [c(S,t) - S^{-qt} + Ke^{-rt}] = 0$$

and conditions on the delta and gamma

$$\lim_{S\to\infty} c_S(S,t) = e^{-qt} \quad \text{and} \quad \lim_{S\to\infty} C_{SS}(S,t) = 0$$

which for numerical methods are frequently enforced at barriers $X_0 \ll K$ and $X_1 \gg K$ for options which behave like a European put near $S = 0$ and like a call as $S \to \infty$.

The bond equation cannot in general be transformed into the heat equation. The existence and uniqueness of its solution must be deduced from the general theory for diffusion equations. However, for special interest rate models the structure of the solution is known and analytic solutions can be found.

Example 1.2. The early exercise boundary for plain American puts and calls.

The solution of an American put will be denoted by $\{P(S,t), S_0(t)\}$ where the price P satisfies (1.1) in the so-called continuation region $S > S_0(t)$ and $S_0(t)$ is the early exercise boundary (a so-called free boundary) below which P takes on its "intrinsic" value

$$P(S,t) = K - S, \quad 0 \le S \le S_0(t).$$

In addition, financial arguments require that $P(S,t)$ be continuously differentiable for $(S,t) \in (0,\infty) \times (0,T]$ which implies the so-called smooth pasting conditions

$$P(S_0(t),t) = K - S_0(t)$$

$$P_S(S_0(t),t) = -1, \quad P_t(S_0(t),t) = 0.$$

We remark that although the Black Scholes equation is a linear equation, the problem for the American put is inherently nonlinear because of the implicit coupling between P and S_0 (see also Section 1.2.4).

In the mathematical literature the free boundary problem for the put (and call) is known as an obstacle problem. $\phi(S) = K - S$ is the obstacle to which $P(S,t)$ attaches itself. It has an alternate formulation as a linear complementarity problem for $P(S,t)$ defined on $(0,\infty) \times (0,T]$ and satisfying

$$\mathcal{L}_{BS}P(S,t)(K-S) = 0$$

$$\mathcal{L}_{BS}P(S,t) \leq 0, \quad P(S,t) \geq K - S$$

$$P(S,0) = \max\{K - S, 0\}.$$

An accessible exposition of the relation between the free boundary and the complementarity formulation, and the connection to a variational inequality, as well as the interpretation of the free boundary problem as an obstacle problem may be found in [27]. The mathematical theory for obstacle problems allows us to prove that a smooth solution $\{P(S,t), S_0(t)\}$ exists so that we can characterize some of its properties by elementary considerations.

Since the maximum principle rules out a negative minimum in the continuation region it follows from $P_S(S_0(t),t) = -1$ that $S_0(t) < K$ for $t > 0$. Since the solution $P(S,t)$ is continuously differentiable on $(0,\infty) \times (0,T]$ and lies either above or on the obstacle $\phi(S) = K - S$ it follows that for all t the function $P(S,t)$ has a relative minimum on $S = S_0(t)$. This implies that

$$\frac{1}{2}\sigma^2 S_0(t)^2 P_{SS}(S_0(t)+,t) = rK - qS_0(t) \geq 0. \tag{1.6}$$

We see that $P(S,t)$ can lift off the intrinsic value only if $S_0(t) \leq \frac{rK}{q}$. Moreover, from $\lim_{t\to 0} P(S,t) = \max\{K-S, 0\}$ we see that $\lim_{t\to 0} P_{SS}(S,t) = 0$ for $S < K$ so that from (1.6) for $r/q \leq 1$

$$\lim_{t\to 0} S_0(t) = \frac{rK}{q}.$$

Since $S_0(t) < K$ we can conclude that

$$\lim_{t \to 0} S_0(t) = K \min\{1, r/q\}.$$

We remark that the early exercise boundary of the American put has been examined in some detail. It is known to be smooth and monotone so that $S_0'(t) < 0$, but also that for a certain parameter range it is not convex near expiry [11]. Note that for any time t the relationship (1.6) must hold which can serve as a check on the consistency of numerical values for $P_{SS}(S_0(t)+, t)$ and $S_0(t)$.

An analogous convexity argument for an American call $\{C(S, t), S_1(t)\}$ with payoff $\max\{S - K, 0\}$ leads to

$$\lim_{t \to 0} S_1(t) = K \max\{1, r/q\}.$$

Example 1.3. Exercise boundaries for options with jump diffusion.

The above arguments can be extended to American options on an asset with jump diffusion. To be specific, let us consider an American call. The Black Scholes equation now takes on the form of a partial-integro-differential equation (PIDE) [64]

$$\mathcal{L}_{BSJ}C \equiv \frac{1}{2}\sigma^2 S^2 C_{SS} + (r - q - \lambda k)SC_S - (r + \lambda)C - C_t$$

$$+ \lambda \int_0^\infty C(yS, t)G(y)dy = 0 \qquad (1.7)$$

where $G(y)$ is a probability density on $(0, \infty)$, $\lambda \geq 0$ and

$$k = \int_0^\infty (y - 1)G(y)dy.$$

The pay-off is

$$C(S, 0) = \max\{S - K, 0\},$$

and the boundary conditions are

$$C(0, t) = 0$$
$$C(S_1(t), t) = S_1(t) - K$$
$$C_S(S_1(t), t) = 1,$$

which also imply that $C_t(S_1(t), t) = 0$ (i.e. the obstacle is time independent). $S_1(t)$ is the early exercise boundary. In the exercise region $S > S_1(t)$ we set

$$C(S, t) = S - K.$$

It is known that this free boundary value problem is equivalent to an obstacle problem and that it has a unique smooth solution [65]. The maximum principle applied to (1.7) yields that $C(S,t)$ cannot have a negative absolute minimum anywhere in $D(t)$, $t \in [0,T]$ so that $S_1(t) > K$ for $t > 0$.

Let $\phi(S,t) = C_S(S,t)$, then differentiating (1.7) we find that

$$\frac{1}{2}\sigma^2 S^2 \phi_{SS} + (r - q - \lambda k + \sigma^2)S\phi_S - (q + \lambda(k+1))\phi - \phi_t$$

$$+ \lambda \int_0^\infty y\phi(yS,t)G(y)dy = 0. \tag{1.8}$$

The Fichera function approach of Section 1.2.1 suggests that equation (1.8) should hold at $S = 0$. It reduces to $-q\phi - \phi_t = 0$ so that $\phi(0,t) = \phi(0,0)e^{-qt} = 0$. $\phi(S,t)$ cannot assume an absolute positive maximum in $(0, S_1(t))$ because if $\phi(S^*, t^*) \geq \phi(S,t)$ for all $S \in D(t)$, $t^* \leq t$, then

$$q\phi(S^*, t^*) > 0, \quad \phi_S(S^*, t^*) = 0, \quad \phi_t(S^*, t^*) \geq 0$$

and

$$\int_0^\infty y\phi(yS,t)G(y)dy \leq \int_0^\infty y\phi(S^*, t^*)G(y)dy = (k+1)\phi(S^*, t^*).$$

Substitution into (1.8) yields that

$$\phi_{SS}(S^*, t^*) > 0$$

which is incompatible with an interior maximum. Hence $\phi(S,t) \leq 1$ and $C(S,t)$ lies on or above $S - K$. Consequently, the function $C(S,t) - (S-K)$ has a relative minimum at $S_1(t)$ which requires that

$$\lim_{S \to S_1(t)} C_{SS}(S,t) \geq 0.$$

From (1.7) and the boundary data follows that at $S = S_1(t)$

$$\frac{1}{2}\sigma^2 S^2 C_{SS}(S,t) = -(r - q - \lambda k)S + (r + \lambda)(S - K)$$

$$- \lambda \int_0^\infty C(yS,t)G(y)dy. \tag{1.9}$$

We shall assume without proof that

$$\lim_{t \to 0} \int_0^\infty C(yS,t)G(y)dy = \int_0^\infty \max\{0, yS - K\}G(y)dy,$$

$$\lim_{t \to 0} C_{SS}(S,t) = 0, \quad S \neq K.$$

Since

$$\int_0^\infty \max\{0, yS - K\}G(y)dy = \int_{K/S}^\infty (yS - K)G(y)dy$$

$$= \int_0^\infty (yS - K)G(y)dy - \int_0^{K/S} (yS - K)G(y)dy$$

$$= (k+1)S - K - \int_0^{K/S} (yS - K)G(y)dy$$

we find from (1.9) that $S_1(0+)$ must satisfy the equation

$$S_1(0+) = \frac{rK + \lambda K \int_0^{K/S_1(0+)} G(y)dy}{q + \lambda \int_0^{K/S_1(0+)} yG(y)dy}$$

provided $S_1(0+) > K$. This condition for the early exercise boundary near expiry is also known from the Fourier transform solution of the jump-diffusion call (see, e.g. [15]). Moreover, if we define

$$f(x) \equiv x \left(q + \lambda \int_0^{K/x} yG(y)dy \right) - \left(rK + \lambda K \int_0^{K/x} G(y)dy \right)$$

it is straightforward to show that $f'(x) > 0$, that $\lim_{x \to 0} f(x) < 0$ and that $\lim_{x \to \infty} f(x) > 0$ if and only if $q > 0$. Hence $f(x) = 0$ for $q > 0$ has a unique solution x^*. If $\lambda = 0$ we obtain the above limit $x^* = rK/q$. Since

$$f(K) = K(q - r) + \lambda K \left(\int_0^1 (y - 1)G(y)dy \right)$$

we also find that $x^* > K$ whenever $f(K) < 0$. Hence for $\lambda > 0$ we see that $S_1(0+)$ can be greater than K even when $r/q < 1$ provided down-jumps occur. Since $S_1(t) > K$ for all $t > 0$ it follows that

$$S(0+) = K \max(1, x^*).$$

Analogous arguments lead to the characterization of the early exercise boundary $S_0(t)$ for a jump American put. The limit of its early exercise boundary is

$$S_0(0+) = K \min\{1, x^{**}\}$$

where x^{**} is a root of the equation

$$f(x) = x \left(q + \lambda \int_{K/x}^\infty yG(y)dy \right) - K \left(r + \lambda \int_{K/x}^\infty G(y)dy \right).$$

A rigorous derivation of this equation by different means may be found in [12].

Example 1.4. The early exercise premium for an American put.

Let $\{P(S, t, X), S_0(t, X)\}$ denote an American put with early exercise boundary $S_0(t, X)$ and barrier condition

$$P(X, t, X) = 0, \quad X \gg K,$$

and let $p(S, t, X)$ be the corresponding European put. The function $P(S, t) - p(S, t)$ is often called the early exercise premium of the American put. The exercise conditions

$$P(S, t, X) = K - S \quad \text{and} \quad P_S(S, t, X) = -1, \quad S \in (0, S_0(t)]$$

imply that

$$\mathcal{L}_{BS}[P(S, t, X) - p(S, t, X)] = \begin{cases} qS - Kr & \text{on } (0, S_0(t)) \\ 0 & \text{on } (S_0(t), X). \end{cases}$$

Since $S_0(t) \leq K \min\{1, \frac{r}{q}\}$ the source term is non-positive so that $P - p$ cannot have an interior negative minimum. Since the initial and boundary data are non-negative we see that

$$P(S, t, X) - p(S, t, X) \geq 0.$$

This conclusion is independent of X and holds as $X \to \infty$. Hence we see that the standard American put is worth more than its European counterpart.

We shall now derive an upper bound for the premium. Let $u(S, t)$ be the solution of the initial value problem

$$\mathcal{L}_{BS} u(S, t) = -rK$$

$$u(S, 0) = 0.$$

If r and q are independent of S we can find a solution of the form

$$u(S, t) = A(t) + B(t)S$$

provided that for all S

$$(r - q)SB(t) - r(A(t) + B(t)S) - (A'(t) + B'(t)S) = -rK.$$

Collecting coefficients of S we find

$$B' = -qB(t), \qquad B(0) = 0$$
$$A' = -rA(t) + rK, \quad A(0) = 0$$

so that for constant r

$$A(t) = K(1 - e^{-rt}), \quad B(t) = 0 \quad \text{and } u(S, t) = A(t).$$

We observe that

$$\mathcal{L}_{BS}[u(S,t) - (P(S,t) - p(S,t))] = \begin{cases} -qS & \text{on } (0, S_0(t)) \\ -rK & \text{otherwise.} \end{cases}$$

The maximum principle rules out interior negative minima for $u - (P - p)$ and the boundary data rule out negative values at $S = 0$, at $t = 0$ and as $S \to \infty$. Hence the early exercise premium of the American put satisfies

$$0 \leq P(S,t) - p(S,t) \leq u(S,t) = K(1 - e^{-rt}).$$

Example 1.5. The early exercise premium for an American call.

If $\{C(S,t), S_1(t)\}$ denotes an American call and $c(S,t,X)$ is the corresponding European call with the barrier condition

$$c_S(X,t,X) = e^{-qt} \quad \text{for a barrier } X > S_1(t)$$

we obtain

$$\mathcal{L}_{BS}[C(S,t,X) - c(S,t,X)] = \begin{cases} -qS + Kr & \text{on } (S_1(t), X) \\ 0 & \text{on } (0, S_1(t)). \end{cases}$$

For a call we know that $S_1(t) \geq \max\{K, Kr/q\}$ so that the source term of the Black Scholes equation is again non-positive. The boundary data rule out an absolute negative minimum at $t = 0$ and on the lateral boundaries, and the maximum principle rules out interior negative minima for $C - c$. Hence again for all $X \gg K$ we find that the early exercise premium for an American call is non-negative. As $X \to \infty$ the barrier conditions reduce to the correct boundary conditions for standard options defined on $0 < S < \infty$.

To bound the premium for a call from above let $v(S,t)$ be the solution of

$$\mathcal{L}_{BS}v(S,t) = -qS$$

$$v(S,0) = 0.$$

It is straightforward to verify that for constant q the solution is

$$v(S,t) = (1 - e^{-qt})S.$$

By inspection

$$\mathcal{L}_{BS}[v(S,t) - (C(S,t) - c(S,t)] = \begin{cases} -qS & 0 < S < S_1(t) \\ -rK & \text{otherwise.} \end{cases}$$

Since $v(0,t) = C(0,t) - c(0,t) = 0$, $v(S,0) = C(S,0) - c(S,0) = 0$ and, from the Black Scholes formula,

$$\lim_{S \to \infty} [v(S,t) - (C(S,t) - c(S,t))]$$
$$= \lim_{S \to \infty} [Se^{-qt}(N(d_1) - 1) + K(1 - e^{-rt}N(d_2))] \geq 0$$

we obtain from the maximum principle

$$0 \leq C(S,t) - c(S,t) \leq v(S,t) = (1 - e^{-qt})S.$$

Example 1.6. Strike price convexity.

As a further application of the maximum principle let us examine the change of a European put with the strike price K. If $p(S,t,K)$ denotes the price of a European put with pay-off

$$p(S,0,K) = \max\{K - S, 0\}$$

then for $\Delta K > 0$ the function

$$V(S,t) = p(S,t,K + \Delta K) - p(S,t,K)$$

satisfies the Black Scholes equation, the initial condition

$$V(S,0) = \begin{cases} \Delta K, & S \leq K \\ \max\{\Delta K + (K - S), 0\}, & S > K \end{cases}$$

and the boundary conditions

$$V(0,t) = \Delta K e^{-rt}, \quad \lim_{S \to \infty} V(S,t) = 0.$$

It can be shown that $V(S,t)$ is a classical solution so that by the maximum principle $V(S,t) \geq 0$. It also can be shown that V varies smoothly with K so that

$$\lim_{\Delta K \to 0} \frac{V(S,t)}{\Delta K} = \frac{\partial p(S,t,K)}{\partial K} \geq 0.$$

Similarly, if we define

$$V(S,t) = p(S,t,K + \Delta K) + p(S,t,K - \Delta K) - 2p(S,t,K)$$

then

$$V(S,0) \geq 0, \quad V(0,t) = 0, \quad \lim_{S \to \infty} V(S,t) = 0$$

and the maximum principle imply that $V(S,t) \geq 0$ for all K and $\Delta K > 0$, while smoothness in K implies that

$$\frac{\partial^2 p(S,t,K)}{\partial K^2} \geq 0.$$

Example 1.7. Put-call parity.

The put-call parity relation in the Black Scholes setting is the function $V(S, t) = p(S, t) - c(S, t)$. It can often be found from arbitrage theory without knowing $p(S, t)$ and $c(S, t)$ explicitly (see [38, 64]) or by solving analytically

$$\mathcal{L}_{BS} V(S, t) = 0$$

subject to the pay-off initial condition

$$V(S, 0) = p(S, 0) - c(S, 0)$$

and to any boundary conditions imposed on the options. For European options without barrier conditions the Black Scholes equation is equivalent to the heat equation on the real line so that the initial condition alone uniquely determines $V(S, t)$. For constant parameters $V(S, t)$ can often be found with elementary calculations. For example, suppose that we have a European put $p(S, t)$ with pay-off

$$p(S, 0) = \max\left\{0, \left(K - \sum_{i=1}^{N} \beta_i S^{\alpha_i}\right)\right\}.$$

Let $c(S, t)$ be the corresponding call with pay-off

$$c(S, 0) = \max\left\{0, \left(\sum_{i=1}^{N} \beta_i S^{\alpha_i} - K\right)\right\}.$$

Then by linearity of the Black Scholes equation we obtain for

$$V(S, t) = p(S, t) - c(S, t)$$

the initial value problem

$$\mathcal{L}_{BS} V(S, t) = 0$$

$$V(S, 0) = K - \sum_{i=1}^{N} \beta_i S^{\alpha_i}.$$

Because, loosely speaking, each S^{α_i} is an eigenfunction of the spatial part of the Black Scholes operator, it is straightforward to find a solution of the form

$$V(S, t) = \gamma_0(t) + \sum_{i=1}^{N} \gamma_i(t) S^{\alpha_i}.$$

Substitution into the Black Scholes equation and equating the coefficients of each S^{α_i} to zero yields

$$-r\gamma_0(t) - \gamma_0'(t) = 0, \quad \gamma_0(0) = K$$

$$\left[\frac{1}{2}\sigma^2\alpha_i(\alpha_i - 1) + \alpha_i(r - q) - r\right]\gamma_i(t) - \gamma_i'(t) = 0, \quad \gamma_i(0) = -\beta_i.$$

Hence for constant financial parameters we obtain

$$V(S,t) = Ke^{-rt} - \sum_{i=1}^{N}\beta_i e^{-\delta_i t}S^{\alpha_i}$$

where

$$\delta_i = \left[\frac{1}{2}\sigma^2\alpha_i(\alpha_i - 1) + \alpha_i(r - q) - r\right].$$

For example, for plain puts and calls with $\alpha_1 = 1$ and $\alpha_i = 0$, $i \geq 2$, we obtain the well known put-call parity expression

$$V(S,t) = p(S,t) - c(S,t) = Ke^{-rt} - \beta_1 Se^{-qt}.$$

It reduces to $V(S,t) = Ke^{-rt}$ for a binary put-call where $\beta_1 = 0$.

A similar argument applies to the multi-dimensional Black Scholes equation. Suppose we consider a European option on a basket of two assets with value $V(S_1, S_2, t)$. For notational convenience let us scale the variables and write

$$x = S/K, \quad y = S/K, \quad u(x,y,t) = V(Kx, Ky, t)/K$$

where K is a convenient parameter, usually taken to be the strike price. u is the solution of the two-dimensional Black Scholes equation

$$\mathcal{L}_{BS}u = \frac{1}{2}\sigma_1^2 x^2 u_{xx} + \rho\sigma_1\sigma_2 xy u_{xy} + \frac{1}{2}\sigma_2^2 y^2 u_{yy} + (r - q_1)xu_x$$

$$+ (r - q_2)yu_y - ru - u_0 = 0. \tag{1.10}$$

For the initial condition

$$u(x,y,0) = \gamma_0 x^\alpha y^\beta$$

substitution into (1.10) shows that the solution of this initial value problem is

$$u(x,y,t) = \gamma(t)x^\alpha y^\beta$$

where

$$\left[\frac{1}{2}\sigma_1^2\alpha(\alpha - 1) + \rho\sigma_1\sigma_2\alpha\beta + \frac{1}{2}\sigma_2^2\beta(\beta - 1)\right.$$

$$+ (r - q_1)\alpha + (r - q_2)\beta - r \Big] \gamma(t) - \gamma'(t) = 0.$$

$$\gamma(0) = \gamma_0.$$

For constant (or only time dependent parameters) this linear ordinary differential equation is solvable. Hence if the payoffs for a (scaled) put $p(x, y, t)$ and call $c(x, y, t)$ are $\max\{f(x, y), 0\}$ and $\max\{-f(x, y), 0\}$, resp., where

$$f(x, y) = \sum_{i,j} \gamma_{ij}(0) x^{\alpha_i} y^{\alpha_j}$$

then by superposition

$$\mathcal{L}_{BS}[c(x, y, t) - p(x, y, t)] = 0$$

$$c(y, 0) - p(x, y, 0) = f(x, y)$$

has the computable solution

$$c(x, y, t) - p(x, y, t) = \sum_{i,j} \gamma_{ij}(t) x^{\alpha_i} y^{\alpha_j}.$$

Thus the put-call parity relation can be establish without knowing the put and call explicitly.

We note that if

$$p_1(S, 0) = \max\{0, K_1 - S^{\alpha_1}\} + \max\{0, K_2 - S^{\alpha_2}\}$$

$$c_1(S, 0) = \max\{0, S^{\alpha_1} - K_1\} + \max\{0, S^{\alpha_2} - K_2\}$$

then $V(S, 0) = p_1(S, 0) - c_1(S, 0)$ is given by

$$V(S, 0) = K_1 + K_2 - S^{\alpha_1} - S^{\alpha_2}$$

which is the same as the put-call parity initial condition for the European put with pay-off

$$p_2(S, 0) = \max\{0, K_1 + K_2 - S^{\alpha_1} - S^{\alpha_2}\}.$$

In general $p_1(S, t) \neq p_2(S, t)$ so that put-call parity does not uniquely define the underlying put and call.

While the definition of the put-call relation as the difference between the put and call can be maintained for American options the resulting problem for V would appear more difficult to solve than either the put or call alone. It is possible, however, to find an upper and lower bound on

$$V(S, t) = P(S, t) - C(S, t)$$

for plain American puts and calls. It follows from

$$P(S,t) - C(S,t) \equiv (P - p) - (C - c) + (p - c)$$

that

$$-(C - c) + (p - c) < P - C < (P - p) + (p - c)$$

because the early exercise premiums are non-negative. If we now substitute the bounds on the premiums derived in Examples 1.4, 1.5 and use put-call parity for plain European options we obtain

$$Ke^{-rt} - S \leq P(S,t) - C(S,t) \leq K - Se^{-qt}.$$

These bounds are also known from arbitrage theory [67, p. 98].

Example 1.8. Put-call symmetry for a CEV and Heston model.

Besides put-call parity there also exists a put-call symmetry relation. It follows from the Black Scholes equation and can be interpreted financially [46, p. 144], [67, p. 72]. We shall derive the symmetry relation with a change of variables, which will also prove useful in the subsequent discussion of permissible boundary values.

Let $C(S, t, r, q, K)$ denote the Black-Scholes call with strike price K, riskfree interest rate r and dividend rate q. It satisfies (1.1). Let us again scale the equation by writing

$$x = S/K, \quad u(x, t) = C(Kx, t, r, q, K)/K.$$

Then the call satisfies

$$\frac{1}{2}\sigma^2 x^2 u_{xx} + (r - q)x u_x - ru - u_t = 0 \tag{1.11}$$

$$u(x, 0) = \max\{x - 1, 0\}.$$

If we make the change of variable

$$z = \frac{1}{x}$$

then the function

$$\tilde{u}(z, t) = u\left(\frac{1}{z}, t\right)$$

satisfies

$$u_x = \tilde{u}_z\left(-\frac{1}{x^2}\right), \quad u_{xx} = \tilde{u}_{zz}\left(\frac{1}{x^4}\right) + \tilde{u}_z\left(\frac{2}{x^3}\right).$$

Substitution into (1.11) shows that $\tilde{u}$ solves

$$\frac{1}{2}\sigma^2 z^2 \tilde{u}_{zz} - (r - q - \sigma^2)z\tilde{u}_z - r\tilde{u} - \tilde{u}_t = 0 \tag{1.12}$$

$$\tilde{u}(z,0) = \max\left\{\frac{1-z}{z}, 0\right\}.$$

If we set

$$w(z,t) = z\tilde{u}(z,t)$$

then

$$w_z = \tilde{u} + z\tilde{u}_z, \quad w_{zz} = 2\tilde{u}_z + z\tilde{u}_{zz}$$

so that

$$z^2\tilde{u}_z = zw_z - w, \quad z^3\tilde{u}_{zz} = z^2 w_{zz} - 2(zw_z - w).$$

If we multiply (1.12) by z and replace $\tilde{u}$ in terms of w we find that w solves

$$\frac{1}{2}\sigma^2 z^2 w_{zz} + (q - r)zw_z - qw - w_t = 0 \tag{1.13}$$

$$w(z,0) = \max\{1 - z, 0\}.$$

If $P(S,t,q,r,E)$ denotes the price of a put with strike price E, interest rate q and dividend rate r then with

$$z = S/E, \quad w(z,t) = P(Ez,t,q,r,E)/E$$

we see that the solution $w(z,t)$ of (1.13) is exactly the scaled price of the put. Hence

$$C(S,t,r,q,K)/K = u(x,t) = \tilde{u}(z,t) = w(z,t)/z = P(zE,t,q,r,E)/(Ez).$$

If S, K, E, r and q are given then $x = S/K$, $z = K/S$ and then

$$EC(S,t,r,q,K) = SP(EK/S,t,q,r,E).$$

If $E = S$ then $C(S,t,r,q,K) = P(K,t,q,r,S)$ [46, p. 144].
If $E = K$ then $KC(S,t,r,q,K) = SP(K^2/S,t,q,r,K)$ [67, p. 72].

Finally, we observe that if $x_c(t)$ is the free boundary of a scaled American call, so that $u(x_c(t),t) = x_c(t) - 1$, $u_x(x_c(t),t) = 1$ and if we set

$$z_p(t) = 1/x_c(t) \tag{1.14}$$

then

$$w(z_p(t),t) = z_p(t)u(x_c(t),t) = 1 - z_p(t)$$

and

$$w_z(z_p(t), t) = u(x_c(t), t) + z_p(t)u_x(x_c(t), t)(-1/z_p(t)^2) = -1.$$

Hence $z_p(t)$ is the early exercise boundary of the scaled put. If $S_1(t, r, q, K)$ denotes the boundary for the unscaled call $C(S, t, r, q, K)$ and $S_0(t, q, r, E)$ is the exercise boundary for the put $P(S, t, q, r, E)$ then (1.14) implies

$$S_0(t, q, r, E)S_1(t, r, q, K) = EK \quad [46, \text{p. } 146].$$

We remark that if $u(x, t, \alpha, \sigma, r, q)$ denotes a scaled call for the CEV equation

$$\mathcal{L}(\alpha, \sigma, r, q)u \equiv \frac{1}{2}\sigma^2 x^{2\alpha}u_{xx} + (r - q)xu_x - ru - u_t = 0$$

with pay-off

$$u(x, 0, \alpha, \sigma, r, q) = \max\{0, x - 1\}$$

then the change of variable $z = \frac{1}{x}$ shows that

$$w(z, t) = z\tilde{u}(z, t) = zu\left(\frac{1}{z}, t, \alpha, \sigma, r, q\right) \tag{1.15}$$

satisfies the scaled CEV equation for a put

$$\mathcal{L}(2 - \alpha, \sigma, q, r)w = 0, \quad w(z, 0) = \max\{1 - z, 0\}.$$

Hence in the CEV setting the put-call symmetry takes on the form

$$u(x, t, \alpha, \sigma, r, q) = xw\left(\frac{1}{x}, t, 2 - \alpha, \sigma, q, r\right). \tag{1.16}$$

If $C(S, t, \alpha, \Sigma_0, r, q, K_0)$ denotes a CEV call with exponent α, volatility Σ_0, interest rate r, dividend rate q and strike price K_0, and $P(S, t, \beta, \Sigma_1, r_1, q_1, K_1)$ is a CEV put then (1.16) is equivalent to

$$K_1C(S, t, \alpha, \Sigma_0, r, q, K_0) = SP(K_0/K_1/S, t, 2 - \alpha, \Sigma_0(K_0/K_1)^{\alpha-1}, q, r, K_1).$$

As $\alpha \to 1$ this put-call symmetry relationship returns to the familiar form for geometric Brownian motion shown above.

The same transformation can also be used to derive a put-call symmetry relationship for the Black Scholes equation for options with stochastic volatility. For example, for the Heston volatility model the pricing equation for a call is

$$\frac{vx^2}{2}u_{xx} + \rho\sigma vxu_{xv} + \frac{\sigma^2 v}{2}u_{vv} + (r - q)xu_x + (\alpha - \beta v)u_v - ru - u_t = 0 \tag{1.17}$$

$$u(x, v, 0) = \max\{0, x - 1\}.$$

For $z = \frac{1}{x}$ and $\tilde{u}(z, v, t) = u\left(\frac{1}{z}, v, t\right)$ we find that (1.17) leads to

$$\frac{vz^2}{2}\tilde{u}_{zz} + \rho\sigma zv\tilde{u}_{zv} + \frac{\sigma^2 v}{2}\tilde{u}_{vv} - (r - q - v)z\tilde{u}_z + (\alpha - \beta v)\tilde{u}_v - r\tilde{u} - \tilde{u}_t = 0$$

$$\tilde{u}(z, v, 0) = \max\left\{0, \frac{1 - z}{z}\right\}.$$

Thus $w(z, v, t) = z\tilde{u}(z, v, t)$ has the pay-off of a put. Since

$$z^2\tilde{u}_z = zw_z - w, \quad (z^2\tilde{u}_z)_v = zw_{zv} - w_v \quad \text{and} \quad z^3\tilde{u}_{zz} = z^2 w_{zz} - 2zw_z + 2w$$

we obtain for w the pricing equation

$$\frac{vz^2}{2}w_{zz} - \rho\sigma zvw_{zv} + \frac{\sigma^2 v}{2}w_{vv} + (q - r)zw_z + [\alpha - (\beta - \rho\sigma)v]w_v - qw - w_t = 0.$$

Thus we have the symmetry relationship for the scaled put and call

$$w(z, v, t) = zu(x, v, t).$$

If $C(S, v, t, \sigma, \rho, r, q, \alpha, \beta, K_0)$ denotes the unscaled price of a call with strike price K_0, and $P(S, v, t, \sigma, -\rho, q, r, \alpha, \beta - \rho\sigma, K_1)$ is a put with strike price K_1 then for $x = S/K_0$ and $z = S/K_1$ we find that

$$u(x, v, t) = \frac{C(K_0 x, v, t, \sigma, \rho, r, q, \alpha, \beta, K_0)}{K_0}$$

and

$$w(z, v, t) = \frac{P(K_1 z, v, t, \sigma, -\rho, q, r, \alpha, \beta - \rho\sigma, K_1)}{K_1}$$

are the scaled solutions of the symmetry relation. Hence we obtain the put-call symmetry relationship

$$K_1 C(S, v, t, \sigma, \rho, r, q, \alpha, \beta, K_0) = SP\left(\frac{K_0 K_1}{S}, v, t, \sigma, -\rho, q, r, \alpha, \beta - \rho\sigma, K_1\right).$$

The formula shows the expected exchange of interest and dividend rates, but the correlation and the mean reversion rates in the CIR model for v are also changed.

An analogous expression would appear to hold for the puts and calls depending on stochastic volatility and interest rate considered in Example 7.12*:

---

*Put-call symmetry also applies to equation (1.7). If $u(x, t)$ is a scaled put with jump integral $\lambda \int u(xy, t)g(y)dy$ then $w(z, t)$ is a call with jump integral $(k + 1)\lambda \int w\left(\frac{z}{y}, t\right)\frac{yg(y)}{k+1}dy$.

Example 1.9. Equations with an uncertain parameter.

As a final application of the maximum principle for elliptic and parabolic problems we shall use it to find sharp upper and lower bounds on option and bond prices when a single coefficient in the pricing equation may vary arbitrarily between known upper and lower bounds. We shall give a formal derivation of the relevant equations first and defer a discussion of the underlying theoretical issues to the end of this exposition.

We start with the general equation (1.3) defined on a domain $Q = \{(x,t)), x \in D(t), t \in (0,T]\}$. We assume that $c(x,t) \le c_0 < 0$ and that $d(x,t) \le 0$ so that the maximum principle rules out an interior positive maximum if $f(x,t) \ge 0$ and a negative relative minimum if $f(x,t) \le 0$.

Since the matrix (a_{ij}) in (1.3) is symmetric, and since for a smooth function u we know that $u_{x_i x_j} = u_{x_j x_i}$ we may assume without loss of generality that (1.3) is written conveniently in the form

$$\mathcal{L}u = \sum_{\substack{i=1 \\ j=i}}^{m} a_{ij} u_{x_i x_j} + \sum_{i=1}^{m} b_i u_{x_i} + cu + du_t = f. \tag{1.18}$$

We shall assume that u is subject to given Dirichlet conditions on $\partial D(t)$ and an initial condition at $t = 0$.

Let us now suppose that one coefficient in equation (1.18) is not known with certainty. For notational convenience we label this coefficient $\alpha(x,t)$. Usually

$$\alpha(x,t) = a_{ij}(x,t) \quad \text{for some } j \ge i, \quad i = 1, \dots, m$$

but it could be any other one coefficient of u and its derivatives appearing in (1.18).

While not known with certainty we shall assume that α satisfies

$$a_0(x,t) \le \alpha(x,t) \le a_1(x,t) \tag{1.19}$$

where $a_0(x,t)$ and $a_1(x,t)$ are known functions. All functions $\alpha(x,t)$ satisfying (1.19) for which (1.18) has a continuously differentiable solution will be called "admissible".

The aim is to find functions $u_0(x,t)$ and $u_1(x,t)$ such that one can assert that

$$u_0(x,t) \le u(x,t) \le u_1(x,t)$$

for all admissible $\alpha(x,t)$, and that there are two admissible functions for which (1.18) has solutions $u_0(x,t)$ and $u_1(x,t)$ so that u_0 and u_1 are sharp lower and upper bounds.

For argument's sake let us suppose that α is the coefficient of $u_{x_k x_l}$ in (1.18).

For an arbitrary admissible α let u_0 denote the solution of the nonlinear equation

$$\mathcal{L}u = f(x,t) + (\alpha - a_0)u^+_{x_k x_l} + (\alpha - a_1)u^-_{x_k x_l} \tag{1.20}$$

subject to the same initial and boundary conditions as the solution u of (1.18). Here $\mathcal{L}u$ is the linear differential operator defined by (1.18) and $a^+ = \max\{a,0\}$, $a^- = \min\{a,0\}$. Since $\mathcal{L}$ is linear we see by inspection that

$$\mathcal{L}(u_0 - u) \geq 0.$$

The maximum principle rules out a positive interior maximum for $u_0 - u$, which together with zero initial and boundary data guarantees that

$$u_0 \leq u.$$

Equation (1.20) is actually solvable regardless of the algebraic sign of $u_{x_k x_l}$ because the uncertain coefficient α cancels out of (1.20). What remains is equation (1.18) provided the uncertain coefficient α is replaced by the coefficient

$$\alpha(x,t,u_{x_k x_l}(x,t)) = \begin{cases} a_0(x,t) & \text{if } u_{x_k x_l} \geq 0 \\ a_1(x,t) & \text{if } u_{x_k x_l} < 0. \end{cases}$$

In other words, u_0 is a solution of the fully nonlinear equation

$$\mathcal{L}u = \sum_{\substack{i=1 \\ j=i \\ i\neq k, j\neq l}}^{m} a_{ij}u_{x_i x_j} + \alpha(x,t,u_{x_k x_l})u_{x_k x_l} + \sum_{i=1}^{m} b_i u_x + cu + du_t = f. \tag{1.21}$$

If (1.21) does indeed have a smooth solution then $\alpha(t,x,u_{x_k x_l})$ is an admissible function so that $u_0(x,t)$ is an attainable lower bound. For the analysis and numerical solution of equation (1.21) we find it advantageous to substitute

$$u^+_{x_k x_l} = \frac{u_{x_k x_l} + |u_{x_k x_l}|}{2}, \qquad u^-_{x_k x_l} = \frac{u_{x_k x_l} - |u_{x_k x_l}|}{2}$$

into the right side of (1.20). The unknown coefficient α again cancels and we are left with a modified equation

$$\mathcal{L}u_0 = f(x,t) + F(x,t,u_{0x_k x_l}) \tag{1.22}$$

where the entry $\alpha(x,t)$ in (1.18) is replaced by

$$a_{kl}(x,t) = \frac{a_0(x,t) + a_1(x,t)}{2}$$

and where

$$F(x, t, u_{x_k x_l}) \equiv \frac{a_1(x,t) - a_0(x,t)}{2} \, |u_{x_k x_l}|.$$

If one can find a continuously differentiable solution u_0 of (1.22) subject to the initial and boundary conditions which apply to u, then one has a sharp lower bound on u for any admissible α.

An analogous argument starting with negative nonlinear terms in (1.20) yields a sharp upper bound $u_1(x, t)$. Its numerical solution can be found from (1.22) when F is replaced by $-F$.

As a first illustration consider the Black Scholes equation (1.1) when the volatility σ is uncertain but known to satisfy

$$\sigma_0 \leq \sigma \leq \sigma_1.$$

Then equations (1.21, 1.22) for the lower bound V_0 become

$$\mathcal{L}(\sigma(V_{SS}))V = 0 \tag{1.23}$$

where $\mathcal{L}(\sigma)$ denotes the differential operator defined by (1.1) with

$$\sigma(V_{SS}) = \begin{cases} \sigma_0 & \text{when } V_{SS} \geq 0 \\ \sigma_1 & \text{when } V_{SS} < 0, \end{cases}$$

and

$$\frac{1}{2}\left(\frac{\sigma_1^2 + \sigma_0^2}{2}\right) S^2 V_{SS} + (r - q)SV_S - rV - V_t = F(\sigma_1, \sigma_0, S, V_{SS}) \tag{1.24}$$

where

$$F(\sigma_1, \sigma_0, S, V_{SS}) = \frac{1}{2}\left(\frac{\sigma_1^2 - \sigma_0^2}{2}\right) S^2 |V_{SS}|.$$

(1.23) is the so-called Black Scholes Barenblatt equation for uncertain volatility introduced in [6], and (1.24) is an equivalent equation. The above derivation is taken from [56]. Its numerical solution is the subject of Example 4.4 below. It may be noted that the Black Scholes Barenblatt version (1.24) has the same form as the Leland model for options with transaction costs.

As a second example, consider the Black Scholes equation (1.10)

$$\mathcal{L}(\rho)u = 0$$

for an option on two assets where $\mathcal{L}(\rho)$ simply indicates that the correlation ρ is the quantity of interest in (1.10). Let us suppose that ρ is uncertain but that

$$-1 < \rho_0 \leq \rho \leq \rho_1 < 1.$$

Then u_0 is the solution of the three equivalent formulations (1.20, 1.21, 1.22) which for this application are

$$\mathcal{L}(\rho)u = \sigma_1\sigma_2 xy \left[(\rho - \rho_0)\, u_{xy}^+ + (\rho - \rho_1)u_{xy}^-\right], \qquad (1.25)$$

$$\mathcal{L}(\rho(u_{xy})) = 0 \qquad (1.26)$$

where

$$\rho(u_{xy}) = \begin{cases} \rho_0 & \text{if } u_{xy} \geq 0 \\ \rho_1 & \text{if } u_{xy} < 0, \end{cases}$$

and

$$\mathcal{L}\left(\frac{\rho_1 + \rho_0}{2}\right) u = F \equiv \left(\frac{\rho_1 - \rho_0}{2}\right) \sigma_1 \sigma_2 \, xy! u_{xy}!. \qquad (1.27)$$

A numerical solution of the pricing problem with uncertain correlation based on the last equation is given in Example 7.10.

As a final example we point out that the uncertain coefficient may multiply several terms in the pricing equation. Consider the equation for jump diffusion (1.7) for Poisson jumps with uncertain intensity. We shall assume that

$$0 \leq \lambda_0 \leq \lambda \leq \lambda_1.$$

The pricing equation is written as

$$\mathcal{L}(\lambda)u(x,t) = \frac{1}{2}\sigma^2 u_{xx} + (r - q)xu_x - ru - u_t + \lambda f(u) = 0$$

where f is the linear function defined by

$$f(u) = \left[\int_0^\infty u(yx,t)G(y)dy - kxu_x - u\right]$$

for a probability density $G(y)$ on $(0, \infty)$ and $k = \int_0^\infty (y - 1)G(y)dy$. It is straightforward to see that $f(u) \geq 0$ at an interior absolute negative minimum of u. Maximum principle arguments can again be invoked to find a bounding solution.

The three equivalent formulations for the lower bound u_0 are:

$$\mathcal{L}(\lambda)u = (\lambda - \lambda_0)f(u)^+ + (\lambda - \lambda_1)f(u)^-, \qquad (1.28)$$

$$\mathcal{L}(\lambda(f(u)))u = 0 \qquad (1.29)$$

for

$$\lambda(f(u)) = \begin{cases} \lambda_0 & \text{if } f(u) \geq 0 \\ \lambda_1 & \text{if } f(u) < 0, \end{cases}$$

and

$$\mathcal{L}\left(\frac{\lambda_1 + \lambda_0}{2}\right) u = \left(\frac{\lambda_1 - \lambda_0}{2}\right) |f(u)|. \tag{1.30}$$

For the upper bound u_1 we interchange f^+ and f^- in (1.28).

A maximum principle based derivation of the equations (1.20, 1.21, 1.22) also shows that when early exercise conditions for an American put or call are imposed, then the free boundaries for u_0 and u_1 bracket the early exercise boundary of u for any admissible uncertain coefficient [56].

The dominant mathematical question is the existence of a continuously differentiable solution of the fully nonlinear equations. Both for analysis and numerical computation the equation (1.22) appears to be most useful. It is possible to show that a solution of the time discrete Black Scholes Barenblatt equation can be obtained from a fixed point iteration by lagging the source term. Its smoothness is a consequence of the continuity of the nonlinear term. It has also been observed that numerical methods based on the same linearization perform reliably for uncertain volatility in (1.24) in a jump-diffusion setting [57] and for an uncertain correlation in (1.27) (see Example 7.10, p. 237). No numerical tests were carried out for jump diffusion with uncertain intensity. It also appears that the concept of static hedging used to narrow bounds for the Black Scholes Barenblatt solutions as in [56] may be applied for other uncertain parameters, but we know of no such studies at this time.

Many other tools of mathematics such as integral identities and inequalities, integral transforms, separation of variables approximations and asymptotic methods have been applied in finance to establish, find and examine analytic and approximate solutions of the pricing equations. Apparently, no jarring discrepancies between mathematical predictions and economic theory have been discovered which disqualify the Black Scholes PDE approach.

1.2 Boundary conditions for the pricing equations

The initial condition

$$u(x, 0) = u_0(x), \quad x \in D(0)$$

represents the pay-off of the option or bond at maturity and is known with certainty. However, in order to be able to solve the diffusion problem for (1.3) we also need boundary conditions on part or all of $\partial D(t)$ which may not be so easy to write down. The difficulties arising in finance are twofold.

1) It is common that there will be a parts of $\overline{D(t)}$ where the coefficient matrix $(a_{ij}(x,t))$ becomes singular. The diffusion equation is said to be degenerate at such points. Degeneracy on $\partial D(t)$ complicates what boundary conditions may be imposed. It also complicates the numerical solution of the problem.

2) The domain $D(t)$ may be unbounded. There may, or may not, be asymptotic conditions known for the solution on the far boundaries. However, in order to solve the problem numerically one may have to restrict oneself to a bounded domain, and it often is difficult to formulate consistent boundary conditions on near boundaries.

Boundary conditions for non-degenerate elliptic and parabolic equations like (1.3) commonly imposed on $\partial D(t)$ are

i) Dirichlet condition: $u = g(x,t)$, $x \in \partial D(t)$.

ii) Neumann condition: $\frac{\partial u}{\partial n} \equiv \langle n(x), \mathrm{grad}\ u \rangle = g(x,t)$ where $n(x)$ is the inward unit normal vector at $x \in \partial D(t)$.

iii) Oblique boundary condition:

$$\langle \vec{\beta}(x,t), \mathrm{grad}\ u \rangle = g(x,t)u + h(x,t)$$

where $\langle \vec{\beta}(x,t), n(x) \rangle \geq 0$, $g(x,t) > 0$ and where $n(x)$ again is the inward unit normal. If $\vec{\beta}(x,t) = n(x)$ the oblique condition is known as a Robin boundary condition.

The algebraic sign requirements imposed on the boundary conditions are generally required for the well-posedness of the resulting boundary value problem for (1.3). A general existence theorem for solutions of elliptic problems with oblique boundary conditions on smooth boundaries may be found in [31, p. 128]

We remark that the oblique boundary condition can be generalized to equations containing u_t [48, p. 96]. When such parabolic problems are approximated by time discrete elliptic problems (as will be done throughout these notes) then the above oblique boundary condition results where $g(x,t)$ grows like $1/\Delta t$.

As we shall see, when (1.3) is degenerate at points of $\partial D(t)$ then the structure of (1.3) determines whether any of the above boundary conditions lead to well-posed problems.

1.2.1   The Fichera function for degenerate equations

The so-called "Fichera function" approach is used to identify those parts of $\partial D(t)$ where the differential equation itself is expected to hold and where no independent boundary conditions can be imposed.

There exists a general theory for the existence, uniqueness and regularity (i.e. smoothness) of solutions for the general second order equation

$$\mathcal{L}u \equiv \sum_{i,j=1}^{m} a_{ij}(y)u_{y_iy_j} + \sum_{i=1}^{m} b_i(y)u_{y_i} + c(y)u = f(y) \qquad (1.31)$$

defined on a bounded open domain $D \subset R_m$ with boundary ∂D, and degeneracy in D and along parts of ∂D. It is generally assumed that $A(y)$ is symmetric and non-negative definite and that $c(y) < 0$. If $A(y)$ is positive definite then (1.31) is said to be an elliptic equation. To apply this general theory to the diffusion equations of finance we identify time with the last component of the vector y. If the submatrix $(a_{ij}(y))$, $1 \leq i,j \leq m-1$ is positive definite and $b_m \neq 0$ then (1.31) is a parabolic equation.

The theory for degenerate equations used here is presented in the monograph [59]. (For a more accessible but early version of the theory see also [29].) It applies to general degenerate equations irrespective of any underlying financial or physical models. Its relevance for financial problems is mentioned but not exploited in [8] in an analytic and numerical study of Asian options. Around the same time it was used in [54] to clarify the boundary conditions for a method of lines solution of a fixed strike Asian option (see also Example 1.16 below). The theory of [59] gives conditions when at points of degeneracy on the boundary ∂D, (i.e. where $A(y)$ has a zero eigenvalue for $y \in \partial D$), one can impose Dirichlet boundary data on (1.31), and when the differential equation itself should hold there. Specifically, it gives sufficient conditions for the existence of weak and classical solutions of (1.31) subject to Dirichlet boundary conditions on the boundary ∂D when $A(y)$ may be singular on parts of ∂D. The theory is quite technical and imposes extensive hypotheses on the structure of the equation (1.31) and the data of the problem which may not be met by financial applications. For example, the application may lead to nonlinar pricing problems as for American options, to a partial-integro-differential equation (a PIDE) as in jump diffusion, to nonlinear terms due to uncertain parameters, or impose derivative boundary conditions like "no convexity" on ∂D rather than Dirichlet conditions. The theory of [59] does not apply to such problems and does not guarantee the existence of a unique solution. However, if its existence can be established by other means, or even if it is simply assumed, then its restriction to ∂D provides Dirichlet data. Similarly, a jump integral then can be considered just a source term for the differential equation and nonlinear terms become data. If the theory of [59] applies to the resulting linear degenerate elliptic Dirichlet problem then its solution must be the same as that of the original problem. In particular, a solution of the pricing problem must satisfy the differential equation on those points of ∂D identified by the theory for degenerate equations. At those points no boundary conditions may be imposed regardless of how sensible they might seem on financial grounds.

We shall assume that the coefficients and the source term are smooth in D, and that the matrix $(a_{ij}(y))$ is symmetric and positive semidefinite so that

$$\langle A(y)z, z \rangle \geq 0 \text{ for every unit vector } z \in R_m,$$

where $\langle w, z \rangle$ denotes the dot product in $\mathbb{R}_m$. Let Σ^0 denote the subset of ∂D where

$$\langle A(y)n, n \rangle = 0$$

where $n = (n_1, \ldots, n_m)$ denotes the inward unit normal at $y \in \partial D$ which is assumed to be defined everywhere on ∂D. $A(y)$ is necessarily degenerate on Σ^0. For each point $y \in \Sigma^0$ we define the so-called Fichera function

$$h(y) = \sum_{i=1}^{m} \left[b_i(y) - \sum_{j=1}^{m} (a_{ij}(y))_{y_j} \right] n_i. \tag{1.32}$$

If we rewrite (1.31) as a diffusion-convection equation

$$\mathcal{L}u \equiv \sum_{j,i=1}^{m} [(a_{ij}(y)u_{y_i}]_{y_j} + \sum_{i,j=1}^{m} \left[b_i(y) - (a_{ij}(y)_{y_j} \right] u_{y_i} + c(y)u = f(y)$$

then the first sum describes the diffusion of the process at y while the second sum collects the convection terms so that (1.32) characterizes the direction of the convection at the point $y \in \partial D$. In particular, the second sum may be related to a directional derivative of u. If we write $\vec{\beta}(y) = (\beta_1(y), \ldots, \beta_m(y))$ where

$$\beta_i(y) = \left[b_i(y) - \sum_{j=1}^{m} a_{ij}(y)_{y_j} \right], \quad i = 1, \ldots, m$$

and if

$$\langle \vec{\beta}(y), n(y) \rangle \leq 0$$

then the convection at $y \in \partial D$ points outward (or is purely tangential). We introduce subsets of Σ^0 defined by

$$\Sigma_0 = \left\{ y \in \Sigma^0 : h(y) = 0 \right\}$$
$$\Sigma_1 = \left\{ y \in \Sigma^0 : h(y) > 0 \right\}$$
$$\Sigma_2 = \left\{ y \in \Sigma^0 : h(y) < 0 \right\}$$
$$\Sigma_3 = \partial D - \Sigma^0.$$

Finally, we shall assume that around each $y \in \partial D$ the boundary can be described by

$$F(y) = 0$$

for a smooth function F with $\nabla F \neq 0$ and $F > 0$ in D.

We shall consider the Dirichlet problem

$$\mathcal{L}u = f \text{ in } D \tag{1.33}$$
$$u = g \text{ on } \Sigma_2 \cup \Sigma_3.$$

Note that no boundary condition is given on $\Sigma_0 \cup \Sigma_1$. Thus the Fichera function identifies the boundary points where the differential equation becomes a consistent boundary condition, provided, of course, all terms of the differential equation have finite limits as one approaches the boundary from within D.

A weak solution of (1.33) is defined to be a bounded measurable function u which for every smooth v vanishing on $\Sigma_1 \cup \Sigma_3$ satisfies the integral identity

$$\int_D u \mathcal{L}^* v \, dy = \int_D f v \, dy - \int_{\Sigma_3} g \left(\frac{\partial v}{\partial \nu} \right) dS + \int_{\Sigma_2} h g v \, dS \tag{1.34}$$

where $\mathcal{L}^*$ is known as the formal adjoint of $\mathcal{L}$ and is defined by

$$\mathcal{L}^* v \equiv \sum_{i,j=1}^{m} a_{ij}(y) v_{y_i y_j} + \sum_{i=1}^{m} b_i^*(y) v_{y_i} + c^*(y) v$$

$$b_i^*(y) = 2 \sum_{j=1}^{m} a_{ij}(y)_{y_j} - b_i(y)$$

$$c^*(y) = \sum_{i,j=1}^{m} a_{ij}(y)_{y_i y_j} - \sum_{i=1}^{m} b_i(y)_y + c(y),$$

and $\frac{\partial v}{\partial \nu}$ is the conormal derivative defined by

$$\frac{\partial v}{\partial \nu} = \sum_{i,j=1}^{m} \left(a_{ij} v_{y_j} \right) n_i$$

((1.34) is obtained by integrating $\int_D v \mathcal{L} u \, dy$ with the divergence theorem and using the degeneracy and imposed boundary conditions on ∂D.)

The following existence theorem may be found in [59]:

Theorem 1.10. *In* (1.31) *suppose that* $c(y) \leq c_0 < 0$ *on* D, *that* f *is a bounded measurable function on* D, *g a bounded measurable function on* $\Sigma_2 \cup \Sigma_3$ *and* $\mathcal{L}F(y) \leq 0$ *at interior points of* $\Sigma_2 \cup \Sigma_0$. *Then there exists a weak solution of the boundary value problem* (1.33).

The hypothesis that $c(y) < c_0 < 0$ is an essential condition used throughout these notes for the analysis and numerical solution of (1.31). If (1.31) is a parabolic equation with $y_m = t$ and

$$b_m(y)u_y = -u_t,$$

or if (1.31) is the time discrete analog of a parabolic equation, then c_0 can be made arbitrarily small through an exponential scaling of u or by taking a sufficiently small time step.

We note that if we choose for v a smooth function with compact support in D (i.e. a function which vanishes in a neighborhood of ∂D) then (1.34) reduces to

$$\int_D u \mathcal{L}^* v \, dy = \int_D f v \, dy. \tag{1.35}$$

It is known that if (1.31) is elliptic or parabolic, and if the coefficients and the source term are smooth, then the weak solution satisfying (1.35) is also smooth in D. In finance the matrix $A(y)$ and f tend to be constant or smooth and bounded so that the weak solution is locally smooth, but it may not be uniquely defined nor need its derivatives be bounded as we approach ∂D.

One may find in [59] conditions under which the weak solution is unique. One may also find there conditions under which the weak solution has bounded derivatives on D guaranteeing that the weak solution satisfies the differential equation on the boundary. These conditions are not straightforward to verify. In addition, corner points on the boundary ∂D may require a sophisticated local analysis. Moreover, we may not know financially sound Dirichlet data on $\Sigma_2 \cup \Sigma_3$. Instead, we may wish to impose

Neumann, reflection, oblique conditions or even tangential diffusion (i.e. a so-called Venttsel boundary condition). In general, there is only limited theory available about the well-posedness of problems with such boundary conditions, and what there is can be quite technical, as may become apparent from the glimpse into this topic given in the next section.

However, if we assume that the problem is well posed then its formulation must be consistent with the Fichera theory for degenerate equations. Hence we need to evaluate the Fichera function to determine the subset $\Sigma_0 \cup \Sigma_1$ of ∂D where no independent boundary conditions can be imposed because the equation has to hold there. To illustrate how this theory might help we shall look at a few examples.

Example 1.11. Boundary conditions for the heat equation.

Given $D = \{(x,t) : 0 < x < 1, 0 < t < T\}$ we shall examine what boundary conditions are required on ∂D to solve the heat equation

$$\mathcal{L}u \equiv u_{xx} - u_t = f, \quad (x,t) \in D.$$

If we set $y = (y_1, y_2) \equiv (x,t)$ then the equation can be rewritten as

$$\mathcal{L}u \equiv u_{y_1 y_1} - u_{y_2} = f(y)$$

so that

$$A = (a_{ij}) = \begin{pmatrix} 1 & 0 \\ 0 & 0 \end{pmatrix}, \quad b_1 = 0, \quad b_2 = -1.$$

Hence in R_2 the heat equation is degenerate everywhere on $\bar{D}$.

The unit normals pointing into D on the boundary ∂D are

$$y_1 \equiv x = 0 : n = (1,0); \quad y_1 \equiv x = 1 : n = (-1,0)$$

$$y_2 \equiv t = 0 : n = (0,1); \quad y_2 \equiv t = T : n = (0,-1).$$

We observe that $\langle An, n \rangle \neq 0$ on $x = 0, 1$ so that these two boundaries belong to Σ_3. Similarly, $\langle An, n \rangle = 0$ on $t = 0, T$ so these two boundaries belong to Σ^0 where the Fichera function needs to be checked. We find on $t = 0$

$$h(y_1, 0) = b_1 n_1 + b_2 n_2 = -1, \quad \text{i.e. } t = 0 \text{ belongs to } \Sigma_2.$$

On $t = T$

$$h(y_1, T) = b_1 n_1 + b_2 n_2 = +1, \quad \text{i.e. } t = T \text{ belongs to } \Sigma_1.$$

If we rewrite the above problem for the new dependent variable $w(x,t)$ defined by

$$u(x,t) = e^{ct}w(x,t)$$

for $c > 0$ we can apply the existence Theorem 1.10 to w and conclude that the heat equation with boundary data

$$u(x,t) = g(x,t) \quad \text{for } x = 0, 1$$
$$u(x,0) = g(x,0) \quad \text{for } 0 < x < 1$$

has a weak solution. In fact, it is well known from the general existence theory for diffusion equations that if f and g are continuous then this solution is also unique and a classical solution. Specifically, this means that on the degenerate boundary $t = T$ the weak solution satisfies the heat equation.

Example 1.12. Boundary condition for the CEV Black Scholes equation at $S = 0$.

The Black Scholes equation for a CEV European put is

$$\frac{1}{2}\sigma^2 x^\alpha u_{xx} + (r - q)x u_x - ru - u_t = 0 \quad \text{for } (x,t) \in (0,X) \times (0,T)$$

where $\sigma, r > 0$, α, $q \geq 0$ and $X \gg 1$ are given constants. We impose the initial and boundary conditions

$$u(x,0) = \max\{1 - x, 0\} \tag{1.36}$$
$$u(0,t) = e^{-\gamma t}, \quad u(X,t) = 0$$

where γ is a constant.

In analogy to Example 1.11 we find

$$A = \begin{pmatrix} \frac{1}{2}\sigma^2 x^\alpha & 0 \\ 0 & 0 \end{pmatrix}, \quad b_1 = (r - q)x, \quad b_2 = -1.$$

Hence the equation is degenerate everywhere in the $x - t$ plane, and for $\alpha > 0$ the boundaries of $(0,X) \times (0,T)$ coinciding with the lines

$$x = 0, \quad t = 0, \quad t = T$$

belong to Σ^0. As above, $x = X$ belongs to Σ_3, $t = 0$ belongs to Σ_2 and $t = T$ belongs to Σ_1.

The boundary $x = 0$ with inward normal $n = (1,0)$ remains to be classified. The Fichera function is

$$h(x,t) = (r - q)x - \frac{1}{2}\sigma^2 \alpha x^{\alpha-1}.$$

Hence for $\alpha > 1$ it follows that in this case

$$\lim_{x \to 0} h(x, t) = 0 \quad \text{so that } x = 0 \text{ belongs to } \Sigma_0.$$

For $\alpha = 1$

$$\lim_{x \to 0} h(x, t) = -\frac{1}{2}\sigma^2 < 0 \quad \text{so } x = 0 \text{ belongs to } \Sigma_2.$$

For $0 < \alpha < 1$

$$h(x, t) \to -\infty \quad \text{as } x \to 0.$$

For $\alpha = 0$ the boundary $x = 0$ belongs to Σ_3.

We conclude that for $\alpha > 1$ the weak solution of the European CEV put is completely specified by the initial and boundary conditions

$$u(x, 0) = \max\{1 - x, 0\}, \quad u(X, t) = 0.$$

If we assume that the weak solution is also unique and smooth (which is known to be the case for $\alpha = 2$), then we require that $u(x, t)$ satisfy the Black Scholes equation on $t = T$, and on $x = 0$ where it reduces to

$$-ru(0, t) - u_t(0, t) = 0$$

so that

$$u(0, t) = u(0, 0)e^{-rt}.$$

Hence the boundary conditions (1.36) can be correct only if $\gamma = r$ whenever $\alpha > 1$.

For $0 < \alpha < 1$ the exposition of [59] gives no information, while for $\alpha = 0$ the boundary $x = 0$ supports Dirichlet data as in Example 1.11. We conjecture that the problem is solvable with Dirichlet data

$$u(0, t) = g(t) \quad \text{for } 0 \leq \alpha \leq 1.$$

For continuity of the solution with respect to the CEV index α a natural choice would be

$$g(t) = u(0, 0)e^{-rt}.$$

Example 1.13. Boundary conditions for a discount bond at $r = 0$.

Suppose the bond equation is of the form

$$\frac{1}{2}\sigma^2 r^\alpha u_{rr} + (\eta - \mu r)u_r - ru - u_t = 0, \quad (r, t) \in (0, R) \times (0, T)$$

defined for $\alpha \geq 0$ with $R \gg 0$. Here again the boundary of $(0, R) \times (0, T)$ belongs to Σ_2 when $t = 0$, to Σ_1 when $t = T$ and to Σ_3 when $r = R$. Hence the demands of the theorem are consistent with the standard conditions imposed on bond prices

$$u(r, 0) = 1$$
$$u(R, t) = e^{-Rt}$$

$u(r, t)$ satisfies the bond equation at $t = T$.

It remains to examine $r = 0$ where $n = (1, 0)$ in the $r - t$ plane. If $\alpha = 0$ then $r = 0$ belongs to Σ_3. If $\alpha > 0$ the Fichera function is

$$h(r, t) = (\eta - \mu r) - \frac{1}{2}\sigma^2 \alpha r^{\alpha - 1}.$$

It follows that

$$\lim_{r \to 0} h(r, t) = \eta > 0 \quad \text{for } \alpha > 1$$

$$\lim_{r \to 0} h(r, t) = \eta - \frac{1}{2}\sigma^2 \quad \text{for } \alpha = 1.$$

Hence at $r = 0$ the bond equation needs no boundary condition when $\alpha > 1$, no boundary condition when $\alpha = 1$ and $\eta \geq \frac{\sigma^2}{2}$, and a boundary condition when $\eta < \frac{\sigma^2}{2}$. We conjecture again that there is a solution for the Dirichlet condition

$$u(0, t) = g(t) \quad \text{when } 0 \leq \alpha < 1. \quad \cdot$$

We point out that the case $\alpha = 1$ describes the bond equation based on the one-factor CIR interest rate model. It has been investigated at length in the financial literature, primarily by exploiting the probabilistic interpretation of the bond equation. The inequality

$$\eta > \frac{1}{2}\sigma^2$$

is known as the Feller condition. If it holds and even if $h(0, t) = 0$, the bond equation must be satisfied at $r = 0$. If it does not hold, one can impose a Dirichlet condition. This Dirichlet condition could be the analytic solution

$$B(r, t) = A(t)e^{B(t)r}\big|_{r=0} \tag{1.37}$$

known for the CIR model which satisfies the bond equation for all $r \geq 0$ and thus yields a solution which is continuous with respect to the parameters of the problem irrespective of the Feller condition. Alternatively, one can impose

$$B_0(0, t) = 0, \quad t > 0$$

for which there also is an analytic solution [35]. (This solution is discontinuous at $t = 0$ since $B_0(0,0) = 1$ but may be thought of as the limit of smooth solutions.) For any other choice with $B(0,t) \geq 0$ it follows from the maximum principle that

$$B(r,t) \geq B_0(r,t).$$

We refer to [35] where these different cases are given a financial interpretation.

For an extensive discussion of the numerical solution of the bond equation for $\alpha = 1$ we refer to [4], where finite difference and Monte Carlo methods are compared, to the finite difference calculation of [25], and to a mathematical analysis of the bond equation for $\alpha = 1$ based on its probabilistic interpretation [26]. We also refer to the numerical approach of Chapter 6 where (1.37) is shown to yield a useful boundary condition for the bond equation for all $\alpha \geq 0$.

Example 1.14. Boundary conditions for the Black Scholes equation on two assets.

Consider the Black Scholes equation for an option on two assets

$$\frac{1}{2}\sigma_1^2 x_1^2 u_{x_1 x_1} + \rho\sigma_1\sigma_2 x_1 x_2 u_{x_1 x_2} + \frac{1}{2}\sigma_2^2 \sigma^2 u_{x_2 x_2}$$

$$+ (r - q_1)x_1 u_{x_1} + (r - q_2)x_2 u_{x_2} - ru - u_t = 0 \qquad (1.38)$$

defined on $(0, X_1) \times (0, X_2) \times (0, T)$. We assume that $|\rho| < 1$. With the identification

$$y = (y_1, y_2, y_3) = (x_1, x_2, t)$$

we see that

$$A(y) = \begin{pmatrix} \frac{1}{2}\sigma_1^2 x_1^2 & \frac{1}{2}\sigma_1\sigma_2 x_1 x_2 & 0 \\ \frac{1}{2}\sigma_1\sigma_2 x_1 x_2 & \frac{1}{2}\sigma_2^2 x_2^2 & 0 \\ 0 & 0 & 0 \end{pmatrix}$$

and

$$h(x_1, x_2, t) = \left((r - q_1)x_1 - \sigma_1^2 x_1 - \frac{1}{2}\rho\sigma_1\sigma_2 x_1 \right) n_1$$

$$+ \left((r - q_2)x_2 - \frac{1}{2}\rho\sigma_1\sigma_2 x_2 - \sigma_2^2 x_2 \right) n_2 - n_3.$$

All points on the boundary of $(0, X_1) \times (0, X_2) \times (0, T)$ are points of degeneracy because $A(y)$ is a singular matrix. Let us consider the boundary coinciding with the plane $y_1 \equiv x_1 = 0$. Here the inward normal is

$$n = (1, 0, 0)$$

so that $\langle An, n \rangle = 0$ and

$$h(0, x_2, t) = 0.$$

We conclude that on $x_1 = 0$ no boundary data should be given. Instead $u(0, x_2, t)$ should satisfy (1.38) for $x_1 = 0$. On the plane $x_1 = X$ we have $n = (-1, 0, 0)$ and $\langle An, n \rangle > 0$ so that a boundary condition can be imposed at $x_1 = X$. Analogous results hold for $x_2 = 0$ and $x_2 = X_2$.

We remark that for American options it seems natural to require that the one-dimensional solutions on $x_1 = 0$ and $x_2 = 0$ satisfy the corresponding early exercise free boundary conditions.

On $t = 0$ we have $n = (0, 0, 1)$ so that $h(x_1, x_2, 0) = -1$. Hence as usual an initial condition (the pay-off) should be given at $t = 0$. At $t = T$ we have $n = (0, 0, -1)$ so that $h(x_1, x_2, T) = 1$ which suggests that Black Scholes equation should hold at $t = T$.

Example 1.15. Boundary conditions for the Black Scholes equation with stochastic volatility v at $S = 0$ and $v = 0$.

Considerations similar to Example 1.13 apply when the volatility in the Black Scholes equation is stochastic. If the Heston square root model

$$dS = (r - q)S\,dt + \sqrt{v}S\,dW_1$$
$$dv = k(\theta - v)dt + \sigma\sqrt{v}\,dW_2$$

is employed, then the pricing equation for an option on a single asset S can be written in the form (see, e.g. [15])

$$\frac{vS^2}{2}V_{SS} + \rho\sigma vSV_{Sv} + \frac{\sigma^2 v}{2}V_{vv} + (r - q)SV_S$$
$$+ (k(\theta - v) - \lambda v)V_v - rV - V_t = 0 \tag{1.39}$$

where r, k, θ and σ are positive parameters, where $q, \lambda \geq 0$, and where $|\rho| < 1$. The equation is defined on

$$0 < S < \infty, \quad 0 < v < \infty, \quad t \in (0, T].$$

The corresponding coefficient matrix is

$$A = \begin{pmatrix} \frac{vS^2}{2} & \frac{\rho\sigma vS}{2} & 0 \\ \frac{\rho\sigma vS}{2} & \frac{\sigma^2 v}{2} & 0 \\ 0 & 0 & 0 \end{pmatrix}$$

which is singular everywhere. For the boundaries $S = 0$, $v = 0$ and $t = 0$ we have the corresponding inward normals $(1, 0, 0)$, $(0, 1, 0)$ and $(0, 0, 1)$, while the inward normal on $t = T$ is $(0, 0, -1)$. We observe that $\langle An, n \rangle = 0$ at all of these boundary points which therefore belong to Σ^0. The Fichera function is

$$h(S, v, t) = \left((r - q)S - \left(vS + \frac{\rho\sigma S}{2} \right) \right) n_1$$
$$+ \left(k(\theta - v) - \lambda v - \left(\frac{\rho\sigma v}{2} + \frac{\sigma^2}{2} \right) \right) n_2 - n_3.$$

On $v = 0$ we obtain the Feller expression

$$h(S, 0, t) = k\theta - \frac{\sigma^2}{2}.$$

A boundary condition can be imposed on $v = 0$ when $h < 0$ while the differential equation should hold on $v = 0$ when $h \geq 0$, i.e.

$$(r - q)SV_S + \kappa\theta V_v - rV - V_t = 0. \tag{1.40}$$

If $h(S, 0, t) < 0$ then a Dirichlet condition could be imposed which is not necessarily consistent with a solution of (1.40) and the resulting solution of (1.40) would not be continuous with respect to the parameters of the Feller expression. However, as shown in Example 1.22 below, equation (1.40) has the correct structure to serve as an admissible oblique boundary condition on $v = 0$ for the pricing equation (1.40) because

$$\langle ((r - q)S, \kappa\theta, -1), n \rangle = \kappa\theta > 0$$

for the inward normal $n = (0, 1, 0)$ in $S - v - t$ space at $v = 0$. If (1.39) can be solved subject to the boundary condition (1.40) on $v = 0$ then, as in Example 1.13, the solution will be expected to be continuous with respect to the parameters regardless of the algebraic sign of $\kappa\theta - \sigma^2/2$.

On $t = 0$ we see that $h(S, v, 0) = 1$ so we can impose the pay-off for the option at maturity as initial condition on (1.39) while at $t = T$ the differential equation holds.

On $S = 0$ we see that $h(0, v, t) = 0$ so that the differential equation

$$\frac{\sigma^2 v}{2} V_{vv} + [k(\theta - v) - \lambda v]V_v(0, v, t) - rV(0, v, t) - V_t(0, v, t) = 0 \tag{1.41}$$

should hold.

As in the constant volatility case one can argue on the basis of the stochastic differential equation for the asset S that if $S(t)$ ever reaches 0 it will remain 0 and hence that the value of a European option on S should just be its discounted pay-off value

$$V(0, v, t) = V_0(0, 0)e^{-rt}$$

whenever $V_0(S, 0)$ is a volatility-independent pay-off.

It may not be obvious that this conclusion is consistent with equation (1.41). However, it is straightforward to show with the maximum principle that a solution of (1.41) cannot have a positive maximum on $0 < v < \infty$ and $t \in (0, T]$. If $\kappa\theta \geq \sigma^2/2$ then the Fichera function $h(v, t)$ associated with (1.41) implies that at $v = 0$ the equation (1.41) has to hold so that

$$\kappa\theta V_v(0, 0, t) - rV(0, 0, t) - V_t(0, 0, t) = 0.$$

This equation rules out that $V(0, 0, t)$ is a positive maximum. Analogous considerations rule out that $V(0, 0, t)$ is a negative minimum. If the boundary condition imposed on (1.41) as $v \to \infty$ likewise rules out a nonzero extremum on $(0, \infty)$ then the solution of (1.41) is unique. If

$$V(0, v, 0) = V_0(0, 0)$$

then this solution is

$$V(0, v, t) = V_0(0, 0)e^{-rt},$$

which can also serve as a solution of (1.41) when $\kappa\theta < \sigma^2/2$. For numerical simulations the boundary condition for (1.39) as $v \to \infty$ is frequently replaced by

$$V_v(S, v_{\max}, t) = 0$$

for $v_{\max} < \infty$ [18]. This condition does rule out a non-zero extremum at $v_{\max}$. Comments on this boundary condition for (1.39) can be found in the next section.

Example 1.16. Boundary conditions for an Asian option.

In the final example we shall consider the Black Scholes equation for an Asian option discussed in [46, p. 286]. Its price is a function of the underlying x, the average a of a price process over $(0, t)$ and the time to expiration t and satisfies:

$$\frac{1}{2}\sigma^2 x^2 u_{xx} + rxu_x + \frac{1}{T}xu_a - ru - u_t = 0, \quad (x, a, t) \in (0, X) \times (0, B) \times (0, T)$$
$$(1.42)$$

with pay-off

$$u(x, a, 0) = \max\{0, a - K\}$$

where X, B and T are finite. If the Fichera theory is applied to $y = (x, a, t)$ then

$$A(x) = \begin{pmatrix} \frac{1}{2}\sigma^2 x^2 & 0 & 0 \\ 0 & 0 & 0 \\ 0 & 0 & 0 \end{pmatrix}$$

$$h(x, a, t) = (rx - \sigma^2 x)n_1 + \left(\frac{1}{T}x\right)n_2 - n_3.$$

The discussion of Example 1.12 shows that the Black Scholes equation (1.42) should hold at $x = 0$ and $t = T$ while at $x = X$ and $t = 0$ data are required. Note that at $x = 0$ the equation (1.42) reduces to

$$-ru - u_t = 0$$

so that

$$u(0, a, t) = u(0, a, 0)e^{-rt}.$$

On the boundary coinciding with the plane $a = 0$ the normal vector is $n = (0, 1, 0)$ so that

$$h(x, 0, t) = \frac{1}{T}x > 0 \quad \text{for } x \in (0, X).$$

Hence we expect the Black Scholes equation to hold for $a = 0$. On the other hand, on $a = B$ the unit vector is $n = (0, -1, 0)$ so that the points (x, B, t) belong to Σ_2 which would call for a boundary condition.

The missing boundary condition at $a = B$ is read off an analytic solution of (1.42)

$$u(x, a, t) = (a - K)e^{-rt} + \frac{1}{Tr}(1 - e^{-rt})x \qquad (1.43)$$

which is assumed to hold for $a \gg K$, while

$$u_x(X, a, t) = \frac{1}{Tr}(1 - e^{-rt})$$

is suggested on financial grounds as an approximation to the delta at $x = X \gg 1$ for $a \in (0, B)$ (see [42] and Example 1.20).

In all examples of parabolic problems where $a_{im} = 0$ for $i = 1, \ldots, m$, the Fichera theory always requires the same behavior at expiration $t = 0$ and at any future time (to expiry) $t > 0$, namely if $y = (x, t)$ then at $t = 0$ we can impose the pay-off u_0 of the option

$$u(x, 0) = u_0(x)$$

while $u(x, t)$ at $t = T$ satisfies the pricing equation for $x \in D(T)$. This, of course, is expected. Therefore, the application of the Fichera function can be simplied if one treats t as a parameter and u_t as data and considers the equation (1.31) as a time independent elliptic equation in the "spatial" variables $x_1, x_2, \ldots, x_{m-1}$. The Fichera function (1.32) now is defined by the first $m - 1$ terms of the sum and the vector $n = (n_1, \ldots, n_{m-1})$ is the inward normal to the boundary $\partial D(t)$ at some fixed t. Alternatively, one can apply the Fichera approach at each time level to the time-discretized pricing equation. In this case the condition of $c(y) \leq c_0 < 0$ in Theorem 1.10 can always be achieved for sufficiently small Δt.

We also would like to mention that there exists an extension of the Fichera theory to problems with Neumann boundary conditions instead of Dirichlet conditions on $\Sigma_2 \cup \Sigma_3$ [58]. The solution of the problem is interpreted to be a stochastic solution, and the tools of probability are used to establish its existence and properties. This theory also ties into problems with Venttsel boundary conditions considered in the next section. The implication of this work for the pricing problem, particularly for multifactor models, remains unexplored.

1.2.2   *The boundary condition at "infinity"*

The Fichera theory can sometimes be adapted to give some insight into consistent boundary conditions for the Black Scholes equation (1.1) as $S \to \infty$. To illustrate this point let us revisit the CEV equation of Example 1.12.

Example 1.17. CEV puts and calls.

We wish to consider the behavior of the solution of

$$\frac{1}{2}\sigma^2 x^\alpha u_{xx} + (r - q)x u_x - ru - u_t = 0$$

as $x \to \infty$. We make the formal change of variable

$$z = \frac{1}{x}$$

so that

$$u_x = u_z \left(-\frac{1}{x^2}\right), \quad u_{xx} = u_{zz}\left(\frac{1}{x^4}\right) + u_z\left(\frac{2}{x^3}\right).$$

The CEV Black Scholes equation is now

$$\frac{1}{2}\sigma^2 z^{4-\alpha} u_{zz} + (\sigma^2 z^{3-\alpha} - (r - q)z)u_z - ru - u_t = 0 \tag{1.44}$$

defined for $0 < z < \infty$ and $t \in (0, T]$. The question of whether the CEV equation needs a boundary condition at infinity or whether the differential equation should hold there now is answered by considering the Fichera function $h(z, t)$ for (1.44) at $z = 0$ where

$$h(z, t) = \left[\sigma^2 \left(1 - \frac{4 - \alpha}{2} \right) z^{3-\alpha} - (r - q)z \right] n_1 - n_2.$$

Suppose that $\alpha < 3$ then at $z = 0$ we have the inward normal $n = (1, 0)$ and find

$$\lim_{z \to 0} h(z, t) = 0$$

so that formally the point at infinity belongs to Σ_0.

If the pay-off $u(z, 0)$ is bounded on $(0, \infty)$ then Theorem 1.10 suggests that the differential equation should hold at $z = 0$, i.e.

$$\lim_{z \to 0} [-ru(z, t) - u_t(z, t)] = 0.$$

This implies that

$$\lim_{z \to 0} u(z, t) = \lim_{z \to 0} u(z, 0)e^{-rt} = \lim_{x \to \infty} u(x, 0)e^{-rt}.$$

For a put we have $u(x, 0) = 0$ for $x > K$ so that we have the familiar condition

$$\lim_{x \to \infty} u(x, t) = 0.$$

For a European call $\lim_{x \to \infty} u(x, 0) = \infty$ so the pay-off is not bounded and Theorem 1.10 does not apply. However, the initial delta is bounded. We may assume that the call price is smooth for $t > 0$. Then formal differentiation of the CEV Black Scholes equation shows that the delta

$$u_x(x, t) \equiv \phi(x, t)$$

satisfies the partial differential equation

$$\frac{1}{2}\sigma^2 x^\alpha \phi_{xx} + (r - q)x\phi_x - r\phi - \phi_t + \frac{1}{2}\sigma^2 \alpha x^{\alpha-1}\phi_x + (r - q)\phi = 0.$$

In terms of the variable $z = 1/x$ we obtain

$$\frac{1}{2}\sigma^2 z^{4-\alpha}\phi_{zz} + \left[\sigma^2 \left(\left(1 - \frac{\alpha}{2} \right) z^{3-\alpha} - (r - q)z \right] \phi_z - q\phi - \phi_t = 0.$$

Again, the Fichera function at $z = 0$ is of interest. We see that

$$h(z, t) = \left\{ \left[\sigma^2 \left(1 - \frac{\alpha}{2} \right) z^{3-\alpha} - (r - q)z \right] - \sigma^2 \frac{4 - \alpha}{2} z^{3-\alpha} \right\} n_1 - n_2.$$

For $\alpha < 3$ we see that $h(0, t) = 0$ so that by Theorem 1.10 the differential equation should hold at $z = 0$. It follows that

$$\lim_{z \to 0} \phi(z, t) = \lim_{z \to 0} \phi(z, 0)e^{-qt} = \lim_{x \to \infty} u_x(x, 0)e^{-qt} = e^{-qt}$$

which is the familiar boundary condition for the delta of a call at infinity.

We emphasize that this conclusion follows from the PDE theory and the pay-off at maturity and not from financial arguments or the Black Scholes formula.

Example 1.18. Puts and calls with stochastic volatility.

In numerical simulations of puts and calls with stochastic volatility following the Heston square root model the scaled pricing equation (1.14) for $x = S/K$, $y \equiv v$ and $u(x, y, t) = V(S, v, t)/K$ is

$$\frac{yx^2}{2}u_{xx} + \rho\sigma xyu_{xy} + \frac{\sigma^2 y}{2}u_{yy} + (r - q)xu_x + [\kappa(\theta - y) - \lambda y]u_y - ru - u_t = 0 \tag{1.45}$$

for $0 < x < \infty$ and $0 < y < \infty$. The initial condition for (1.45) is unambiguously determined by the option, and for an American put and call the boundary condition for large x is also known. Moreover, according to Example 1.15 the equation

$$\frac{\sigma^2 y}{2}u_{yy}(0, y, t) + [\kappa(\theta - y) - y]u_y(0, y, t) - ru(0, y, t) - u_t(0, y, t) = 0$$

has to hold on $x = 0$. We already observed that $u(0, y, t)$ cannot have a positive maximum on $[0, \infty)$ for $t > 0$. If at $y = y_{\max} < \infty$ we know $u(0, y_{\max}, t)$ or that $\frac{\partial u}{\partial y}(0, y_{\max}, t) = 0$ then

$$u(0, y, t) = u(0, y_{\max}, 0)e^{-rt}.$$

The problem now is to determine what boundary condition is admissible as $y_{\max} \to \infty$. We shall examine whether the Fichera function approach can yield any insight.

As in the previous example we shall write

$$z = \frac{1}{y}, \quad \tilde{u}(x, z, t) = u\left(x, \frac{1}{z}, t\right).$$

Then

$$u_y = -z^2\tilde{u}_z, \quad u_{yy} = z^4\tilde{u}_{zz} + 2z^3\tilde{u}_z.$$

Substitution into (1.45) leads to

$$\frac{x^2}{2}\tilde{u}_{xx} - \rho\sigma xz^2\tilde{u}_{xz} + \frac{\sigma^2}{2}\left[z^4\tilde{u}_{zz} + 2z^3\tilde{u}_z\right] + (r - q)xz\tilde{u}_x$$

$$- [\kappa(\theta z - 1) - \lambda] z^2 \tilde{u}_z - rz\tilde{u} - z\tilde{u}_t = 0 \tag{1.46}$$

It is clear by inspection that the equation (1.46) is degenerate on the boundary $z = 0$.

The associated Fichera function (considering t a parameter) is

$$h(x, z) \equiv [(r - q)xz - x + \rho\sigma xz]n_1$$

$$+ \left[-\kappa((\theta z - 1) - \lambda)z^2 + \sigma^2 z^3 + \frac{1}{2}\rho\sigma z^2 - 2\sigma^2 z^3 \right] n_2.$$

Since $n = (0, 1)$ at $z = 0$ in the $x - z$ plane we see that

$$h(x, 0) = 0.$$

This would suggest that the differential equation hold for $z = 0$ so that

$$\tilde{u}_{xx} = 0, \quad \text{or} \quad \tilde{u}(x, 0, t) = a(t)x + b(t), \quad x > 0.$$

The boundary conditions for a scaled European call and put

$$\lim_{y \to \infty} c(x, y, t) = e^{-qt}x$$

and

$$\lim_{y \to \infty} p(x, y, t) = e^{-rt}$$

which are read off the Black Scholes formulas as the volatility increases, would be consistent with this equation.

Unfortunately, the coefficient $-rz$ of $\tilde{u}$ in (1.46) is not strictly negative for $z \geq 0$, so Theorem 1.10 does not necessarily apply. It would apply to the time discrete problem if the term $z\tilde{u}_t$ in (1.46) were perturbed to

$$\alpha(z)\tilde{u}_t \text{ for } \alpha(z) = \max\{\epsilon, z\}, \quad \epsilon > 0.$$

For each $\epsilon > 0$ the European and call and put boundary conditions would hold. However, it is not obvious whether they remain valid for $\epsilon = 0$.

It is doubtful that the boundary conditions for a European put or call can be applied at some computational boundary $y_{\max} < \infty$. They also rule out early exercise and would therefore be incorrect for American options defined on $0 \leq y \leq y_{\max}$. For additional comments see Example 1.22.

Example 1.19. The European max option.

Consider the European max option described by equation (1.38) and the pay-off

$$u(x, y, 0) = \max\{\max(x, y) - K, 0\}$$

for some strike price $K > 0$ and $0 < x < \infty$, $0 < y < \infty$, $t \in (0, T]$.

Since the pay-off is unbounded we deduce from Example 1.17 that the Fichera theory will yield little information about $u(x, y, t)$ as $x \to \infty$ or $y \to \infty$. Let us consider instead the delta

$$u_x(x, y, t) \equiv \phi(x, y, t).$$

It follows from the pay-off that

$$\phi(x, y, 0) = \begin{cases} 1, & \text{if } x > \max\{K, y\} \\ 0, & \text{otherwise.} \end{cases}$$

Assuming again that $u(x, y, t)$ is smooth for $t > 0$ we differentiate (1.38) with respect to x and obtain the equation

$$\frac{1}{2}\sigma_1^2 x^2 \phi_{xx} + \rho\sigma_1\sigma_2 xy\phi_{xy} + \frac{1}{2}\sigma_2^2 y^2 \phi_{yy}$$
$$+ (r - q_1 + \sigma_1^2)x\phi_x + (r - q_2 + \rho\sigma_1\sigma_2)y\phi_y - q_1\phi - \phi_t = 0. \tag{1.47}$$

In order to consider the behavior of ϕ as $x \to \infty$ we make the change of variable

$$z = \frac{1}{x}.$$

In terms of (z, y, t) equation (1.47) becomes

$$\frac{1}{2}\sigma_1^2 z^2 \phi_{zz} - \rho\sigma_1\sigma_2 zy\phi_{zy} + \frac{1}{2}\sigma_2^2 y^2 \phi_{yy}$$
$$- (r - q_1)z\phi_z + (r - q_2 + \rho\sigma_1\sigma_2)y\phi_y - q_1\phi - \phi_t = 0.$$

The coefficient matrix $A(z, y, t)$ is given by

$$A(z, y, t) = \begin{pmatrix} \frac{1}{2}\sigma_1^2 z^2 & -\frac{1}{2}\rho\sigma_1\sigma_2 zy & 0 \\ -\frac{1}{2}\rho\sigma_1\sigma_2 zy & \frac{1}{2}\sigma_2^2 y^2 & 0 \\ 0 & 0 & 0 \end{pmatrix}$$

and the Fichera function is

$$h(z, y, t) = \left[-(r - q_1)z - \sigma_1^2 z + \frac{1}{2}\rho\sigma_1\sigma_2 z \right] n_1$$
$$+ \left[(r - q_2)y + \frac{3}{2}\rho\sigma_1\sigma_2 y - \sigma_2^2 y \right] n_2 - n_3.$$

On $z = 0$ where $n = (1, 0, 0)$ we have

$$h(0, y, t) = 0$$

which suggests that the differential equation should hold at $z = 0$. Hence

$$\lim_{x \to \infty} u_x(x, y, t) = \phi(0, y, t)$$

where $\phi(0, y, t)$ is a solution of

$$\frac{1}{2}\sigma_2^2 y^2 \phi_{yy} + (r - q_2 + \rho\sigma_1\sigma_2)y\phi_y - q_1\phi - \phi_t = 0$$

$$\phi(0, y, 0) = \lim_{x \to \infty} u_x(x, y, 0) = 1. \tag{1.48}$$

We note that the initial value problem (1.48) has the solution

$$\lim_{x \to \infty} u_x(x, y, t) = \phi(0, y, t) = e^{-q_1 t}.$$

Hence the boundary condition for the delta u_x of the max option as $x \to \infty$ is the same as the delta for a simple European call. Analogous results can be derived for $u_x(x, y, t)$ as $y \to \infty$ and for $u_y(x, y, t)$ as $x, y \to \infty$.

Example 1.20. An Asian average price call.

We conclude with a qualitative discussion of the boundary condition

$$\lim_{x \to \infty} u_x(x, a, t) = \frac{1}{\text{Tr}}(1 - e^{-rt}) \tag{1.49}$$

suggested in [42] for the Asian option of Example 1.16. It follows from equation (1.42) and the pay-off that

$$u_x(x, a, t) = \phi(x, a, t)$$

satisfies

$$\frac{1}{2}\sigma^2 x^2 \phi_{xx} + \sigma^2 x\phi_x + rx\phi_x + r\phi + \frac{x}{T}\phi_a + \frac{1}{T}u_a - r\phi - \phi_t = 0$$

$$\phi(x, a, 0) = 0.$$

With the change of variable

$$z = \frac{1}{x}$$

the equation is transformed into

$$\frac{1}{2}\sigma^2 z^3 \phi_{zz} - rz^2 \phi_z + \frac{1}{T}\phi_a - z\phi_t = -\frac{z}{T}u_a(z, a, t).$$

The Fichera function is

$$h(z, a, t) = \left[-rz^2 - \frac{3}{2}\sigma^2 z^2\right]n_1 + \frac{1}{T}n_2 - zn_3.$$

For $z = 0$ we have $n = (1, 0, 0)$ so that

$$h(0, a, t) = 0.$$

Hence $z = 0$ belongs to Σ_0 and the differential equation should hold. If we assume that the function $u_a(x, a, t)$ is bounded then the differential equation reduces to

$$\phi_a(0, a, t) = 0.$$

Thus $\lim_{x \to \infty} u_x(x, a, t)$ is a function of time only so that (1.49) is consistent with the demands of the Fichera theory.

1.2.3   The Venttsel boundary conditions on "far but finite" boundaries

When boundary conditions for the pricing equation are known at infinity then it is common to impose them, or a rational modification of them, on the far boundaries of a finite computational domain. For example, for numerical work a put with strike price K defined in $(0, \infty) \times (0, T]$ with boundary condition

$$\lim_{S \to \infty} P(S, t) = 0$$

is typically replaced with a barrier put on $(0, 3K) \times (0, T]$ with boundary condition

$$P(3K, t) = 0.$$

Similarly, a bond with boundary condition

$$\lim_{r \to \infty} B(r, t) = 0$$

can be solved numerically over $(0, R) \times (0, T]$ with boundary condition

$$B(R, t) = e^{-Rt}.$$

Finally, Example 1.19 suggests that the European max option can be solved on a bounded interval $0 < x < X$ with the boundary condition

$$u_x(X, y, t) = \phi(y, t)$$

where $\phi(y, t)$ is a solution of equation (1.48) subject to the initial condition

$$\phi(y, 0) = u_x(X, y, 0) = \begin{cases} 1, & y < X \\ 0, & y \geq X. \end{cases}$$

The problem is more complicated when no boundary conditions at infinity are known. In this case it is often suggested that the differential equation itself can be used to define a boundary condition on the boundary of a finite computational domain. For example, one can postulate that the gamma of the option is negligible and then impose the remaining terms of the equation as a boundary condition (see, e.g. [63, p. 120]). We would like to point out again that one has to insure that the financial considerations underlying such approximation are consistent with the mathematical requirements of the theory that guarantees the existence, uniqueness and computability of the solution of the resulting boundary value problem.

The pricing equation itself or some simplification of it can sometimes be justified as a boundary condition if it is a so-called Venttsel boundary condition. To introduce the concept in a simple but still useful setting for pricing equations consider equation (1.3) on the domain $D(t) \subset R_m$. Let us assume that a part of the boundary of $D(t)$ coincides with the plane $x_m = c$ where c is a constant and x_m is the last component of the vector $x = (x_1, \ldots, x_m)$.

Definition. The equation

$$\mathcal{L}_V u = \sum_{i,j=1}^{m-1} \alpha_{ij}(x,t) u_{x_i x_j} + \sum_{i=1}^{m} \beta_i(x,t) u_{x_i} + \gamma(x,t) u - u_t = f(x,t) \quad (1.50)$$

for $\gamma \leq 0$ defines a Venttsel boundary condition on $x_m = c$ for (1.3) if the $(m-1) \times (m-1)$ matrix (α_{ij}) is symmetric and non-negative definite, and if the vector

$$\beta(x,t) = (\beta_1(x,t), \ldots, \beta_m(x,t))$$

points inward into $D(t)$ at all points of $\partial D(t) \cap \{x : x_m = c\}$, i.e. if for an inward normal vector $n(x)$ at the boundary point x the dot product $\langle n, \beta \rangle$ satisfies

$$\langle n(x), \beta(x,t) \rangle \geq 0. \quad (1.51)$$

Thus in the boundary operator $\mathcal{L}_V$ only tangential second order derivatives occur while the convective terms define a so-called oblique derivative of u along an inward pointing vector $\beta(x,t)$. (We remark that the concept of Venttsel boundary conditions extends naturally to boundaries of the form

$$x_m = f(x_1, \ldots, x_{m-1}).)$$

It follows from the theory for parabolic problems with Venttsel boundary conditions given in [66], [3] that if (1.3) is a uniformly parabolic equation and the matrix (α_{ij}) is positive semi-definite then depending on technical smoothness assumptions on the data and the domain $D(t)$ the equation (1.3) with the Venttsel boundary condition and a smooth initial condition has a unique weak or classical solution.

For applications in finance we usually find a mixture of Venttsel, oblique, Neumann and Dirichlet conditions on the boundary $\partial D(t)$ of the computational domain, which is only piecewise smooth. Moreover, (1.3) is often degenerate on parts of $\partial D(t)$. This more general setting has apparently not been considered yet in the PDE literature. Nonetheless, wherever Venttsel boundary conditions are imposed one would expect that the convective terms define an admissible oblique derivative so that (1.51) holds whenever u_t is present in the boundary conditions.

To provide a glimpse into Venttsel boundary conditions for equations in finance we shall consider in detail for two examples the boundary conditions obtained from the pricing equation itself. We emphasize that our discussion can only give some qualitative insight into computational practice because our rectangular computational domain does not satisfy the smoothness assumptions required for the Venttsel theory. In particular, an analysis of the correct behavior of the solution at the corner points is lacking. It is not clear if requiring only continuity of the solution in the corners will give a well-posed problem, or to what extent financial information leading to Dirichlet or Neumann conditions can be incorporated.

Example 1.21. A defaultable bond.

The pricing equation for a defaultable bond [63] or a mortgage [60] based on a CIR interest rate model is of the following form

$$\mathcal{L}u = a_{11}(x,r,t)u_{xx} + a_{12}(x,r,t)u_{xr} + a_{22}(x,r,t)u_{rr}$$
$$+ (r-q)xu_x + k(\theta - r)u_r - \gamma u - u_t = f(x,r,t) \qquad (1.52)$$

where

$$a_{11}(x,r,t) = \frac{1}{2}\sigma_x^2 x^2, \quad a_{12}(x,r,t) = \rho\sigma_x\sigma_r x\sqrt{r}, \quad a_{22}(x,r,t) = \frac{1}{2}\sigma_r^2 r$$

and

$$0 < x < X, \quad 0 < r < R, \quad t \in (0,T].$$

Numerical experiments are reported in [63, p. 225] where (1.52) is solved with finite difference stencils which depend on whether the mesh point is in the interior or on the boundary of the computational domain. No external boundary data are provided.

By inspection $\mathcal{L}u$ is degenerate on $x = 0$ and $r = 0$. In order to apply the concept of Venttsel boundary conditions, and consistent with the computational practice of Chapter 7, we shall regularize the equation by allowing a small diffusion on $x = 0$ and $r = 0$. We shall set

$$a_{11}(x,r,t) = \max\left\{\frac{1}{2}\sigma_x^2 x^2, \epsilon\right\}, \quad a_{22}(x,r,t) = \max\left\{\frac{1}{2}\sigma_r^2 r, \epsilon\right\}$$

for $0 < \epsilon \ll 1$. For $|\rho| < 1$ the regularized equation (1.52) is non-degenerate on the entire computational domain and can sustain Dirichlet, Neumann or reflection boundary conditions on parts of the boundary. We shall now see how the pricing equation itself can be used to define admissible Venttsel boundary conditions.

$x = 0$: The inward normal in the $x - r$ plane is $n = (1,0)$. The oblique derivative is

$$\langle (0, k(\theta - r)), (1,0) \rangle = 0.$$

Hence

$$a_{22}(0,r,t)u_{rr} + k(\theta - r)u_r - \gamma u - u_t = f(0,r,t)$$

is an admissible Venttsel boundary condition. In other words, equation (1.52) itself applies on $x = 0$.

$r = 0$: The inward normal is $n = (0,1)$. The oblique derivative is

$$\langle ((r - q)x, k\theta), (0,1) \rangle = k\theta > 0$$

so that (1.52) on $r = 0$

$$a_{11}(x,0,t)u_{xx} + (r - q)xu_x + k\theta u_r - \gamma u - u_t = f(x,0,t)$$

is an admissible Venttsel boundary condition.

$x = X$: The inward normal is $n = (-1,0)$. The oblique derivative is

$$\langle (r - q)X, k(\theta - r)), (-1,0) \rangle < 0 \quad \text{for } r > q$$

so that (1.52) with only the tangential second order derivative $a_{22}(X,r,t)\, u_{rr}(X,r,t)$ is not an admissible Venttsel boundary condition if $r > q$.

We note that in [60] the term $(r-q)Xu_x$ is dropped for financial reasons. The resulting boundary condition

$$a_{22}(X,r,t)u_{rr} + k(\theta - r)u_r - \gamma u - u_t = 0$$

is an admissible Venttsel boundary condition.

$r = R$: The inward normal is $n = (0, -1)$ so that

$$\langle (R - q)X, k(\theta - R)), (0, -1) \rangle = k(R - \theta) > 0$$

for sufficiently large R. Hence

$$a_{11}(x, R, t)u_{xx} + (R - q)xu_x + k(\theta - R)u_r - \gamma u - u_t = f(x, R, t)$$

is an admissible Venttsel boundary condition.

We note the current theory for Venttsel boundary conditions does not allow the inclusion of the cross-derivative u_{xr} in the boundary PDE, but it is not clear that this restriction is essential. However, use of the entire equation at $x = X$ as a boundary condition, including the term $\lim_{x \to X} u_{xx}$, seems risky because two distinct solutions of (1.52) defined on $[0, Y] \times [0, R]$ with $X < Y$ whose boundary values differ only for $x \in (X, Y]$ would satisfy (1.52) at $x = X$. So the problem with the entire equation on the boundary cannot be well posed. Moreover, if only tangential second order derivatives are allowed but the oblique derivative defined by the convective terms points outward, then maximum principles no longer apply and the solution may again no longer be unique.

Example 1.22. The Black Scholes equation with stochastic volatility.

The pricing equation (1.39) considered in Example 1.15 is degenerate on $S = 0$ and $v = 0$. We shall regularize it as in Example 1.21 by writing

$$a_{11}(S, v)V_{SS} + \rho\sigma vSV_{Sv} + a_{22}(S, v)V_{vv} + (r - q)SV_v$$
$$+ (k(\theta - v) - \lambda v)V_v - rV - V_t = 0, \qquad (1.53)$$

where

$$a_{11}(S, v) = \max \left\{ \frac{vS^2}{2}, \epsilon \right\}, \quad a_{22}(S, v) = \max \left\{ \frac{\sigma^2 v}{2}, \epsilon \right\}$$

for $0 < \epsilon \ll 1$, $|\rho| < 1$.

In the $S - v$ plane on $v = 0$ the inward normal vector for the computational domain $[0, S] \times [0, v_{\max}]$ is $n = (0, 1)$ so that

$$\langle n, \beta(S, 0) \rangle = \langle ((r - q)S, \kappa\theta), n \rangle = \kappa\theta > 0.$$

Hence

$$a_{11}(S, 0)V_{SS} + (r - q)SV_S - rV - V_t = 0$$

is an admissible Venttsel boundary condition for all $\epsilon > 0$. This equation is the same as (1.40) except for the regularization.

In Example 1.15 we saw that this equation has to be in effect when $k\theta \geq \sigma^2/2$. Now we see that this equation can always be imposed regardless of the Feller condition. Hence (1.39) is an admissible boundary condition on $S = 0$ and $v = 0$. One would expect continuity in the solution with respect to the parameters in (1.39) as the Fichera function $h(S, v, t)$ changes its algebraic sign which makes (1.39) the natural boundary condition for this problem.

On $S = 0$ we have $n = (1, 0)$ so that

$$\langle n, \beta(0, v)\rangle = \langle (1, 0), (0, \kappa(\theta - v) - \lambda v)\rangle = 0.$$

It follows that

$$a_{22}(0, v)V_{vv} + (\kappa(\theta - v) - \lambda v)V_v - rV - V_t = 0$$

is an admissible Venttsel boundary condition. This equation is, except for the regularization, the same as equation (1.41).

Let us now consider an appropriate boundary condition for (1.53) at $v = v_{\max} < \infty$. We saw in Example 1.18 of the last section that the Fichera theory leads to the boundary condition

$$V_{SS} = 0 \quad \text{as } v \to \infty \tag{1.54}$$

which suggests the boundary condition

$$\lim_{v \to \infty} V(S, v, t) = Se^{-qt}$$

for a European call. Numerical experiments show that it can also be applied at sufficiently large $v_{\max} < \infty$ since the boundary data appear to have little influence on prices for $v \ll v_{\max}$. However, (1.54) cannot hold for an American call because it rules out early exercise for all $q > 0$. In numerical simulations of American calls with a Heston stochastic volatility the boundary condition

$$\partial V(S, v_{\max}, t)/\partial v = 0 \tag{1.55}$$

is frequently imposed, with the oft repeated justification that the call price becomes insensitive to v as $v \to \infty$ [18]. Alternatively, we can drop non-tangential second derivatives from (1.53) and impose on $v = v_{\max}$

$$a_{11}(S, v_{\max})V_{SS} + (r-q)SV_S + (\kappa(\theta - v_{\max}) - \lambda v_{\max})V_v - rV - V_t = 0. \tag{1.56}$$

On $v = v_{\max}$ we have $n(S, v) = (0, -1)$ so that

$$\langle n(S, v), \beta(S, v)\rangle = -[\kappa(\theta - v_{\max}) - \lambda v_{\max}] > 0$$

provided $(\kappa + \lambda)v_{\max} > \kappa\theta$. In this case (1.56) is a valid Venttsel boundary condition and we can expect that it leads to a well posed boundary value problem for (1.53). A comparison of American calls obtained with boundary conditions (1.55) and (1.56) is given in Example 7.1. The early exercise conditions for a call are applied to (1.53) for $v < v_{\max}$ and to (1.56) at $v = v_{\max}$.

In the final Example 7.12 of these notes we solve the Black Scholes equation with stochastic volatility and interest rate for Venttsel like boundary conditions which also contain the correlation terms. The inclusion of cross derivatives seems to yield better numerical results than those based on strictly tangential Venttsel second order derivatives. The theoretical studies of well-posedness of problems with Venttsel boundary conditions do not consider cross derivatives and hence do not rule out well-posedness. But for the reasons stated following Example 1.21 we do not favor using the complete pricing equation as a boundary condition on a far away computational boundary.

1.2.4   *Free boundaries*

American options involve the concept of early exercise boundaries which are examples of so-called free boundaries. Free boundary problems arise in many different contexts but share the feature that differential equations are defined on domains with boundaries or interfaces which are not specified but part of the solution of the problem. Degeneracy of the equation, and the choice of boundary conditions on the free boundary are generally not an issue for applications in finance. Instead, difficulties arise because the problems are nonlinear.

The best known examples of free boundary problems in finance are American puts and calls. For example, an American call for (1.1) would satisfy

$$\mathcal{L}_{BS}u = 0$$
$$u(x,0) = \max\{0, x-1\}$$
$$u(0,t) = 0$$
$$u(s(t),t) = s(t) - 1$$
$$u_x(s(t),t) = 1$$

where $u(x,t) = V(S,t)/K$ and $x = S/K$ and $s(t) = S(t)/K$ is the free boundary which is known to exist if the dividend rate q is positive. The domain of validity of the Black Scholes equation $D(T) = \{(x,t) : 0 < x < s(t), t \in (0,T]\}$ is commonly called the continuation region of the option.

The Dirichlet condition $u(s(t), t) = s(t) - 1$ and the Neumann condition $u_x(s(t), t) = 1$, referred to as the "smooth pasting condition", together will determine the unknowns $\{u(x, t), s(t)\}$ of the problem.

Although the Black Scholes equation for the call is linear, the resulting free boundary problem is inherently nonlinear. This becomes obvious when the problem is rewritten for the new variables

$$y = \frac{x}{s(t)}, \quad \tau = t.$$

If $U(y, \tau) = u(ys(\tau), \tau)$ the Black Scholes equation becomes

$$\frac{1}{2}\sigma^2 y^2 U_{yy} + \left[(r - q) + \frac{s'(\tau)}{s(\tau)}\right] yU_y - rU - U_\tau = 0, \quad 0 < y < 1, \quad \tau \in (0, T],$$

subject to

$$U(y, 0) = \max\{0, ys(0) - 1\}$$
$$U(0, \tau) = 0$$
$$U(1, \tau) = s(\tau) - 1$$
$$U_y(1, \tau) = s(\tau).$$

By inspection this is a nonlinear problem in the unknowns $\{U(y, \tau), s(\tau)\}$ which usually will require an iterative solution algorithm. We remark that the change of variable $y = x/s(t)$, known as a Landau transformation in the early literature on free boundary problems, can be combined with numerical methods to solve free boundary problems. For an application of the Landau transformation to options see, e.g. [67, p. 408].

As stated in Example 1.2, obstacle problems give rise to variational inequalities on the fixed domain $[0, X] \times [0, T]$ and to a related complementarity formulation. The existence and uniqueness of solutions for multidimensional elliptic and parabolic variational inequalities have been studied in great detail (see, e.g. [30, 44]). Moreover, the theory has been applied repeatedly to analyze American options (see, e.g. [1]).

It is characteristic of variational inequality and complementarity problems that they need not have smooth connected free boundaries. Even so, effective algorithms exist for their numerical solution because the free boundary is not explicitly approximated in this setting. However, the a posteriori determination of the free boundaries as level sets of the solution of the variational inequality often requires careful interpolation and is not always straightforward (see, e.g. [67, Chapter 6] for applications in finance). Numerical methods which explicitly find the free boundary are known as front tracking methods. The method of lines, which is the subject of this text, is one such method.

It also should be noted that variational and complementarity formulations break down without smooth pasting. If, for example, we intend to exercise an American put suboptimally when

$$u(s(t), t) = K - s(t)$$

$$u_x(s(t), t) = -\alpha \quad \text{for } 0 < \alpha \leq 1$$

then we no longer attach smoothly to the obstacle and the complementarity formulation breaks down. As shown in Example 5.2, front tracking is not affected as long as the free boundary exists.

In these notes we restrict ourselves to problems with free boundaries which are piecewise graphs in a suitably chosen coordinate system and which can be tracked explicitly. The variational or complementarity structure of an obstacle problem is helpful for the analysis but not relevant for the application of the method of lines [51]. What is relevant for our approach is the existence of the free boundaries and their smoothness and topological properties. Even for a standard American put such properties can be difficult to establish rigorously [11]. For more complicated applications the computed free boundaries in subsequent chapters are deemed acceptable only because they appear stable, comparable and believable as the computational meshes are refined.

Chapter 2

The Method of Lines (MOL) for the Diffusion Equation

The method of lines refers to an approximation of one or more partial differential equations with ordinary differential equations in just one of the independent variables. The assumption is that the ordinary differential equations are easier to analyze and solve than the partial differential equations. The approximation can be based on finite differences, finite elements, collocation or Fourier series like expansions. A method of lines obtained with finite differences seems easiest to apply and will be used exclusively in these notes.

In order to introduce the basic ideas used later for pricing options let us consider the diffusion equation

$$a(x,t)u_{xx} + b(x,t)u_x - c(x,t)u - d(x,t)u_t = f(x,t) \qquad (2.1)$$

and the boundary and initial conditions

$$u(0,t) = \alpha(t), \qquad u(L,t) = \beta(t)$$
$$u(x,0) = u_0(x).$$

Options, bonds and their Greeks are described by equations like (2.1).

Consistent with these applications we shall make the assumption that all coefficients in (2.1) are continuous in x and t and that

$$a(x,t) > 0 \qquad \text{for } 0 \le x \le L \text{ and all } t,$$
$$d(x,t) \ge 0 \qquad \text{for } 0 < x < L \text{ and all } t.$$

The coefficients b and c may change sign in specific problems.

The two independent variables are x and t. In later applications the variable x will stand for an asset price or an interest rate. We shall call x the "spatial" variable. t stands for "time", usually time to expiry of the option or bond.

It is our choice whether to approximate this problem with ordinary differential equations in x or t. In subsequent chapters we shall always retain x as the continuous variable and discretize t. However, in the engineering literature the term MOL invariably refers to ordinary differential equations in t. This version is sometimes called the vertical method of lines. For completeness, we shall give first a brief exposition of a method of lines approximation of (2.1) valid for all t and at discrete values of x, and then turn to the MOL in x.

2.1   The method of lines with continuous time (the vertical MOL)

We define a mesh

$$0 = x_0 < \cdots < x_I = L$$

with

$$\Delta x = L/I \quad \text{and} \quad x = i\Delta x, \qquad i = 0, 1, \ldots, I,$$

and approximate (2.1) along the line $x = x_i$ with the ordinary differential equation

$$a(x_i, t) \frac{u_{i+1}(t) + u_{i-1}(t) - 2u_i(t)}{\Delta x^2}$$
$$+ b(x_i, t) \frac{u_{i+1}(t) - u_{i-1}(t)}{2\Delta x} - c(x_i, t)u_i(t) - u_i'(t) = f(x_i, t)$$

for $i = 1, \ldots, I - 1$, where $u_0(t) = \alpha(t)$ and $u_I(t) = \beta(t)$, and where

$$u_i(0) = u_0(x_i).$$

It is possible to write these $I - 1$ ordinary differential equations for the vector $\vec{u}(t) = (u_1(t), \ldots, u_{I-1}(t))$ in matrix form

$$\vec{u}'(t) = A(t)\vec{u} + \vec{b}(t) \qquad (2.2)$$
$$\vec{u}(0) = \vec{u}_0$$

where $A(t)$ is a tridiagonal matrix and the vector $\vec{b}(t)$ is determined by the source term $f(x, t)$ and the boundary conditions $\{\alpha(t), \beta(t)\}$. The initial condition $\vec{u}_0 = (u_{0,1}, \ldots, u_{0,I-1})$ is defined by

$$u_{0i} = u_0(x_i).$$

Taylor expansions can be used to show that (2.2) is a consistent approximation of (2.1). Moreover, it can be shown that under reasonable hypotheses on the data of problem (2.1) the analytic solution of (2.2) satisfies

$$|u(x_i, t) - u_i(t)| \leq K\Delta x^2, \qquad i = 1, \ldots, I - 1$$

where $u(x, t)$ is the analytic solution of (2.1) and K depends on the smoothness of u and the interval of integration $[0, T]$.

Of course, in general an analytic solution of (2.2) is not available. Then the system must be solved numerically. It is possible to define a numerical integrator for (2.2), for example a backward Euler method or the trapezoidal rule, so that the resulting algebraic equations are identical to standard finite difference approximations to (2.1). In this case nothing has been gained by introducing the method of lines. The attraction of (2.2) is due to the fact that the theory of ordinary differential equations yields insight into the analytic solution of (2.2), and that many efficient adaptive black box numerical codes exist for the approximate solution of initial value problems for linear and non-linear ordinary differential equations. Thus, in principle, a highly accurate numerical of solution of (2.2) is obtainable. Coupled with the fact that the MOL discretization is readily extended to nonlinear problems and to other classes of equations, it is natural that this two step solution approach to time dependent problems has become commonplace and the basis of software for the numerical solution of time dependent partial differential equations.

For a discussion of the method of lines leading to initial value problems for ordinary differential equations, and some caveats against its thoughtless application we refer the reader to [61] and [62].

The transformation of a so-called parabolic initial/boundary value problem like (2.1) to (2.2) is not so straightforward when the domain of the equation changes with time, e.g. when the boundary conditions are given in the form

$$u(S_0(t), t) = \alpha(t), \qquad u(S_1(t), t) = \beta(t) \tag{2.3}$$

where $x = S_0(t)$ and $x = S_1(t)$ describe curved boundaries. The problem is exacerbated when $S_0(t)$ or $S_1(t)$ is not known a priori but a free boundary like an early exercise boundary in an American option. It is possible to map the irregular domain into a rectangle at the expense of complicating the differential equation (2.1). For this approach in a financial setting see [67] where the resulting equations are solved with finite differences. We should point out, however, that for sufficiently exotic options these boundaries need not be monotone or stay separated. For example, Fig. 2.1 shows the computational domain for an in-the-money American power strangle where the left free boundary $S_0(t)$ of the put twice reverses its motion. Also, the free boundaries for a standard American straddle can approach each other as $t \to 0$. Such problems in their free boundary formulation do not appear to be good candidates for a method of lines solution in continuous time.

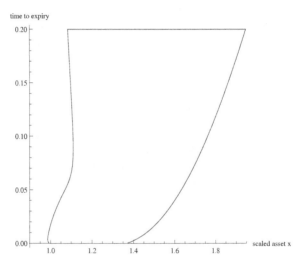

Fig. 2.1. Continuation region D for a Black Scholes American power strangle with early exercise conditions

$$u(x,t) = 3 - x^4, \quad 0 \le x \le S_0(t)$$

$$u(x,t) = \sqrt{x} - 1, \quad S_1(t) \le x$$

$\sigma = .3$, $r = .05$, $q = .04$, $T = .2$ (see Example 5.5).

We have no experience with the time-continuous MOL for financial applications and can give no insight into how well it solves, for example, American option problems. In this book, our goal is to work as much as possible with the original equation in the natural variables of the application. We believe that we can reach this goal readily by discretizing t instead of x.

2.2   The method of lines with continuous x (the horizontal MOL)

For options with discontinuous pay-off, barriers, early exercise features or jumps, the solution of the Black Scholes equation can vary strongly with x at any given time. In this setting it is useful to base the method of lines on discretizing time and solving the resulting ordinary differential equation in x to a high degree of accuracy. This approach, also known as Rothe's method [42], will be followed consistently throughout the remainder of this book.

Assuming that problem (2.1) is to be solved over the time interval $[0, T]$, where T is arbitrary but fixed (usually the time to expiry of the option), we introduce a partition in time

$$0 = t_0 < t_1 < \cdots < t_N = T$$

where

$$\Delta t_n = t_n - t_{n-1}$$

is usually, but not necessarily, constant with respect to n.

For a method of lines approximation of (2.1) at $t = t_n$ we simply replace u_t by a time implicit (i.e. backward) difference quotient. Two approximations are used repeatedly. If $u_n(x)$ denotes the approximation of the solution $u(x, t_n)$ then we employ either the backward Euler approximation

$$u_t(x, t_n) \cong Du_n(x) = \frac{u_n(x) - u_{n-1}(x)}{\Delta t_n} \tag{2.4}$$

or the three-level backward difference formula

$$u_t(x, t_n) \cong Du_n(x) = c_n \frac{u_n(x) - u_{n-1}(x)}{\Delta t_n} + d_n \frac{u_{n-1}(x) - u_{n-2}(x)}{\Delta t_{n-1}}. \tag{2.5}$$

A Taylor series expansion of the right hand side of (2.5) shows that the weights $\{c_n, d_n\}$ should be chosen such that

$$\begin{pmatrix} \dfrac{1}{\Delta t_n} & \dfrac{1}{2\Delta t_n + \Delta t_{n-1}} \end{pmatrix} \begin{pmatrix} c_n \\ d_n \end{pmatrix} = \begin{pmatrix} 1 \\ 0 \end{pmatrix}.$$

In most applications the time step is constant (i.e. $\Delta t_n = \Delta t_{n-1}$). For this case the weights are

$$c_n = \frac{3}{2}, \qquad d_n = -\frac{1}{2}.$$

In general it follows from Taylor expansions applied to (2.4) that for any smooth function $\phi(x, t)$

$$|\phi_t(x, t_n) - D\phi(x, t_n)| \leq K_1 \Delta t_n$$

so that the approximation of ϕ_t is "of order Δt", or of "first order". Similarly it follows from (2.5) that

$$|\phi_t(x,t) - D\phi(x,t_n)| \leq K_2 \max\{\Delta t_n^2, \Delta t_{n-1}^2\}$$

so that the approximation of ϕ_t is of order Δt^2, i.e. of second order. Here K_1 and K_2 are constants which depend only on the smoothness of ϕ.

The method of lines approximation of (2.1) at time $t = t_n$ is given by the two point boundary value problem

$$a(x,t_n)u_n''(x) + b(x,t_n)u_n'(x) - c(x,t_n)u_n(x) - d(x,t_n)Du_n(x) = f(x,t_n)$$
$$(2.6)$$

subject to

$$u_n(0) = \alpha(t_n), \qquad u_n(L) = \beta(t_n).$$

$u_0(x) = g(x)$ is the given initial condition. It is well known that standard finite difference methods based on a backward Euler or an implicit three-level time discretization are unconditionally stable. As the spatial mesh size in the finite difference approximation decreases to zero the equation (2.6) results. Hence we may infer that both (2.4) and (2.5) yield a stable numerical method for the solution of the diffusion equation (2.1). A direct proof of stability is provided in Appendix 2.2. We note that at the first time level $t = t_1$ the equation (2.6) is only defined for the backward Euler quotient (2.4). Once $u_1(x)$ is found then for $n \geq 2$ the equation (2.6) is defined for either difference quotient $Du_n(x)$.

If equation (2.1) is to be solved subject to boundary data like (2.3) then the boundary conditions for (2.6) simply become

$$u_n(S_0(t_n)) = \alpha(t_n), \qquad u_n(S_1(t_n)) = \beta(t_n).$$

However, if the interval $[S_0(t_{n-1}), S_1(t_{n-1})]$ does not contain the interval $[S_0(t_n), S_1(t_n)]$ then $u_{n-1}(x)$ must be extended beyond its boundary points in order to be able to define $Du_n(x)$ on $[S_0(t_n), S_1(t_n)]$. For example, if $S_1(t_n) > S_1(t_{n-1})$ then we would use the (smooth pasting) linear extension

$$u_{n-1}(x) = u_{n-1}(S_1(t_{n-1})) + u_{n-1}'(S_1(t_{n-1}))(x - S_1(t_{n-1})), \quad x > S_1(t_{n-1}).$$

Analogous extensions apply to $u_{n-2}(x)$ and at the lower boundary $S_0(t)$.

The accuracy of the approximation of u_t generally implies the same accuracy for the solution of (2.1), meaning that for an analytic solution of (2.6) we can assert that

$$|u(x,t_n) - u_n(x)| \leq K \max_k \Delta t_k^{1 \text{ or } 2} \quad \text{for all } n$$

where K depends solely on the smoothness of the analytic solution $u(x,t)$ of (2.1). A second order method is preferable, and in fact essential for an efficient MOL code for problems in finance. It comes basically for free because numerical methods for (2.6) differ little whether (2.4) or (2.5) is used. Numerical experiments verify that the performance of the method of lines is greatly improved by switching over to a second order method for $n \geq 3$. In applications we shall routinely approximate $u_t(x,t)$ with the backward quotient (2.4) for $n = 1$ and $n = 2$, and then change over to the three level quotient (2.5) for $n \geq 3$.

The reader familiar with the Crank-Nicolson method for the diffusion equation will be aware that one could equally well define an MOL approximation involving the spatial differential operator at times t_{n-1} and t_n. However, the Crank-Nicolson approximation requires care when initial data are non-smooth (typical for options) or the boundary and initial data are discontinuous (typical for barrier options). In fact, even though self-starting in principle, it often has to be combined with a few implicit Euler steps (sometimes referred to as Rannacher's method) to suppress unwarranted initial oscillations. Hence the self-starting feature is lost. The three level scheme appears simpler to apply and to give comparable results. For this reason a Crank-Nicolson based MOL will not be considered here.

Appendix 2.2

Stability of the time discrete three-level scheme for the heat equation

The proof of stability of the algebraic three-level finite difference scheme will be adapted to the boundary value problem

$$u_{xx} - u_t = f(x,t)$$

$$u(0,t) = u(L,t) = 0$$

$$u(x,0) = u_0(x).$$

We suppose it is approximated at time t_n with the method of lines equations

$$\mathcal{L}u_n \equiv u_n'' - \frac{3}{2\Delta t}u_n = -\frac{4}{2\Delta t}u_{n-1} + \frac{1}{2\Delta t}u_{n-2} + f(x,t_n). \qquad \text{(A2.2.1)}$$

We observe that the Sturm-Liouville eigenvalue problem

$$\mathcal{L}\phi = \mu\phi, \quad \phi(0) = \phi(L) = 0$$

has eigenvalues and eigenfunctions

$$\mu_m = -\left[\frac{3}{2\Delta t} + \left(\frac{m\pi}{L}\right)^2\right], \quad \phi_m(x)\sin\frac{m\pi}{L}x, \quad m \geq 1.$$

For each time level t_n let $u_n(x) = \sum_{m=1}^{\infty} A_{m,n}\phi(x)$ be the Fourier series solution of the boundary value problem. Then the Fourier coefficients of each eigenfunction in (A2.2.1) must add up to zero so that

$$\mu_m A_{m,n} + \frac{4}{2\Delta t}A_{m,n-1} = \frac{1}{2\Delta t}A_{m,n-2} + f_{m,n}$$

where $f_{m,n}$ is the mth Fourier coefficient of $f(x,t_n)$.

This three-level recursion relation can be expressed as

$$B_m\begin{pmatrix}A_{m,n}\\A_{m,n-1}\end{pmatrix} = C\begin{pmatrix}A_{m,n-1}\\A_{m,n-2}\end{pmatrix} + d_m$$

where

$$B_m = \begin{pmatrix}\mu_m & \frac{4}{2\Delta t}\\0 & 1\end{pmatrix} \quad C = \begin{pmatrix}0 & \frac{2}{2\Delta t}\\1 & 0\end{pmatrix}, \quad d_m = \begin{pmatrix}f_{m,n}\\0\end{pmatrix}.$$

Stability of the three-level method follows from the recursion relation if the spectral radius $\rho(B_m^{-1}C)$ is less than one for all Δt as $\Delta t \to 0$. The eigenvalues $\lambda_{1,2}$ of $B^{-1}C$ are readily found from

$$\mathrm{Det}(C - \lambda B) = 0.$$

They turn out to be

$$\lambda_{1,2} = \frac{2 \pm \sqrt{\alpha_m}}{4 - \alpha_m}, \quad \alpha_m = 1 - 2\Delta t\left(\frac{m\pi}{L}\right)^2 \in (-\infty, 1) \quad \text{for } \Delta t \geq 0$$

so that $\rho(B^{-1}C) < 1$ for $\Delta t > 0$ and all m.

2.3   The method of lines with continuous x for multi-dimensional problems

Asian and basket options, stochastic volatility models and multi-factor interest rate bond options lead to multi-dimensional diffusion equations. For such equations the simplicity of the MOL described in Section 2.2 is retained, in principle, if we combine the MOL with an analog of standard line iterative methods known for algebraic approximations of multi-dimensional diffusion equations. In practice, such approach is limited to very low-dimensional problems, and we shall treat applications which usually involve only two "spatial" variables x and y.

We shall consider problems of the form

$$a_{11}(x,y,t)u_{xx} + a_{12}(x,y,t)u_{xy} + a_{22}(x,y,t)u_{yy}$$
$$+ b_1(x,y,t)u_x + b_2(x,y,t)u_y - c(x,y,t)u$$
$$- d(x,y,t)u_t = f(x,y,t) \tag{2.7}$$

on a domain $D_T = \{(x,y,t) : (x,y) \in \mathcal{D}(t), t \in (0,T]\}$ where

$$\mathcal{D}(t) = \{(x,y) : S_0(y,t) < x < S_1(y,t), \quad y_0 < y < Y\}, \quad t > 0.$$

y_0 and Y are given numbers and S_0 and S_1 are smooth curves in y and t. The boundary of $\mathcal{D}(t)$ will be denoted by $\partial\mathcal{D}(t)$.

In applications we impose boundary conditions on $u(x,y,t)$ on all or part of the boundary $\partial\mathcal{D}(t)$, and an initial condition on $u(x,y,0)$. For ease of exposition we shall use so-called Dirichlet boundary data

$$u(x,y,t) = \alpha(x,y,t), \qquad (x,y) \in \partial\mathcal{D}(t)$$

and the initial condition

$$u(x,y,0) = u_0(x,y)$$

where α and u_0 are given functions.

As in the preceding section we begin by discretizing time in (2.7). Let $u_n(x,y)$ denote an approximation to $u(x,y,t_n)$ at time t_n. We employ the difference quotients introduced in Section 2.2

$$u_t(x,y,t_n) \simeq Du_n(x,y) = \begin{cases} \frac{u_n - u_{n-1}}{\Delta t} & \text{for } n = 1,2 \\ \frac{3}{2}\frac{u_n - u_{n-1}}{\Delta t} - \frac{1}{2}\frac{u_{n-1} - u_{n-2}}{\Delta t} & \text{for } n = 3,\dots,N \end{cases}$$

when $\Delta t = t_n - t_{n-1}$ is assumed to be constant for all n. For notational convenience the argument (x,y) of u_n will generally be suppressed. Moreover, if the time index n does not appear explicitly it is assumed to be the index n of the latest time step so that

$$u(x,y) \equiv u_n(x,y).$$

The time index will be written only when it is needed for clarity.

The (parabolic) initial/boundary value problem for (2.7) at time t_n is approximated by the sequence of time discrete (elliptic) problems

$$a_{11}(x,y,t_n)u_{xx} + a_{12}(x,y,t_n)u_{xy} + a_{22}(x,y,t_n)u_{yy} + b_1(x,y,t_n)u_x$$
$$+ b_2(x,y,t_n)u_y - \hat{c}(x,y,t_n)u = \hat{f}(x,y,t_n) \tag{2.8}$$

where

$$\hat{c}(x,y,t_n) = c(x,y,t_n) + \begin{cases} d(x,y,t_n)\frac{1}{\Delta t} & \text{for } n = 1,2 \\ d(x,y,t_n)\frac{3}{2\Delta t} & \text{for } n = 3,\dots,N \end{cases}$$

and

$$\hat{f}(x, y, t_n) = f(x, y, t_n)$$
$$- \begin{cases} d(x, y, t_n) \frac{u_{n-1}(x,y)}{\Delta t} & \text{for } n = 1, 2 \\ d(x, y, t_n) \left[\frac{3u_{n-1}(x,y)}{2\Delta t} + \frac{u_{n-1}(x,y) - u_{n-2}(x,y)}{2\Delta t} \right] & \text{for } n = 3, \ldots, N \end{cases}$$

$u_0(x, y)$ is given and the boundary data are evaluated at t_n.

In order to approximate (2.8) with ordinary differential equations in x we impose a uniform partition

$$y_0 < y_1 < \cdots < y_M = Y.$$

The points $\{y_m\}$ of the partition will always be indexed by m. Next we replace derivatives with respect to y in (2.8) by central difference quotients. If $u_m(x)$ ($\equiv u_{m,n}(x)$) denotes an approximation to $u(x, y_m, t_n)$ then with $\Delta y = y_m - y_{m-1}$ we write

$$u_y(x, y_m, t_n) \cong \frac{u_{m+1}(x) - u_{m-1}(x)}{2\Delta y}$$

$$u_{yy}(x, y_m, t_n) \cong \frac{u_{m+1}(x) + u_{m-1}(x) - 2u_m(x)}{\Delta y^2}$$

$$u_{xy}(x, y_m, t_n) = \frac{u'_{m+1}(x) - u'_{m-1}(x)}{2\Delta y}$$

The method of lines approximation to (2.7) with continuous x at discrete time t_n along the line $y = y_m$ for $m = 1, \ldots, M - 1$ takes on the form

$$\mathcal{L}u_m(x) = a_{11}(x, y_m, t_n)u''_m(x) + b_1(x, y_m, t_n)u'_m(x) - \tilde{c}(x, y_m, t_n)u_m(x)$$
$$= F(x, y_m, t_n, u_{m-1}(x), u_{m+1}(x), u'_{m-1}(x), u'_{m+1}(x),$$
$$u_{m,n-1}(x), u_{m,n-2}(x)) \tag{2.9}$$

where

$$\tilde{c}(x, y_m, t_n) = \hat{c}(x, y_m, t_n) + a_{22}(x, y_m, t_n)\frac{2}{\Delta y^2}$$

and

$$F(x, y_m, t_n) = \hat{f}(x, y_m, t_n) - a_{22}(x, y_m, t_n)\frac{u_{m+1}(x) + u_{m-1}(x)}{\Delta y^2}$$
$$- b_2(x, y_m, t_n)\frac{u_{m+1}(x) - u_{m-1}(x)}{2\Delta y}$$
$$- a_{12}(x, y_m, t_n)\frac{u'_{m+1}(x) - u'_{m-1}(x)}{2\Delta y}$$

(We recall the notation: $u_m \cong u(x, y_m, t_n)$, $u_{m,n-1}(x) \cong u(x, y_m, t_{n-1})$). The initial condition yields $\{u_{m,0}(x)\}_{m=0}^{M}$ and the boundary conditions give $\{u_m(S_0(y_m, t_n))\}$ and $\{u_m(S_1(y_m, t_n))\}$, as well as $u_0(x)$, $u_M(x)$ and their derivatives.

Equations (2.9) represent a boundary value problem for a system of $M-1$ coupled ordinary differential equations. If $S_0(y, t_n)$ and $S_1(y, t_n)$ are not constant with respect to y then the equations are defined over different x-intervals and the boundary value problem is a so-called multipoint boundary value problem. Its numerical solution is often as complicated as the numerical solution of the partial differential equation (2.8). However, for problems arising in finance it generally is possible to solve the system (2.9) iteratively as a sequence of scalar second order equations like (2.6).

We introduce a new index k for the iteration count. It appears as a superscript of u so that $u_m^k(x)$ stands for the kth iterate approximating $u(x, y_m, t_n)$. At time t_n let $\{u_m^0(x)\}_{m=1}^{M-1}$ denote an initial guess for the solution $\{u_m(x)\}$ of (2.9). Typically one would choose the solution from the preceding time step

$$u_m^0(x) = u_{m,n-1}(x).$$

In the kth iteration for $k \geq 1$ we compute a solution $\{u_m^k(x)\}$ for $m = 1, \ldots, M-1$ by solving

$$\mathcal{L}_m u_m^k(x) = F(x, y_m, t_n, u_{m-1}^k, u_{m+1}^{k-1}, u'^k_{m-1}, u'^{k-1}_{m+1}, u_{m,n-1}, u_{m,n-2}).$$
$$(2.10)$$

If necessary, smooth pasting extension of the arguments of F are used so that F is a known source term on $[S_0(y_m, t_n), S_1(y_m, t_n)]$.

Assuming that the sequence $\{u_m^k(x)\}$ converges as $k \to \infty$ we obtain

$$u_{m,n}(x) = \lim_{k \to \infty} u_m^k(x) \quad \text{for } m = 1, \ldots, M-1.$$

The reader familiar with iterative methods for linear algebraic systems will recognize that our iterative method is a line Gauss-Seidel iteration, except that along each line $y = y_m$ a two point boundary value problem for a second order ordinary differential equation has to be solved instead of a matrix problem. In practice we set

$$u_{m,n}(x) = u_m^K(x)$$

where K is an integer such that

$$\max_m |u_m^K(x) - u_m^{K-1}(x)| \leq \epsilon.$$

On occasion the more stringent condition

$$\max\left\{\left|u_m^K(x) - u_m^{K-1}(x)\right| + \left|{u'}_m^K(x) - {u'}_m^{K-1}(x)\right|\right\} \leq \epsilon$$

will be imposed in Chapter 7.

The choice of the convergence tolerance ϵ is dictated by the accuracy required by the application and the computer time it takes for convergence. There does not appear to exist a mathematical proof for the convergence of the line Gauss Seidel iteration for a real financial application, but it always was observed throughout the numerical simulations reported in this book. Indeed, whenever there arose a problem with the iterative solution of a multi-dimensional Black Scholes equation, it pointed to conceptual and programming errors rather than non-convergence of the system (2.10). In Appendix 2.3 at the end of this section we demonstrate for a simple model problem that the underlying structure of the two-dimensional MOL approximation is suitable for a line iterative Gauss-Seidel solution method.

On occasion spurious oscillatory solutions can arise from the central difference approximation of $u_y(x, y, t)$. They can be suppressed by either decreasing Δy, or if that is infeasible, by replacing

$$b_2(x, y_m, t_n)u_y(x, y_m, t_n)$$

with a lower order one-sided difference quotient. For example, if $b_2 \geq 0$ we would choose

$$u_y(x, y_m, t_n) = \frac{u_{m+1} - u}{\Delta y},$$

if $b_2 < 0$ we would use

$$u_y(x, y_m, t_n) = \frac{u - u_{m-1}}{\Delta y}.$$

These first order quotients represent an "upwinding" of the convection term $b_2 u_y$ in (2.7). Upwinding is a well understood and important tool in the theory of numerical methods for partial differential equations. However, in most simulations no oscillations are observed when calculations are based on second order central difference quotients for the convective terms of (2.7).

We also remark that if Δt is very large or if perpetual options are priced then the convergence of the line Gauss Seidel iteration may be unacceptably slow. In this case a line SOR modification of the Gauss Seidel method may prove helpful. We consider the solution of (2.10) an intermediate solution and denote it by $\tilde{u}$. The desired solution u_m^k is found from

$$u_m^k = u_m^{k-1} + \omega[\tilde{u}_m - u_m^{k-1}]$$

for some $\omega \in [1, 2]$. The optimum relaxation factor ω is not known a priori but can be found by trial and error. $\omega = 1$ yields again the Gauss Seidel iteration.

Finally, we remark that it is straightforward to generalize this approach to multi-dimensional equations like

$$\sum_{i,j=1}^{p} a_{ij} u_{x_i x_j} + \sum_{i=1}^{p} b_i u_{x_i} - cu - du_t = f(\vec{x}, t)$$

where $\vec{x} = (x_1, \ldots, x_p)$. Such equation would arise, for example, in connection with basket options depending on p assets. We discretize t and then $x_1, \ldots, x_{p-1}$ and replace all derivates with respect to these variables by appropriate finite difference quotients. Assuming M discrete values for each coordinate x_j, $j \le p - 1$, a system of the order of M^{p-1} coupled second order ordinary differential equations in the independent variable x_p results to which a line Gauss Seidel iteration can be applied. Some parallelization of the line Gauss Seidel method is possible, but we have no practical experience with financial applications for $p > 2$.

Appendix 2.3

Convergence of the line Gauss Seidel iteration for a model problem

We shall consider the Dirichlet problem

$$u_{xx} + \rho u_{xy} + u_{yy} - cu = f(x, y), \quad (x, y) \in D = (0, 1) \times (0, 1)$$
$$u(x, y) = g(x, y) \quad (x, y) \in \partial D. \tag{A2.3.1}$$

This equation has the essential structure of the time discretized Black Scholes equation, in which case the coefficient c can be identified with $1/\Delta t$ and can be made large for small Δt. If y is the continuous variable and

$$0 = x_0 < \cdots < x_{J+1} = 1$$

defines a uniform mesh on $[0, 1]$ then the system (2.10) takes the form

$$\mathcal{L}u_j^k \equiv u''{}_j^k(y) + \rho \frac{u'{}_{j+1}^{k-1}(y) - u'{}_{j-1}^k(y)}{2\Delta x}$$
$$+ \frac{u_{j+1}^{k-1}(y) + u_{j-1}^k(y) - 2u_j^k(y)}{\Delta x^2} - cu_j^k = f(x_j, y).$$

Let $\{u_j^0(y)\}$ be any smooth initial guess. We assume that subsequent iterates $\{u_j^k(y)\}$ are computable. If we set

$$w_j^k(y) = u_j^k(y) - u_j^{k-1}(y)$$

then for $k \geq 2$ we see that for all j

$$\mathcal{L}w_j^k(y) = 0$$

$$w_j^k(0) = w_j^k(1) = w_0^k(y) = w_{J+1}^k(y) = 0.$$

Integrating by parts

$$\int_0^1 \mathcal{L}w_j^k(y)w_j^k(y)dy = 0$$

we obtain

$$-\int_0^1 \left[(w'^k_j)^2 + \left(\frac{2}{\Delta x^2} + c \right)(w_j^k)^2 \right] dy = -\frac{1}{\Delta x^2} \int_0^1 [w_{j-1}^k w_j^k + w_j^{k-1} w_j^k]dy$$

$$-\frac{\rho}{2\Delta x} \int_0^1 [w_{j-1}^k - w_{j+1}^{k-1}]w'^k dy. \qquad (A2.3.2)$$

Applying the algebraic geometric mean inequality to each integral on the left, and using the notation

$$\|g\|^2 = \int_0^1 g^2(y)dy,$$

we find the estimate

$$\|w'^k_j\|^2 + \left(\frac{2}{\Delta x^2} + c \right) \|w_j^k\|^2 \leq \frac{\|w_{j-1}^k\|^2 + \|w_{j+1}^{k-1}\|^2}{2\Delta x^2} + \frac{1}{\Delta x^2}\|w_j^k\|^2$$

$$+ \left(\frac{\rho^2}{4} \right) \frac{\|w_{j-1}^k\|^2 + \|w_{j+1}^{k-1}\|^2}{2\Delta x^2} + \|w'^k_j\|^2.$$

Thus

$$\left(\frac{1}{\Delta x^2} + c \right) \|w_j^k\|^2 \leq \left(\frac{1}{\Delta x^2} + \frac{\rho^2}{4\Delta x^2} \right) \frac{\|w_{j-1}^k\|^2 + \|w_{j+1}^{k-1}\|^2}{2}. \qquad (A2.3.3)$$

If we set $C^k = \max_j \|w_j^k\|^2$ then it follows from (A2.3.3) that

$$C^k \leq \alpha C^{k-1} \quad \text{for some } \alpha < 1 \qquad (A2.3.4)$$

provided that the constant c in the model problem satisfies

$$c > \frac{\rho^2}{4\Delta x^2}. \qquad (A2.3.5)$$

We remark that if $\rho = 0$ then convergence is guaranteed by (A2.3.2) with $c = 0$ because

$$\|w_j^k\|^2 \leq \beta \|w'^k\|^2$$

for some $\beta > 0$.

The inequality (A2.3.4) insures that $\|w_j^k\| \to 0$ so that $\{u_j^k\}$ is a Cauchy sequence in the mean square sense. Equation (A2.3.2) can now be used to infer that $\|w_j'^k\| \to 0$ for each j so that u_j^k converges pointwise as $k \to \infty$.

The significance of the estimate (A2.3.5) is that it suggests that for sufficiently small Δt the MOL line Gauss Seidel iteration can be made to converge. The estimate is sufficient for convergence. For $|\rho| < 2$ where equation (A2.3.1) is elliptic, numerical experiments indicate convergence for all $c \geq 0$, although it may be unacceptably slow. For example, starting from a randomly chosen initial guess

$$w_j^0(x_j, y) = 10 + (x_j y)^5$$

we find numerically that for

$$\Delta x = 10^{-2}, \quad \rho = 1 \text{ and } c = 0$$

$$\max_j |w_j^{6766}(y) - w_j^{6765}(y)| < 10^{-7} \text{ but } \max_j |w_j^{6766}(y)| = 5.35 \ 10^{-5},$$

while for

$$\Delta x = 10^{-2}, \quad \rho = 1 \text{ and } c = 1000$$

we obtain

$$\max_j |w_j^{170}(y) - w_j^{169}(y)| < 10^{-7} \text{ and } \max_j |w_j^{170}(y)| = 9.06 \ 10^{-7}.$$

2.4   Free boundaries and the MOL in two dimensions

Let us suppose that the solution $u(x, y)$ of (2.7) (at a fixed time and with continuous x) is differentiable and satisfies the free boundary condition

$$u(x, y) = \phi(x, y) \tag{2.11}$$

$$u_x(x, y) = \phi_x(x, y) \tag{2.12}$$

on $x = S(y)$ where $\phi(x, y)$ is the height of a smooth obstacle and $x = S(y)$ is a smooth function of y over some interval $[0, Y]$. Then it follows from (2.11) that

$$\frac{d}{dy} u(S(y), y) = u_x(S(y), y)S'(y) + u_y(S(y), y)$$

$$= \phi_x(S(y), y)S'(y) + \phi_y(S(y), y)$$

$$= u_x(S(y), y)S'(y) + \phi_y(S(y), y)$$

so that

$$u_y(S(y), y) = \phi_y(S(y), y).$$

Hence the two contact conditions (2.11, 2.12) suffice to insure that u satisfies the smooth pasting conditions

$$\begin{aligned} u &= \phi \\ \nabla u &= \nabla \phi \end{aligned} \quad \text{on } x = S(y).$$

For the method of lines on $y = y_m$ we can find an approximate free boundary $S_m \equiv S(y_m)$ by imposing on (2.10) the boundary conditions

$$u_m(S_m) = \phi(S_m, y_m)$$

$$u'_m(S_m) = \phi_x(S_m, y_m).$$

Each $\{u_m(x), S_m\}$ will be found with the method of Chapter 3.

A more complicated free boundary problem arises when the free boundary $x = S(y)$ is characterized by

$$u(x, y) = g(x, y)$$

$$\frac{\partial u}{\partial n} \equiv u_x n_1 + u_y n_2 = h(x, y)$$

where g and h are unrelated smooth functions and $n = (n_1, n_2)$ is the outward unit normal to the curve $x - S(y) = 0$. Since smooth pasting is not assumed the derivative u_y is not readily approximated at $(S(y), y)$. Its algebraic elimination from the free boundary condition is suggested instead.

Assuming that u and $S(y)$ are smooth up to the free boundary we obtain from $u = g$

$$u_x(S(y), y)S'(y) + u_y(S(y), y) = \frac{d}{dy} g(S(y), y)$$

$$= g_x(S(y), y)S'(y) + g_y(S(y), y).$$

Since $n = (1, -S'(y))/\sqrt{1 + S'(y)^2}$ we can eliminate $u_y(S(y), y)$ from $\frac{\partial u}{\partial n} = h$ and obtain the free boundary condition

$$u = g(x, y)$$

$$u_x = \frac{1}{1 + S'(y)^2} \left[\sqrt{1 + S'(y)^2} h(x, y) + S'(y) \frac{dg}{dy}(S(y), y) \right]. \qquad (2.13)$$

If we apply the method of lines on $y = y_m$ then the free boundary S_m for (2.10) is found from the boundary condition

$$u_m(S_m) = g(S_m, y_m)$$

$$u'_m(S_m) = H(S_m, y_m, S_{m-1}, S_{m+1})$$

obtained by replacing $S'_m(y)$ with $(S_{m+1} - S_{m-1})/\Delta y$ in (2.13). Alternatively, $dg(S(y), y)/dy$ can be approximated with a central difference quotient at $x = S_m$. In line Gauss-Seidel iteration k we use S^k_{m-1} and S^{k-1}_{m+1} to approximate $S'(y_m)$. These more general boundary conditions arise in phase change problems but also can occur in finance when smooth pasting conditions are violated. For a simple illustration we refer to the American call with suboptimal early exercise discussed in Example 5.2. In this case the free boundary problem is not an obstacle problem, does not have an equivalent linear complementarity or variational inequality formulation and is not solvable with the PSOR formulation [46]. A line Gauss Seidel iteration remains applicable, in principle [52].

The simple MOL approach will break down when the free surface cannot be expected to be a single valued function with respect to y or when it becomes tangent to the lines. For example, a two-component put $u(x, y, t)$ with pay-off

$$u(x, y, 0) = \max\{0, 1 - \min(x, y)\}$$

will have an early exercise boundary which approaches the lines

$$x = 1 \text{ for } y > x \quad \text{and} \quad y = 1 \text{ for } x > y$$

as $t \to 0$. It would seem a daunting task to find a free boundary numerically on lines of constant x or y as we get close to expiration. However, the free boundary can be expected to be a well behaved function with respect to polar coordinates centered at some point (X, X) for sufficiently large X. Front tracking in two (and more) dimensions may well require working in non-financial coordinates. Several numerical option problems in polar coordinates are solved in Chapter 7. Whether this approach is worth the effort compared to alternate methods like PSOR for the complementarity formulation of the equivalent obstacle problem remains to be seen.

The simple MOL approach will also break down when disjoint early exercise regions occur as in the American max call with pay-off

$$u(x, u, 0) = \max\{0, \max(x, y) - 1\}.$$

An MOL solution is computed in Example 7.6 where the two exercise boundaries are found iteratively with an alternating direction MOL method. While relatively simple to implement, this approach likewise needs to be compared with the PSOR method.

In summary then, the method of lines appximation for the parabolic equation describing financial derivatives is reduced at each time level to a single linear second order differential equation (2.6), or to a sequence of such equations. This is a sensible approach only if such second order equation can be solved accurately and efficiently. As stated in Section 2.1, a standard approach would be to replace the derivatives in (2.6) by their finite difference analogs and to set up a matrix system. The resulting algorithm is again a standard finite difference algorithm for the diffusion equation found in every textbook on numerical methods for partial differential equations. Such method would not merit the detour via the method of lines approximation.

Here we shall employ a less familiar algorithm for the solution of (2.6), but one which is readily adapted to the class of problems associated with American options. This algorithm is the subject of the next chapter.

Chapter 3

The Riccati Transformation Method for Linear Two Point Boundary Value Problems

The solution algorithm for two point boundary value problems to be employed here has been derived from different points of view and has had different names at different times. It has been called the method of invariant imbedding, a factorization method, a sweep method, and last but not least, a Riccati transformation method. Since Count Riccati's work in the early 18th century predates all other efforts we shall refer to our algorithm as the Riccati transformation method.

Any boundary value problem for an Nth order ordinary differential equation can always be rewritten in many ways as an N-dimensional first order system. For example, the two point boundary value problem (2.6) can be transformed into a system of two first order equations. Suppose we are working at time level t_n. For notational convenience we shall partially suppress the subscript n and write

$$u(x) \equiv u_n(x)$$
$$v(x) \equiv u_n'(x).$$

Then the linear two point boundary value problem (2.6) with $Du_n(x)$ given by (2.4) can be rewritten as

$$u'(x) = v \tag{3.1}$$
$$v'(x) = \frac{1}{a(x, t_n)} \left[\left(c(x, t_n) + \frac{1}{\Delta t_n} \right) u - b(x, t_n)v + h(x, t_n) - \frac{1}{\Delta t_n} u_{n-1}(x) \right]$$
$$u(0) = \alpha(t_n), \qquad u(L) = \beta(t_n).$$

The Riccati transformation method can be defined for general N-dimensional first order systems. For a detailed discussion of the many theoretical, practical and historical aspects of the Riccati approach, viewed as a factorization method for such equations, we refer to [5]. However, all subsequent applications involve only systems of two scalar equations like (3.1). In this case the Riccati transformation is readily obtained from an implicit shooting method as outlined in [50]. This point of view will prove useful for free boundary problems and for boundary value problems for difference equations.

3.1   The Riccati transformation on a fixed interval

The equations (3.1) and the appropriate boundary conditions are a special case of the general scalar two point boundary value problem

$$u'(x) = A(x)u + B(x)v + f(x), \qquad u(s) = \Gamma v(s) + \alpha \qquad (3.2)$$
$$v'(x) = C(x)u + D(x)v + g(x), \qquad G(u(S), v(S)) = 0$$

where Γ and α are constants and where G is a general function of two variables. G may well be nonlinear. We do not assume that $s < S$. In fact, s may lie below or above S. It is essential, however, that one of the two boundary conditions is linear. In our exposition the linear (actually affine) boundary condition is given at $x = s$.

The solution method for two point boundary value problem will be stated for the general system (3.2) and hence work for the MOL approximation in x of any linear scalar diffusion equation.

It is the essence of the solution method to be applied to (3.2) that the functions $\{u(x), v(x)\}$ are related through the Riccati transformation

$$u(x) = R(x)v(x) + w(x) \qquad (3.3)$$

where R and w are solutions of the well defined initial value problems

$$R' = B(x) + A(x)R - D(x)R - C(x)R^2, \qquad R(s) = \Gamma \qquad (3.4)$$
$$w' = [A(x) - C(x)R(x)]w - R(x)g(x) + f(x), \qquad w(s) = \alpha.$$

Under the hypotheses imposed on the coefficients of (2.1) the data are continuous functions of x. The theory of initial value problems for ordinary differential equations assures us that the equation for R with its quadratic right hand side, a so-called Riccati equation, has a unique local solution, and that the linear inhomogeneous equation for w has a solution as long as $R(x)$ exists.

For the systems (3.2) stemming from the MOL for diffusion equations the Riccati equation always has uniformly bounded solutions so that the initial value problem (3.4) has a unique solution over the interval. The integration of (3.4) from $x = s$ to $x = S$ is called the "forward sweep".

Let us assume that $R(S)$ and $w(S)$ have been found. When we use the Riccati transformation (3.3) in the boundary condition $G(u(S), v(S)) = 0$ we see that $v = v(S)$ must be chosen such that

$$G(R(S)v + w(S), v) = 0. \tag{3.5}$$

This is a scalar equation. Any solution v^* of this equation defines a solution of (3.2) obtained by setting

$$v(S) = v^*$$

and integrating from $x = S$ to $x = s$ the linear equation

$$v' = [C(x)R(x) + D(x)]v + C(x)w(x) + g(x), \qquad v(S) = v^*. \tag{3.6}$$

The integration of (3.6) from $x = S$ to $x = S$ is called the "reverse sweep". Once $v(x)$ is known then $\{u(x) = R(x)v(x) + w(x), v(x)\}$ is a solution of (3.2).

A derivation of this algorithm based on an implicit shooting method may be found in [50]. Here it suffices to verify by substituting the differential equations for R, w and v that

$$u'(x) = R'(x)v(x) + R(x)v'(x) + w'(x)$$
$$= A(x)[R(x)v(x) + w(x)] + B(x)v(x) + f(x)$$

which together with (3.6) shows that $\{u(x), v(x)\}$ solves (3.2).

In summary, the Riccati transformation for the linear inhomogeneous system (3.2) consists of three steps: the forward sweep (3.4), the determination of the boundary values $\{u(S), v(S)\}$ from (3.5), and the reverse sweep (3.6). In essence, the two point boundary value problem has been converted to two well-defined initial value problems. As was stated in connection with the method of lines for continuous t, initial value problems with bounded solutions are generally considered straightforward to solve numerically.

A notational difficulty arises if the system (3.2) is subject to

$$v(s) = \Gamma u(s) + \alpha$$

$$G(u(S), v(S)) = 0.$$

If $\Gamma = 0$ then we cannot solve for $u(s)$ and use (3.4). This case will arise, for example, when the delta is given at s for the forward sweep with the time discretized Black Scholes equation. In this case we reorder the equations of (3.2) and write

$$v' = D(x)v + C(x)u + g(x) \qquad v(s) = \Gamma u(s) + \alpha$$

$$u' = B(x)v + A(x)u + f(x)$$

and employ the inverse Riccati transformation

$$v(x) = RI(x)u(x) + wi(x)$$

where the forward sweep requires the solution

$$RI' = C(x) + D(x)RI - A(x)RI - B(x)RI^2, \qquad RI(s) = \Gamma$$
$$wi' = [D(x) - B(x)RI(x)]wi - RI(x)f(x) + g(x), \qquad wi(s) = \alpha.$$

A boundary value of u at $x = S$ is necessarily a root of

$$G(u, RI(S)u + wi(S)) = 0.$$

Once a root u^* is known then the reverse sweep requires the integration of

$$u' = B(x)[RI(x)u + wi(x)] + A(x)u + f(x), \qquad u(S) = u^*.$$

Alternatively, we use the inverse of the Riccati transformation

$$v(x) = R^{-1}(x)u(x) - R^{-1}(x)w(x).$$

By observing that $R(x)[R^{-1}(x)]' + R'(x)R^{-1}(x) = 0$ we can find the differential equation for $R^{-1}(x)$ and verify by direct computation that $RI(x) \equiv R^{-1}(x)$ and $wi(x) \equiv -R^{-1}(x)w(x)$.

The success of the Riccati transformation for time discretized diffusion problems is due to the following general properties:

1) The solution of the Riccati equation behaves like $\tanh x$; i.e. it is smooth and bounded.

2) The fundamental solution of the forward sweep equation for w is exponentially decreasing and hence readily computable numerically.

3) The second boundary condition is uncoupled from the forward sweep. Only the numerical values of $R(S)$ and $w(S)$ are required.

4) Once the boundary condition at the second boundary is known the backward sweep equation again has an exponentially decreasing fundamental solution in the direction of integration.

To illustrate these points consider the simple problem

$$u''(x) - u(x) = g(x) \qquad (3.7)$$
$$u(0) = 1, \qquad u'(1) = -u^4(1).$$

An equivalent first order system and boundary conditions are

$$u' = v, \qquad u(0) = 1$$

$$v' = u + g(x), \qquad G(u(1), v(1)) \equiv u^4(1) + v(1) = 0.$$

The forward sweep requires the solution of

$$R' = 1 - R^2, \qquad R(0) = 0$$
$$w' = -R(x)w - R(x)g(x), \qquad w(0) = 1.$$

Since $R'(x) = 1$ whenever $R(x) = 0$ and $R'(x) < 0$ whenever $R(x) > 1$ it follows that $0 \leq R(x) \leq 1$ for all x. (In fact, in this case $R(x) = \tanh x$.) The positivity of $R(x)$ then assures that w has an exponentially decreasing fundamental solution with increasing x. The boundary value $v(1)$ is found from the scalar equation

$$u^4(1) + v(1) \equiv (R(1)v + w(1))^4 + v = 0.$$

This quartic equation may have up to four real roots. If this equation has no real solution then the nonlinear boundary value problem likewise has no real solution. All real solutions v^* of this equation can serve as initial values for the backward sweep equation

$$v' = R(x)v + w(x) + g(x), \quad v(1) = v^*.$$

Since we integrate from $x = 1$ toward $x = 0$ we see from $R(x) \geq 0$ that this equation likewise has an exponentially decreasing fundamental solution. As long as the source term stays bounded the exponentially decreasing fundamental solution will assure that the linear equations for w and v have bounded solutions. We can expect that the sweep equations are easy to solve numerically.

3.2 The Riccati transformation for a free boundary problem

The independence of the forward sweep from the boundary condition at $x = S$ makes the Riccati transformation approach attractive for free boundary value problems. We again consider the system (3.2) with the affine boundary condition

$$u(s) = \Gamma v(s) + \alpha$$

and free boundary conditions

$$G_1(u(S), v(S), S) = 0$$
$$G_2(u(S), v(S), S) = 0$$

at an a priori unknown point S. From the application we generally know whether S should lie above or below s. For definiteness we shall assume that $S > s$.

Three boundary conditions are necessary for a second order ordinary differential equation (and the equivalent first order system) to be able to pin down the two constants of integration and the free boundary.

The forward sweep required in the Riccati method is independent of the far boundary and we begin by integrating the differential equations (3.4). We shall assume that $R(x)$ and $w(x)$ are available over some interval (s, X). If X were the free boundary then $u(X)$, $v(X)$ and X must satisfy

$$u(X) = R(X)v(X) + w(X)$$
$$G_1(u(X), v(X), X) = 0$$
$$G_2(u(X), v(X), X) = 0.$$

We have three equations in the three unknowns u, v, and X. We can eliminate u and reduce the system to

$$G_1(R(X)v + w(X), v, X) = 0$$
$$G_2(R(X)v + w(X), v, X) = 0.$$

In most applications it is possible to also eliminate v from the system and end up with a single scalar equation

$$\phi(X) \equiv \phi(X, R(X), w(X)) = 0. \tag{3.8}$$

If so we integrate (3.4) forward from $x = s$. At every point x we monitor the function $\phi(x)$. Where it has a zero we can place the free boundary S. Once S is known we can compute $v(S)$ and carry out the reverse sweep by integrating (3.6) from $x = S$ to $x = s$. Its solution $v(x)$ in the Riccati transformation (3.3) then determines $u(x)$.

To illustrate the process we return to (3.7) and assume that the free boundary conditions are like the early exercise conditions of an American call

$$u(S) = S - 1$$
$$v(S) = 1.$$

It follows from the Riccati transformation $u(x) = R(x)v(x) + w(x)$ that S must be a root of

$$\phi(x) \equiv x - 1 - (R(x)(1) + w(x)) = 0.$$

It is conceivable that ϕ has multiple roots. Each root leads to a solution of the free boundary problem. Which root to choose as the correct free boundary is dictated by the application and will be commented on in later chapters.

3.3   The numerical solution of the sweep equations

It is tempting to turn over the numerical solution of the forward and backward sweep equations (3.4) and (3.6) to a highly accurate adaptive ODE solver for an N-dimensional first order (generally nonlinear) system of the form

$$u' = F(x, u), \qquad u(x_0) = u_0 \qquad (3.9)$$

which can be found in most scientific program libraries. This approach may not be advisable in our MOL setting. The main difficulty is that the forward sweep depends on the numerical solution $u_{n-1}(x)$ from the preceding time level which only is available at discrete points $\{x_i\}$. Similarly, the backward sweep depends on R and w from the forward sweep which likewise are available at discrete points only. Since adaptive ODE solvers for (3.9) require a function F defined for all x, our data would have to be interpolated to an order consistent with the accuracy of the integrator. To avoid this complexity, and in view of the fact that our time discretization already introduces an error of order Δt or Δt^2, and that financial parameters (i.e. the coefficients in the sweep equations) are not known with great certainty, we have consistently applied the second order trapezoidal rule on a fixed but not necessarily uniform mesh. The method is simple, implicit, stable, and, as we intend to demonstate, sufficiently accurate and fast that the solutions of the sweep equations can be found to any degree of accuracy simply by reducing the mesh size.

It is likely that many of the cited advantages of the trapezoidal rule are retained when higher order methods like Adams and BDF integrators are applied on a time invariant fixed mesh. They would require comparable effort per mesh point but fewer mesh points and thus be advantageous for the higher dimensional pricing problems of Chapter 7 where the trapezoidal rule can require fine grids and lots of memory. So far, no computational experience with other integrators for the equations of the Riccati transformation in a Black Scholes setting has been reported in the financial literature.

We recall the trapezoidal rule for the system (3.9). We define a partition

$$x_0 < \cdots < x_J$$

of the interval of integration where

$$x_0 = \min\{s, S\}, \qquad x_J = \max\{s, S\}.$$

The points of the partition are not necessarily evenly spaced. Then given a numerical solution u_{j0} of (3.9) at the point x_{j0} we find the numerical solution u_j at a neighboring point x_j from the system

$$\frac{u_j - u_{j0}}{x_j - x_{j0}} = \frac{1}{2}\left[F(x_j, u_j) + F(x_{j0}, u_{j0})\right].\tag{3.10}$$

Note that x_j may be to the right or left of the data point x_{j0}.

When the trapezoidal rule is applied to the Riccati equation (3.4) the following algebraic equation results

$$\frac{R_j - R_{j0}}{x_j - x_{j0}} = \frac{1}{2}\left\{\left[B_j + (A_j - D_j)R_j - C_j R_j^2\right]\right.$$

$$\left. + \left[B_{j0} + (A_{j0} - D_{j0})R_{j0} - C_{j0}R_{j0}^2\right]\right\}$$

where $A_j = A(x_j)$, $B_j = B(x_j)$ etc. This is a quadratic equation of the form

$$\alpha_j R_j^2 + \beta_j R_j + \gamma_j = 0$$

where

$$\alpha_j = \frac{C_j}{2}$$

$$\beta_j = \frac{1}{x_j - x_{j0}} - \frac{(A_j - D_j)}{2}$$

and

$$\gamma_j = \frac{C_{j0}}{2}R_{j0}^2 - \left[\frac{1}{x_j - x_{j0}} + \frac{(A_{j0} - D_{j0})}{2}\right]R_{j0} - \frac{(B_j + B_{j0})}{2}.$$

It is solved by formula

$$R_j = \frac{-\beta_j \pm \sqrt{\beta_j^2 - 4\alpha_j\gamma_j}}{2\alpha_j}.\tag{3.11}$$

Up to this point the algebraic sign of $x_j - x_{j0}$, i.e. the direction of integration, does not matter. However, it determines the branch of the root in (3.11). In all of our subseqent applications it is the case that $B(x) > 0$ for all x. It follows from the Riccati equation that $R'(x_{j0}) = B(x_{j0}) > 0$ whenever $R(x_{j0}) = 0$ so that $R(x) > 0$ for $x > x_{j0}$ and $R(x) < 0$ for $x < x_{j0}$. If $0 < x_j - x_{j0} \to 0$ then $\beta_j \to \infty$ and $\gamma_j < 0$. It follows that $R_j > 0$ only if the positive branch of (3.11) is chosen. Similarly, if $0 > x_j - x_{j0} \to 0$ then $\beta_j \to -\infty$ and $\gamma_j < 0$. In this case $R_j < 0$ requires the negative branch in (3.11).

We note that for very small step size (3.11) requires the subtraction of two nearly equal large numbers which can lead to loss of accuracy due to subtractive cancellation. For this reason the formula (3.11) is rewritten as

$$R_j = \frac{-2\gamma_j}{\beta_j + \sqrt{\beta_j^2 - 4\alpha_j\gamma_j}} \quad \text{if } x_j > x_{j0} \tag{3.12a}$$

$$R_j = \frac{-2\gamma_j}{\beta_j - \sqrt{\beta_j^2 - 4\alpha_j\gamma_j}} \quad \text{if } x_j < x_{j0}. \tag{3.12b}$$

Once $\{R_j\}$ is known for all j then $\{w_j\}$ is found from the linear algebraic equation

$$\frac{w_j - w_{j0}}{x_j - x_{j0}} = \frac{1}{2}\Big\{ [A_j - C_j R_j]\, w_j + [A_{j0} - C_{j0} R_{j0}]\, w_{j0} \tag{3.13}$$

$$- (R_j g_j + R_{j0} g_{j0}) + (f_j + f_{j0}) \Big\}.$$

Similarly, if $\{R_j, w_j\}$ are known then we obtain $\{v_j\}$ in the reverse sweep from

$$\frac{v_j - v_{j0}}{x_j - x_{j0}} = \frac{1}{2}\Big\{ [C_j R_j + D_j]\, v + [C_{j0} R_{j0} + D_{j0}]v_{j0} \tag{3.14}$$

$$+ (C_j w_j + C_{j0} w_{j0}) + (g_j + g_{j0}) \Big\}.$$

It is straightforward to solve these equations explicitly for w_j and v_j.

Although the trapezoidal is stable it does have a de facto step size limitation for the sweep equations obtained from the method of lines. Formula (3.11) requires real roots which can always be assured by taking $|x_j - x_{j0}|$ sufficiently small. In practice we have rarely seen this limitation. However, the linear equations (3.13), (3.14) also impose a constraint on $|x_j - x_{j0}|$. Numerical experience suggests that the step size should be so small that monotone analytic solutions of

$$w' = [A(x) - R(x)C(x)]w \quad \text{for } A(x) - R(x)C(x) \neq 0$$

and

$$v' = [C(x)R(x) + D(x)]v \quad \text{for } C(x)R(x) + D(x) \neq 0$$

are approximated by non-oscillating numerical solutions $\{w_j\}$ and $\{v_j\}$. For the numerical solution of these homogeneous equations we see from (3.13) that

$$w_j = \frac{1 + \frac{x_j - x_{j0}}{2}(A_{j0} - C_{j0}R_{j0})}{1 - \frac{x_j - x_{j0}}{2}(A_j - C_j R_j)}\, w_{j0} \equiv \mathcal{M}_j w_{j0}.$$

w_j will be monotone in j only if $\mathcal{M}_j > 0$. This will be the case if

$$\frac{x_j - x_{j0}}{2} (A_{j0} - C_{j0} R_{j0}) > -1 \tag{3.15}$$

and

$$\frac{x_j - x_{j0}}{2} (A_j - C_j R_j) < 1. \tag{3.16}$$

For the reverse sweep we obtain the formula

$$v_j = \frac{1 + \frac{x_j - x_{j0}}{2} (C_{j0} R_{j0} + D_{j0})}{1 - \frac{x_j - x_{j0}}{2} (C_j R_j + D_j)}.$$

$\{v_j\}$ will not oscillate if

$$\frac{x_j - x_{j0}}{2} (C_{j0} R_{j0} + D_{j0}) > -1 \tag{3.17}$$

and

$$\frac{x_j - x_{j0}}{2} (C_j R_j + D_j) < 1. \tag{3.18}$$

Failure to enforce these inequalities can lead to oscillations in $\{w_j\}$ and $\{v_j\}$ which will degrade the accuracy of the MOL solution. In all subsequent applications $|x_j - x_{j0}|$ is small enough to satisfy (3.15)–(3.18). To give some meaning to these inequalities consider the solution of the model problem

$$u_{xx} - u_t = 0$$

$$u(0, t) = u(1, t) = 0$$

$$u(x, 0) = u_0(x)$$

with an implicit Euler time discretization and the integration of the sweep equations on an equidistant grid with mesh size Δx. The time discretized problem at time t_n is

$$u' = v, \qquad\qquad u(0) = 0$$

$$v' = \frac{1}{\Delta t} u - \frac{1}{\Delta t} u_{n-1}(x), \qquad u(1) = 0$$

so that $A(x) = 0$, $B(x) = 1$, $C(x) = \frac{1}{\Delta t}$, $D(x) = 0$ and $g(x) = -\frac{1}{\Delta t} u_{n-1}(x)$. The Riccati equation

$$R' = 1 - \frac{1}{\Delta t} R^2, \qquad R(0) = 0$$

has the solution $R(x) = \sqrt{\Delta t} \tanh \frac{x}{\sqrt{\Delta t}}$ which we shall take to be also the numerical solution. The forward sweep proceeds from $x = 0$ to $x = 1$ so that $x_j - x_{j0} = \Delta x > 0$. For the reverse sweep we have $x_j - x_{j0} = -\Delta x < 0$.

By inspection the inequalities (3.16) and (3.18) hold for all Δx, while (3.15) requires

$$-\frac{\Delta x}{2\sqrt{\Delta t}} \tanh \frac{x_{j0}}{\sqrt{\Delta t}} > -1$$

which can be assured if

$$\frac{\Delta x}{2\sqrt{\Delta t}} < 1.$$

The same estimate is obtained from (3.17). We note that for a given Δt the inequality

$$\frac{\Delta x^2}{\Delta t} < 4$$

gives an upper bound on the acceptable Δx (which is sort of the reverse of the well known stability constraint

$$\frac{\Delta t}{\Delta x^2} < \frac{1}{2}$$

for the explicit Euler finite difference method for the heat equation). (For a demonstration of the effect of too large a space mesh near a discontinuity of the solution we refer to Figs. 7.3, 7.4.)

Little additional work is required to treat a free boundary if the boundary conditions and the Riccati transformation can be combined to characterize the location of the free boundary as the root of a single scalar equation

$$\phi(x, R(x), w(x)) \equiv \phi(x) = 0.$$

We shall assume that the free boundary S is located somewhere in the interval $[x_0, x_J]$. The initial point for the forward sweep is one of the endpoints of this interval. As above we carry out the forward sweep and compute $\{R_j, w_j\}$ for successive points of the partition. At every point x_j we evaluate $\phi(x_j, R_j, w_j)$. If ϕ changes sign between x_{j0} and x_j for some j then by continuity $\phi(x, R(x), w(x)) = 0$ at some point S between x_{j0} and x_j. We accept as the numerical free boundary S the zero of an interpolant to ϕ. In the numerical examples of this book the interpolant is a cubic through $\{\phi(x_j)\}$ at the nearest two meshpoints above and below the zero of ϕ. For example, if the forward sweep proceeds in the direction of decreasing x (as in a put) and ϕ changes sign between x_j and x_{j+1} for some j then the interpolant is the cubic through $\{\phi(x_{j+1})\}_{i=-1}^{i=2}$. The zero of this cubic is found with Newton's method starting from the zero of the linear interpolant, i.e. from the solution of

$$\phi(x_j)\,\frac{x_{j+1} - x}{x_{j+1} - x_j} + \phi(x_{j+1})\,\frac{x - x_j}{x_{j+1} - x_j} = 0.$$

On rare occasions Newton's method will fail to converge. Then S is taken to be the zero of the linear (instead of the cubic) interpolant.

One further complication has to be resolved. The reverse sweep should start at S. However, S is generally not a point of the partition $\{x_j\}$ and thus not a data point where $v'(S)$ is defined. To approximate $v'(S)$ we linearly interpolate C, D, R, w and g in (3.6) and use the trapezoidal rule to get from S back to the nearest regular mesh point.

In summary, if the method of lines with continuous x is applied then at each time level we work on a fixed grid $\{x_j\}$ plus one floating point S which describes the location of the free boundary at that time level. The forward and backward sweeps are carried out just once at each time level, while the determination of the free boundary is reduced to finding the zero of a well defined but discretely evaluated function. If ϕ has no zero then there is no free boundary and two point conditions at the ends of a given interval must apply. If ϕ has multiple zeros then the application generally dictates which is the correct free boundary.

There are applications in finance, for example American straddles, where the x-interval is bounded above and below by a free boundary. The problem is genuinely nonlinear and requires iteration. A simple modification of the above algorithm is the following approach.

We assume that x_0, x_I and x_J are chosen such that

$$x_0 < s < x_I < S < x_J$$

where s and S denote the unknown lower and upper free boundary at time t_n. We compute the Riccati solution $\{R_j\}$ with the trapezoidal rule by integrating the Riccati equation in (3.4) from x_I to x_J and from x_I to x_0 subject to

$$R(x_I) = 0.$$

We make an initial guess $w(x_I) = w_I^0$. Given w_I^k for $k \geq 0$ we

1) carry out the forward sweep (3.4) starting with $w_I = w_I^k$ from x_I to x_J and determine S^k as described above.

2) carry out the backward sweep (3.6) from S^k to x_I to generate the solution $\{V_j^k\}$ over $[x_I, S^k]$.

3) carry out the forward sweep (3.4) starting with $w_I = w_I^k$ from x_I to x_0 and determine s^k as described above.

4) carry out the backward sweep (3.6) from s^k to x_I to generate the solution $\{v_j^k\}$ over $[s^k, x_i]$.

The problem is solved if $u(x) = R(x)v(x) + w(x)$ is continuously differentiable at $x = x_I$, i.e. if $v(x)$ is continuous at x_I. Thus we need an initial value w_I^k such that

$$\psi(w_I^k) \equiv v_I^k - V_I^k = 0.$$

When $\psi(w_I^k) \neq 0$ we need a method to generate an updated value w_I^{k+1}. In the application given in Chapter 3 it is possible to find w_I^0 and w_I^1 such that $\psi(w_i^0)\psi(w_I^1) < 0$. In this case w_I^{k+1} can be found with the bisection method.

Alternatively, a discrete Newton's method can be applied to $\psi(w_I) = 0$ where

$$w_I^{k+1} = w_I^k - \frac{\psi(w_I^k)\Delta w}{\psi(w_I^k + \Delta w) - \psi(w_I^k)}$$

for a sufficiently small Δw. For an implementation of this approach we refer to the pricing of an American strangle of power options in Example 5.5.

A different approach to multiple free boundaries would be a repeated back and forth iteration between right and left free boundaries. For widely separated boundaries and slow diffusion this can be an effective method as the next application illustrates.

Example 3.1. A real option for interest rate sensitive investments.

An investment-divestment real option model is discussed in [22] which leads to the following two-sided free boundary problem

$$\frac{1}{2}\sigma^2 r^{2\gamma} V''(r) + \kappa(\theta - r)V'(r) - rV(r) + 1 = 0 \qquad (3.19)$$

$$V(r_0) = I, \quad V'(r_0) = 0; \quad V(r_1) = \alpha I, \quad V'(r_1) = 0.$$

V is the value function for an investment initiated at interest rate r_0 with initial investment I, and a recovery of αI on divestment at interest rate r_1. $V(r)$ is valued as a perpetual with coupon rate $C = 1$ for the one factor interest rate model

$$dr = k(\theta - r) + \sigma r^\gamma dW.$$

A numerical solution of (3.19) with the Riccati transformation for the CIR model with $\gamma = .5$ and a Vasicek model with $\gamma = 0$ starting with an initial guess of $r_1^0 = 2$ and $V(r_1^0) = \alpha I$ yields the iterates

CEV index γ	left boundary	right boundary	analytic [22]	
.5	$r_0^1 = .072269;$	$r_1^1 = .237541$		
.5	$r_0^2 = .072336:$	$r_1^2 = .237541$	.0723	.2375
subsequent iterates stay the same				
0	$r_0^1 = -.005511;$	$r_1^1 = .268415$		
0	$r_0^2 = .002645:$	$r_1^2 = .268249$		
0	$r_0^3 = .002645:$	$r_1^3 = .268249$		
subsequent iterates stay the same				

$\sigma = .0854, I = 10, \alpha = .75, \kappa = .2339, \theta = .0808.$

The analytic results in [22] are obtained numerically with the aid of the general solution of (3.19) in the form

$$V(r) = c_1 V_1(r) + c_2 V_2(r) + V_p(r)$$

where V_1, V_2 are hypergeometric fundamental solutions of (3.19) and V_p is a hypergeometric particular integral. We do not know whether there exists an analogous special function solution for the Vasicek interest rate model. The Riccati numerical solution of this problem is obtained instantaneously for any $\gamma \geq 0$.

We should point out that if negative left boundaries are generated during the iteration, such as r_0^1 in the Vasicek case, then general one-factor models are extended to (negative) r below an a-priori chosen threshhold r^* as a mean reverting model as discussed in Chapter 6. The extension does not affect the final result whenever the converged left free boundary r_0 lies inside (r^*, r_1).

Appendix 3.3
Connection between the Riccati transformation,
Gaussian elimination and the Brennan-Schwartz method

It is known that the Riccati transformation applied to a boundary value problem for a second order linear equation is closely related to the LU factorization of the tridiagonal algebraic system obtained from a finite difference approximation of the differential equation. In fact, all arguments can be extended to block tri-diagonal matrix equations [2], but for ease of exposition we shall illustrate the connection for the simple model problem

$$u'' - u = g(x) \qquad \text{(A3.1.1)}$$
$$u(0) = \alpha, \quad u(X) = \beta.$$

It can be solved efficiently with finite differences. For a uniform grid $\{x_i\}$ with

$$0 = x_0 < \cdots < x_{I+1} = X$$

we obtain the algebraic equations

$$u_{i+1} + u_{i-1} - 2u_i - \Delta x^2 u_i = \Delta x^2 g(x_i) \equiv \Delta x^2 g_i, \quad i = 1, \ldots, I \quad \text{(A3.1.2)}$$

which can be written compactly in matrix form

$$AU = F$$

where $U = (u_1, \ldots, u_I)$ and F depends on the source terms and the boundary data. The matrix A is tri-diagonal and strictly diagonally dominant. Hence the linear system can be solved rapidly with the so-called Thomas algorithm, a particular implementation of Gaussian elimination.

In the algorithm one recursively computes scalars $\{c_i'\}$ and $\{d_i'\}$ in a "forward sweep" for $i = 1, \ldots, I$. The method then implies that

$$u_I = d_I' \quad \text{(A3.1.3)}$$

and that the remaining components of U can be found from the reverse sweep

$$u_i = d_i' - c_i' u_{i+1}, \quad i = I - 1, I - 2, \ldots, 1. \quad \text{(A3.1.4)}$$

Details of this method may be found, for example, in the Wikipedia entry for the Thomas algorithm.

An alternate derivation of Gaussian elimination for the finite difference equations can be based on an implicit shooting method for the difference equations (A3.1.2) [50]. It leads to a discrete Riccati transformation.

For our model problem if we set

$$\frac{u_{i+1} - u_i}{\Delta x} = v_{i+1} \quad \text{(A3.1.5)}$$

then the algebraic equation (A3.1.2) can be written in the form

$$\frac{v_{i+1} - v_i}{\Delta x} = u_i + g_i. \quad \text{(A3.1.6)}$$

Since the solution of (A3.1.2) is unique, any solution of (A3.1.5), (A3.1.6) subject to $u_0 = \alpha$ and $u_{I+1} = \beta$ will be the same as the the Gaussian elimination solution.

The equations (A3.1.5), (A3.1.6) can be written in matrix form as

$$\begin{pmatrix} 1 & -\Delta x \\ 0 & 1 \end{pmatrix} \begin{pmatrix} u_{i+1} \\ v_{i+1} \end{pmatrix} = \begin{pmatrix} 1 & 0 \\ \Delta x & 1 \end{pmatrix} \begin{pmatrix} u_i \\ v_i \end{pmatrix} + \begin{pmatrix} 0 \\ \Delta x g_i \end{pmatrix}$$

so that

$$\begin{pmatrix} u_{i+1} \\ v_{i+1} \end{pmatrix} = \begin{pmatrix} 1 + \Delta x^2 & \Delta x \\ \Delta x & 1 \end{pmatrix} \begin{pmatrix} u_i \\ v_i \end{pmatrix} + \begin{pmatrix} \Delta x^2 g_i \\ \Delta x g_i \end{pmatrix}.$$

If the second equation is used to eliminate v_i from the first we see that u_i and v_i for $i = 2, \ldots, I + 1$ are related through an affine transformation of the form

$$u_i = R_i v_i + w_i \qquad (A3.1.7)$$

where from (A3.1.5)

$$R_1 = \Delta x, \quad w_1 = \alpha.$$

(A3.1.7) will be called a discrete Riccati transformation. Since u_i and v_i must solve the system (A3.1.5), (A3.1.6) we can substitute (A3.1.7) into (A3.1.5), eliminate v_{i+1} with (A3.1.6) and obtain

$$\begin{aligned} &\left[R_{i+1} - R_i - \Delta x + \Delta x R_i R_{i+1} - \Delta x^2 R_i \right] v_i \\ &= \left[w_i - w_{i+1} - \Delta x w_i (R_{i+1} - \Delta x) - \Delta x g_i (R_{i+1} - \Delta x) \right]. \end{aligned}$$

This equation will hold for all data and any choice of v_1 if both sides are set to zero. We obtain

$$R_{i+1} - R_i - \Delta x + \Delta x R_i R_{i+1} - \Delta x^2 R_i = 0, \quad R_1 = \Delta x \qquad (A3.1.8)$$

$$w_{i+1} - w_i + \Delta x w_i (R_{i+1} - \Delta x) + \Delta x g_i (R_{i+1} - \Delta x) = 0, \quad w_1 = \alpha$$

which lead to the simple recursion formulas for $i = 1, \ldots, I$

$$R_{i+1} = x + \frac{R_i}{1 + \Delta x R_i} \qquad (A3.1.9)$$

$$w_{i+1} = w_i - \Delta x R_{i+1}(w_i + g_i) + \Delta x^2 (w_i + g_i).$$

We observe that $R_1 = \Delta x$ and $w_1 = \alpha$ are consistent with $u_0 = R_0 v_0 + w_0$ if we set $R_0 = 0$, $w_0 = \alpha$ so that (A3.1.9) holds for $i = 0, \ldots, I$. (A3.1.9) is the forward sweep for the discrete Riccati transformation.

At the endpoint $x_{I+1} = X$ we require

$$R_{I+1} v_{I+1} + w_{I+1} = u_{I+1} = \beta$$

which determines v_{I+1}. The values of $\{v_i\}$ are now determined from (A3.1.5) together with $u_i = R_i v_i + w_i$ from

$$(1 + \Delta x R_i) v_i = v_{i+1} - \Delta x (w_i + g_i), \quad i = I, I - 1, \ldots, 1. \qquad (A3.1.10)$$

Using (A3.1.7) again we can rewrite this equation in the form

$$u_i = d_i - c_i u_{i+1} \qquad (A3.1.11)$$

(A3.1.10), (A3.1.11) define the backward sweep for the discrete Riccati transformation.

Since by construction the $\{u_i\}$ just found solves the system (A3.1.5), (A3.1.6) and thus (A3.1.2), and assume the correct boundary values at x_0 and X, the constants $\{d_i\}$, $\{c_i\}$ must be the same as in the backward sweep with the Thomas algorithm.

Alternatively, one can show algebraically that c_1 and d_1 coincide with c_1' and d_1', that $\{c_i\}$ and $\{d_i\}$ satisfy the recursion relations of the Thomas algorithm, and that the boundary value $u_{I+1} = R_{I+1}v_{I+1} + w_{I+1} = \beta$ implies that $u_I = d_I'$.

The algebra also shows that for our model problem

$$c_i' = \frac{\Delta x}{R_{i+1}} - 1, \quad d_i' = \frac{\Delta x}{R_{i+1}w_{i+1}}$$

so that, for example, with (A3.1.9)

$$c_i' = \frac{1}{-(2 + \Delta x^2) - c_{i-1}'}.$$

This is the recursion relation for c_i' of the Thomas algorithm. We conclude that the discrete Riccati transformation solution for a tridiagonal system is algorithmically identical to Gaussian elimination.

We now observe that if $\Delta x \to 0$ then the equations (A3.1.5), (A3.1.6) become

$$u' = v, \qquad\qquad u(0) = \alpha$$
$$v' = u + g(x), \qquad u(X) = \beta$$

while (A3.1.8) become

$$R' = 1 - R^2, \qquad\qquad R(0) = 0$$
$$w' = -R(x)w - R(x)g(x), \qquad w(0) = \alpha$$

and (A3.1.10), (A3.1.11) become

$$v' = R(x)v + w(x) + g(x), \quad v(X) = \frac{\beta - w(X)}{R(x)}$$
$$u(x) = R(x)v(x) + w(x).$$

For this reason the Riccati transformation method is sometimes called the "closure" of Gaussian elimination as $\Delta x \to 0$ [65].

When the ordinary differential equations of the Riccati transformation are solved on $[0, X]$ with the trapezoidal rule, a different approximate solution $\{u_i\}$ is obtained because R_{i+1} is found as the root of a quadratic.

It does not appear easy to discover what difference equation equivalent to (A3.1.2) it solves. However, solving a quadratic by formula will have no significant computational cost over solving the rational function in (A3.1.9) required in the Thomas algorithm.

Although given here specifically for the equations (A3.1.2) the Thomas algorithm and the discrete Riccati transformation apply also to the difference equations obtained from the time discrete Black Scholes equation. In this context it may be noted that the forward sweep continues until the boundary X is reached, but X need not be known a priori for the forward sweep. When for an American call X is chosen large enough to fall into the exercise region, and the back substitution is combined with an upward projection onto the intrinsic value then the Brennan Schwartz algorithm results (for a recent discussion of the Brennan Schwartz algorithm interpreted as an LU decomposition see [39]). Alternatively, since the forward sweep may be terminated at any mesh point, one can search during the forward sweep for that mesh point x_{I+1} where the smooth pasting delta $v_{I+1} = 1$ yields (approximately) the intrinsic option value $u_{I+1} = X - K$. At this point the forward sweep is terminated and the backward sweep begins. The Riccati approach to free boundary problems mirrors this approach. The forward and backward sweeps with the trapezoidal rule require computations similar to those of the Brennan Schwartz algorithm, but the projections in the exercise regions are avoided because the exercise boundary is known.

Similar comments apply to the American put where the forward sweep proceeds from X toward 0 and the back-substitution (also called a backward sweep in these notes) from the early exercise boundary toward X. Again, the early exercise boundary found corresponds to that mesh point x_{i0} where the smooth pasting delta $v_{i0} = -1$ yields the correct intrinsic value of the put.

The computational cost of the Thomas algorithm is a linear function of the number of mesh points and the same is true when the trapezoidal rule is used to solve the equations of the continuous Riccati transformation. Hence the Riccati method is comparable to the Brennan Schwartz method in computational efficiency.

Chapter 4

European Options

European option prices governed by the Black Scholes equation can often be found analytically from a so-called Black Scholes formula. Such closed form solutions are useful to analyze and calibrate numerical methods so that they can be employed with confidence for related problems where no exact solutions are known. Here we shall compare the MOL solution with the analytic solution for some typical European options.

We shall consider first the standard scaled Black Scholes equation for the price V of a plain European option

$$\frac{1}{2}\sigma^2 x^2 u_{xx} + (r - q)xu_x - ru - u_t = F(x, t), \qquad (4.1)$$

where $u = V/C$, $x = S/K$. C is a scaling factor and for most options is equal to K, where K denotes the strike price. S is the value of the underlying asset, and σ, r and q are the volatility of the asset price, the risk-free interest rate and the dividend rate. $t = T - \tau$ stands for the time to expiry of the option where τ is calendar time. For plain puts and calls $F \equiv 0$. In addition, σ, r and q in (4.1) are initially assumed to be constant which allows the transformation of (4.1) to the standard heat equation, and which ultimately leads to analytical solutions in terms of error integrals.

Equation (4.1) is subject to boundary conditions at $x = 0$ and as $x \to \infty$ or at some finite barriers, and to a pay-off condition at expiry which we shall write as

$$u(x, 0) = u_0(x).$$

Desired are the value of the option

$$V(S, t) = Cu(x, t),$$

the delta of the option

$$V_S(S, t) = C/K u_x(x, t),$$

and the gamma of the option

$$V_{SS}(S,t) = C/K^2 u_{xx}(x,t)$$

where $x = S/K$. Other Greeks are computed from equations similar to (4.1) obtained by differentiating (4.1) with respect to problem parameters. In this case we find in general that $F \not\equiv 0$.

The challenge to the numerical solution of (4.1) typically comes from three sources:

(1) Severe numerical problems arise when the initial condition and the boundary conditions are discontinuous. Binary and barrier options are common examples leading to discontinuities in u at $t = 0$ at isolated points of x, and to large changes in the delta and gamma for $t > 0$ near such points. Numerical methods have to take note of such points, either by "subtracting out" a function which shows similar singular behavior [67, p. 260], or by refining the approximations near such points. The method of lines coupled with the sweep method will also depend on refined approximations near singularities (see Example 4.2).

(2) A second source of problems arises when equation (4.1) has to be solved for $x \in (0, \infty)$. A numerical method typically is affected by the vanishing coefficient of u_{xx} at $x = 0$ and by the unbounded domain. Fortunately, for the Black Scholes equation (4.1) the coefficient $\frac{1}{2}\sigma^2 x^2$ vanishes fast enough as $x \to 0$ that it has little influence on the computation as long as the numerical method reduces to a consistent approximation of (4.1) for $x = 0$. Alternatively, we can sometimes impose a boundary condition derived from the Black Scholes equation. For example, as discussed in Example 1.12, equation (4.1) has to hold at $x = 0$. It reduces to

$$-ru(0,t) - u_t(0,t) = 0$$

which leads to the boundary condition

$$u(0,t) = u_0(0)e^{-rt}.$$

For an application of the MOL on $0 < x < \infty$ with a boundary condition given at $x = 0$ we avoid the degeneracy at $x = 0$ either by replacing (4.1) with the regularized equation

$$con(x)u_{xx} + (r-q)xu_x - ru - u_t = F(x,t) \qquad (4.2)$$

where

$$con(x) = \max\left\{\epsilon, \frac{1}{2}\sigma^2 x^2\right\}, \quad \epsilon \ll 1,$$

or by imposing the left boundary condition at some barrier $x = x_0 \ll 1$ instead of at $x = 0$.

If (4.1) is also subject to a boundary condition as $x \to \infty$ then the right boundary condition is imposed instead at a barrier $x = X$, i.e. at $S = XK$. The influence of X on option prices needs to be examined in each case. For most of our numerical examples we find $X = 3$ (i.e. a barrier at 3 times the strike price) to be sufficiently large to have negligible impact on V near $S = K$ (see again Example 4.2).

We note that a computational domain $[x_0, X]$ for (4.1) with $x_0 > 0$ is equivalent to a finite computational domain which is routinely employed when the Black Scholes equation is transformed to a constant coefficient equation with the transformation $y = \ln x$ and then solved numerically. In these notes we usually solve the regularized equation (4.2) or its analog in higher dimensions on a fixed grid. It is generally straightforward to determine a threshhold for ϵ below which the regularization has no discernible influence on the solution near x-values of practical interest.

(3) A third class of problems arises near points where the convective term rxu_x in (4.1) dominates the diffusive term $\frac{1}{2}\sigma^2 x^2 u_{xx}$. Attention has been paid in the PDE based financial literature on how to cope with the almost hyperbolic aspects of this problem [68]. It is easy to recognize when a method fails to solve a convection dominated diffusive problem because the numerical solution will show unacceptable oscillations. We can often eliminate the oscillations simply by refining the spatial mesh used for the Riccati method (see Example 4.3 below).

The method of lines approximation at $t = t_n = n\Delta t = nT/N$ of (4.2) is

$$con(x)u'' + (r - q)xu' - ru - Du_n(x) = F(x, t_n) \qquad (4.3)$$

where

$$Du(x) = \begin{cases} \dfrac{u - u_{n-1}(x)}{\Delta t}, & n = 1, 2 \\[2ex] \dfrac{3}{2}\dfrac{u - u_{n-1}(x)}{\Delta t} - \dfrac{1}{2}\dfrac{u_{n-1}(x) - u_{n-2}(x)}{\Delta t}, & n = 3, \dots, N. \end{cases}$$

The first order systems are

$$u' = v \qquad n = 1, 2 \qquad (4.4)$$

$$v' = \frac{1}{con(x)}\left[\left(r + \frac{1}{\Delta t}\right)u - (r - q)xv - \frac{1}{\Delta t}u_{n-1}(x) + F(x, t_n)\right]$$

and

$$u' = v \qquad\qquad n = 3, \ldots, N \qquad\qquad (4.5)$$

$$v' = \frac{1}{con(x)} \left[\left(r + \frac{3}{2\Delta t} \right) u - (r - q)xv - \frac{3}{2\Delta t} u_{n-1}(x) \right.$$

$$\left. - \frac{1}{2\Delta t} \left(u_{n-1}(x) - u_{n-2}(x) \right) + F(x, t_n) \right].$$

The approximation introduced in (4.2) assures that all coefficients are bounded.

The direction of the sweep is dictated by the boundary conditions imposed on (4.3). We recall that a non-iterative forward/backward sweep method results whenever we have an affine boundary condition of the form

$$c_1 u + c_2 v = c_3$$

at one endpoint of the interval. The forward sweep then proceeds from that endpoint to the opposite endpoint.

We shall examine the quality of the MOL solution for some representative non-trivial applications when the equations (4.4) and (4.5) are solved with the sweep method and the trapezoidal rule as described in the previous chapter. The objective is to show that for many options the numerical solution of the time-discrete equations can be computed economically to such an accuracy that it is indistinguishable from the analytical solution of the MOL equation.

Example 4.1. A plain European call.

The Black Scholes model for a European call requires the solution of (4.1) with $F(x,t) = 0$ and $C = K$ for $x \in (0, \infty)$ subject to the initial condition

$$u(x, 0) = \max\{x - 1, 0\}.$$

We know from Example 1.1 that its solution is given by the Black Scholes formula

$$u_{BS}(x, t) = xe^{-qt} N(d_1) - e^{-rt} N(d_2)$$

where

$$d_1 = \frac{\ln x + \left(r - q + \frac{\sigma^2}{2} \right) t}{\sigma \sqrt{t}}$$

and

$$d_2 = d_1 - \sigma\sqrt{t}.$$

There is, of course, no need to solve (4.1) numerically to price a call (and its counterpart — the European put). This simple option is chosen solely to illustrate the method of lines for options and to outline some of the decision which must be made to implement the sweep method.

The Black Scholes formula is the unique solution of this problem, and by inspection we see that $u(x,t)$ is continuous for $t \geq 0$ and infinitely differentiable for $t > 0$. However,

$$\lim_{t \to 0} u_x(x,t) = H(x-1) \quad \text{for } x \geq 0$$

and

$$\lim_{t \to 0} u_{xx}(x,t) = \delta(x-1)$$

where H and δ denote the Heaviside (step) function and the (mathematical) delta or impulse function. Thus for $t \ll 1$, i.e. near expiry of the option, we expect steep gradients in the (financial) delta $u_x(x,t)$ and (scaled) gamma $u_{xx}(x,t)$ around $x = 1$. Since the delta and gamma are often required information any numerical method for solving the Black Scholes equation must demonstrate that it also delivers reliable Greeks. Discontinuities in the boundary/initial data exacerbate the numerical problem because the delta itself is large near discontinuities.

The call is defined for $x \in (0, \infty)$ and $t \in [0, T]$, and its analytic solution is determined by the initial condition only. For a time implicit numerical solution we generally need a finite computational domain $[x_0, x_J] \times [0, T]$ and boundary conditions at x_0 and x_J.

Financial considerations (as well as the arguments of Example 1.12) dictate that

$$\lim_{x \to 0} u(x,t) = 0$$

and that $u(x,t)$ grow linearly as $x \to \infty$, i.e. that

$$\lim_{x \to \infty} u_{xx}(x,t) = 0.$$

We remark that this boundary condition, rather than the growth condition

$$\lim_{x \to \infty} u_x(x,t) = e^{-qt}$$

derived in Example 1.17, is chosen simply in order to illustrate how it can be incoporated into the Riccati approach. The numerical MOL results are identical for both boundary conditions at $x = X$. These conditions are, of course, consistent with the Black Scholes formula. It is natural to impose these asymptotic limits at x_0 and x_J.

The numerical solution of the European call will show errors due to

a) the regularization at $x_0 = 0$ (or, alternatively, a barrier condition at $x_0 > 0$),
b) the imposition of barrier boundary conditions at x_J,
c) the time discretization chosen for the MOL approximation of the Black Scholes equation, and
d) the numerical solution of the MOL approximation on $[x_0, x_J]$ with the sweep method.

We shall examine the performance of the method of lines coupled with the sweep method for the call considered in [63, p. 126]. The parameters are

$$T = 1, \quad r = .05, \quad q = .025, \quad \sigma = .35.$$

Our implementation of the sweep method for this call uses an a priori chosen grid with mesh widths

$$\Delta x = \frac{.9 - x_0}{j1} \quad \text{on } [x_0, .9]$$

$$\Delta x = \frac{1.1 - .9}{j2} \quad \text{on } [.9, 1.1]$$

and

$$\Delta x = \frac{x_J - 1.1}{j3} \quad \text{on } [1.1, x_J]$$

so that $J = j1 + j2 + j3$. The mesh size is smallest around $x = 1$ because of the lack of smoothness of the solution near $x = 1$ as $t \to 0$.

The time step is chosen to be uniform with

$$\Delta t = T/N,$$

and two initial backward Euler steps are followed by the three level method.

At every time step the boundary value problem for the first order system (4.4) and (4.5) is solved with the sweep method of section 2.1. For time levels 1 and 2 a comparison of (4.4) and (3.2) shows that

$$A(x) = 0, \qquad B(x) = 1$$

$$C(x) = \frac{1}{\text{con}(x)}\left(r + \frac{1}{\Delta t}\right), \qquad D(x) = \frac{-1}{\text{con}(x)}(r - q)x$$

$$f(x) = 0, \qquad g(x) = \frac{-1}{\text{con}(x)}\frac{u_{n-1}(x)}{\Delta t}$$

where $\text{con}(x) = \max\left\{10^{-6}, \frac{1}{2}\sigma^2 x^2\right\}$.

The forward sweep proceeds from $x = x_0$ with initial conditions

$$\Gamma = \alpha = 0$$

to $x = x_J$. The reverse sweep calls for the integration of (3.6) from x_J to x_0. The initial condition for $v(x_J)$ is found from

$$u_{xx}(x_J, t_n) \cong v'(x_J) = 0,$$

i.e.

$$C(x_J)u(x_J) + D(x_J)v(x_J) + g(x_J) = 0.$$

Since

$$u(x_J) = R(x_J)v(x_J) + w(x_J)$$

it follows that

$$v(x_J) = \frac{-[C(x_J)w(x_J) + g(x_J)]}{C(x_J)R(x_J) + D(x_J)}.$$

For $n \geq 3$ we make the change

$$C(x) = \frac{1}{\text{con}(x)}\left(r + \frac{3}{\Delta t}\right)$$

$$g(x) = \frac{1}{\text{con}(x)}\left(\frac{-4u_{n-1}(x) + u_{n-2}(x)}{2\Delta t}\right).$$

Note that the Riccati equation needs to be solved only for $n = 1$ and $n = 3$. At all other time levels the Riccati solution from the preceding time level can be used.

Numerical results are given for

$$x_0 = .005 \quad \text{(i.e. } S_{\min} = Kx_0; \text{ note that } \text{con}(x_0) = 1.53 \cdot 10^{-6})$$

$$x_J = 3.5 \quad \text{(i.e. } S_{\max} = Kx_J),$$

$$j1 = 179, \ j2 = 80, \ j3 = 480 \text{ and } N = 200.$$

Maximum observed errors over the interval $.5 < x < 2$ (i.e. away from the barriers) are

$$\max_x |u(x,T) - u_{BS}(x,T)| = 2.169 \ 10^{-6} \quad \text{at } x = 1.445$$

$$\max_x |u_x(x,T) - u_{BSx}(x,T)| = 8.043 \ 10^{-6} \quad \text{at } x = .5$$

$$\max_x |u_{xx}(x,T) - u_{BSxx}(x,T)| = 6.436 \ 10^{-5} \quad \text{at } x = .605.$$

The error in the option price is about the same as reported in [63] for a finite difference solution of the Black Scholes equation. Mesh refinements

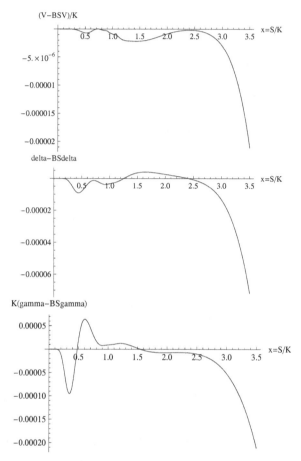

Fig. 4.1. The error in the scaled option price $u(x, T) = V(S, T)/K$, in the delta $u_x(x, T) = V_S(S, T)$ and in the scaled gamma $u_{xx}(x, T) = K V_{SS}(S, T)$ for $x = S/K$ compared with the corresponding analytic Black Scholes solutions. The MOL results exhibited in Fig. 4.1 are obtained instantaneously with a desktop computer of Table 7.15.

in x and t lead to errors of the same order which suggests that the MOL equations are a good approximation of the Black Scholes equation and that they are solved accurately with the trapezoidal rule for the sweep method on the chosen grid.

Computing with the same mesh size on the interval $[.1, 3]$ (when $con(.1) = 6.13 \cdot 10^{-4}$) gave the same errors on $.5 < x < 2$ as above. Hence for most of the following examples we shall use $x_J = 3$. However, if option prices deep in the money are required then the choice of x_J becomes critical. For example, if $x_0 = .005$ then (see also [63])

$$u(1.5, 1) - u_{BS}(1.5, 1) = -2.4387 \ 10^{-2} \quad \text{if } x_J = 1.5$$
$$u(1.5, 1) - u_{BS}(1.5, 1) = -2.1660 \ 10^{-6} \quad \text{if } x_J = 3.$$

We should point out that the quality of the numerical solution is greatly aided by the choice of $T = 1$. Near expiration, say at $t = \Delta t$, the delta and gamma change rapidly near $x = 1$ so that discretization errors become dominant. The next example indicates that only the time discretization is troublesome.

Example 4.2. A binary cash or nothing European call.

This example and its numerical challenge are representative for all options with discontinuous initial and/or boundary data such as binary and barrier options, but with significant volatility, say $\sigma \geq .05$.

The price of a cash or nothing call (for notational convenience with payout $C = K$) is obtained from (4.1) with $F \equiv 0$ subject to the initial condition

$$u_0(x) = H(x - 1), \qquad 0 < x < \infty,$$

where H is the standard Heaviside function

$$H(x) = \begin{cases} 0, & x < 0 \\ 1, & x \geq 0. \end{cases}$$

The boundary conditions are

$$u(0, t) = 0, \quad \lim_{x \to \infty} u(x, t) = e^{-rt}.$$

Because the initial condition is discontinuous at $x = 1$ the solution of the time discrete approximation at $n = 1$ will be the most difficult to find numerically. At subsequent time levels the MOL solutions will be smoother and therefore easier to compute. Hence we shall focus on the solution of (4.4) for $n = 1$.

The method of lines approximation of (4.1) at $t = \Delta t$ is

$$\frac{1}{2} \sigma^2 x^2 u'' + rxu' - \left(r + \frac{1}{\Delta t}\right) u = \begin{cases} 0 & x < 1 \\ -\frac{1}{\Delta t} & x \geq 1 \end{cases}$$

$$u(0) = 0, \quad \lim_{x \to \infty} u(x) = \exp(-r\Delta t). \tag{4.6}$$

Standard solution techniques for ordinary differential equations tell us that the analytic solution of (4.6) is of the form

$$u(x) = \begin{cases} c_1 x^{\gamma_1} + c_2 x^{\gamma_2}, & x < 1 \\ d_1 x^{\gamma_1} + d_2 x^{\gamma_2} + \dfrac{1}{1 + r\Delta t}, & x \geq 1 \end{cases} \tag{4.7}$$

where γ_1 and γ_2 are the positive and negative root of

$$\frac{1}{2}\sigma^2\gamma(\gamma - 1) + r\gamma - \left(r + \frac{1}{\Delta t}\right) = 0.$$

The boundary conditions and the continuity of u and u' at $x = 1$ yield four conditions to determine the coefficients $c_{1,2}$ and $d_{1,2}$. (We observe in passing that the analytic MOL solution is bounded at $x = 0$ and as $x \to \infty$ if and only if $c_2 = d_1 = 0$. This implies that

$$\lim_{x \to \infty} u(x) = \frac{1}{1 + r\Delta t},$$

in other words, that the problem (4.6) does not have a solution at all unless the boundary condition at infinity is approximated by

$$e^{-rt} \cong \frac{1}{1 + r\Delta t}.)$$

To avoid the singularity at $x = 0$ and the infinite interval in the numerical solution of (4.6) we shall impose on (4.6) the boundary (i.e. barrier) conditions

$$u(.005, t) = 0, \qquad u(3, t) = e^{-rt}. \tag{4.8}$$

For these boundary conditions it is simple to compute algebraically the coefficients of the solution (4.7). We are then able to compare the numerical solution of the MOL approximation at $t = \Delta t$ with the analytic solution of the MOL approximation. This will give insight how well the sweep method coupled with a trapezoidal rule can solve the boundary value problem for the time discretized Black Scholes equation. In addition we shall compare the analytic MOL solution with the Black Scholes solution for a cash or nothing call to examine the effect of the time discretization and of the barrier at $x = 3$.

For the numerical simulation we use the following data:

$$\sigma = .3$$
$$r = .05$$
$$t = .001.$$

Hence we wish to price the cash or nothing call about 9 hours before expiration.

The analytic MOL solution (4.7) will have a steep delta and a discontinuous gamma at $x = 1$. To cope with this lack of smoothness we shall use a predefined variable grid on the interval of computation $[.005, 3]$ with grid size

$$\Delta x = \begin{cases} (.9 - .005)/100 & \text{on } [.005, .9] \\ (1.1 - .9)/500 & \text{on } [.9, 1.1] \\ (3 - 1.1)/100 & \text{on } [1.1, 3]. \end{cases}$$

Numerical and analytic solutions are collected in Figs. 4.2(a)–(f). Note that only scaled values are plotted. Actual prices and Greeks require the strike price K and the cash payment C as described above.

Figure 4.2(a) shows a plot of the numerical MOL solution $un(x)$ and of the analytic MOL solution $uan(x)$ given by (4.7). To plotting accuracy these two curves coincide. The maximum absolute error between these two solutions occurs at $x = 1$ where

$$|un(1) - uan(1)| = .01448$$

which amounts to an error of about 3%. Doubling the mesh points on each subinterval halves the error.

We also show in Fig. 4.2(a) the analytic Black Scholes solution $ubs(x, t)$ given for the cash or nothing call by

$$ubs(x, t) = e^{-rt} N(d_2), \qquad d_2 = \frac{(\ln x + (r - \sigma^2/2)t}{\sigma \sqrt{t}}$$

(see [33, p. 88]). There is a noticeable difference between the MOL and the Black Scholes solutions. The maximum error is found at $x = 1.0044$ where

$$|un(1.0044) - ubs(1.0044, .001)| = .06945$$

which corresponds to a relative error of about 10%.

Figure 4.2(b) shows the corresponding curves for the delta. Again, to plotting accuracy the numerical and analytic MOL solutions coincide but differ markedly from the Black Scholes delta. Clearly, the MOL delta has no significance at the first time step for the cash or nothing option.

Figure 4.2(c) shows the corresponding gamma. The numerical and analytic MOL solutions coincide in the plot. The maximum error occurs again at $x = 1$ where

$$|un''(1\pm) - uan''(1\pm)| = 324.123$$

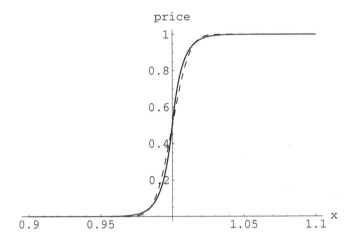

Fig. 4.2. (a) Solid line: Analytical and numerical MOL price at $t = \Delta t = .001$. Broken line: Black Scholes price at $t = .001$.

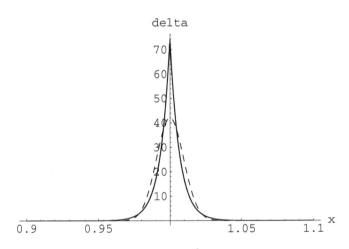

Fig. 4.2. (b) Solid line: Analytical and numerical MOL delta at $t = \Delta t = .001$. Broken line: Black Scholes delta at $t = .001$.

which also amounts to an error of about 3%. As above, doubling the mesh points halves this error. A comparison with the Black Scholes gamma is meaningless because the MOL gamma is discontinuous while the Black Scholes gamma is necessarily smooth.

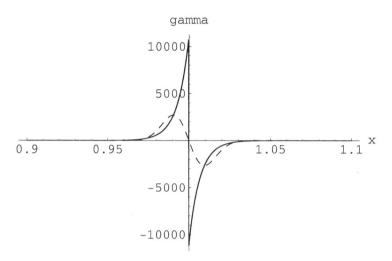

Fig. 4.2. (c) Solid line: Analytical and numerical MOL gamma at $t = \Delta t = .001$. Broken line: Black Scholes gamma at $t = .001$.

The conclusion from these graphs is that the spatial resolution of the MOL equation with the sweep method and the trapezoidal integrator is good enough that numerical errors in x can essentially be suppressed for sufficiently small Δx. Since no large matrices are stored in the sweep method one can refine Δx until the computed answers at a given time level no longer change. There are neither oscillations nor overshoot at the points of discontinuity. Hence for sufficiently small Δx the error in the numerical MOL solution is governed only by the time discretization of the Black Scholes equation.

If an accurate solution in x at $t = .001$ is desired then the time step must be reduced further. Figures 4.2(d)–(f) show the numerical MOL solution, the delta and the gamma and the corresponding analytical Black Scholes functions again at

$$t = .001$$

obtained after ten time steps with $\Delta t = .001/10$ and the spatial resolution used for Fig. 4.2(a). The backward Euler discretization (4.4) is used for the first two time steps, followed by the 3-level scheme (4.5). (It is also possible to find the analytic MOL solution after ten time steps, but the calculation is cumbersome and not carried out here.)

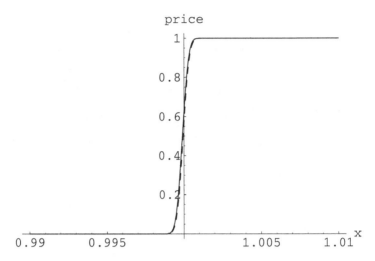

Fig. 4.2. (d) Solid line: Numerical MOL price at $t = .001$ after ten time steps. Broken line: Black Scholes price at $t = .001$.

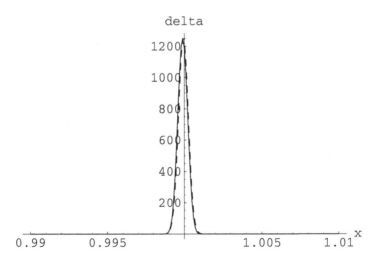

Fig. 4.2. (e) Solid line: Numerical MOL delta at $t = .001$ after ten time steps. Broken line: Black Scholes delta at $t = .001$.

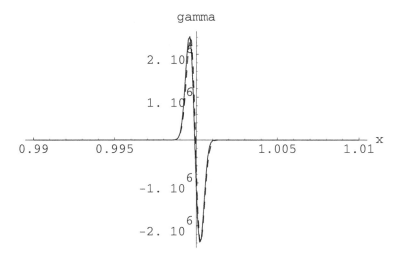

Fig. 4.2. (f) Solid line: Numerical MOL gamma at $t = .001$ after ten time steps. Broken line: Black Scholes gamma at $t = .001$.

The good agreement with the analytical solution indicates that the artificial barrier at $x = 3$ does not degrade the solution. This is not surprising. It follows from the Black Scholes formula for the cash or nothing call that for our parameters

$$u_{bs}(3, t) \cong e^{-rt}$$

for all $t \leq .5$.

Example 4.3. A binary call with low volatility.

Convection dominated diffusion has been observed when pricing bonds for low interest rates with certain mean reversion one factor models [68]. We can illustrate this phenomenon also with Example 4.2 when we choose a low volatility and a very high interest rate. For our calculation we use

$$\sigma = .01$$
$$r = 1.0$$
$$q = 0.$$

The convective term rxu_x dominates $\frac{1}{2}\sigma^2 x^2 u_{xx}$ in equation (4.1) on $0 < x < 1$ and we expect a wave-like propagation of the Heaviside payoff function toward $x = 0$ with time. Since we still have the Black Scholes equation the formulas of Example 4.2 allow us to compare the analytical and the computed MOL solution, while a comparison with the analytical Black Scholes

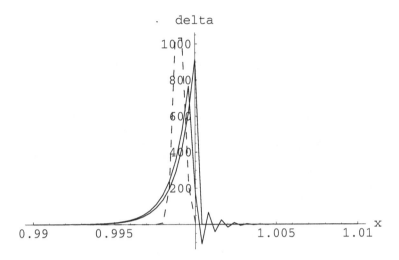

Fig. 4.3. (a) Solid lines: Analytical and numerical MOL delta at $t = \Delta t = .001$ coarse grid with 700 points. Broken line: Black Scholes delta.

formula gives insight into how well the MOL approximation reproduces the analytical solution of the cash or nothing calls for low volatility.

The same number of mesh points as in Example 4.2, i.e. 100 evenly spaced points in $[.005, .9]$ and in $[1.1, 3]$, and 500 evenly spaced points in $[.9, 1.1]$ cannot resolve the problem after one time step with $t = .001$. The computed price shows oscillations near $x = 1$ which are reflected in the jagged delta shown in Fig. 4.3(a). Repeating the calculation with a fine mesh of 800 points on $[.005, .9]$ and on $[1.1, 3]$ and with 4000 points on $[.9, 1.1]$ gave agreement in the plots for the computed and analytical MOL price, delta, and gamma. The new delta is shown in Fig. 4.3(b).

As in Example 4.2 the MOL solution differs from the analytical Black Scholes solution reflecting the influence of the time discretization. A better fit is obtained for smaller Δt. Figures 4.3(c), (d), (e) show the price, delta and gamma at $t = .001$ obtained after 20 time steps with $\Delta t = .001/20$ with the fine x-grid of 5600 points.

The plots appear to show good agreement, but the MOL results are at the limit of their reliability. For example, the maximum error in the scaled price occurs at $x = S/K = .99875$ where

$$|un(.99875) - ubs(.99875, .001)| = .23645 - .21359 = 2.286 \cdot 10^{-2}$$

which misprices the cash or nothing call by about 11%. Smaller time steps yield the same maximum error which suggests that the space discretization

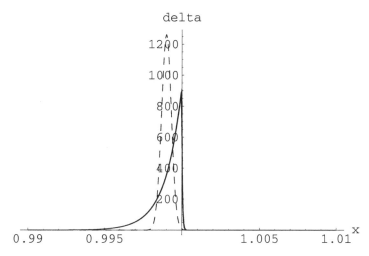

Fig. 4.3. (b) Solid lines: Analytical and numerical MOL delta at $t = \Delta t = .001$ fine grid with 5600 points. Broken line: Black Scholes delta.

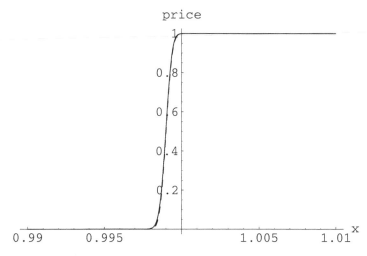

Fig. 4.3. (c) Solid line: Numerical MOL price at $t = .001$ after 20 time steps. Broken line: Black Scholes price at $t = .001$.

is limiting the accuracy. Increasing the number of points in $[.9, 1.1]$ to 18000 and using 100 time steps yields a maximum error

$$|un(.999) - ubs(.999, .001)| = 6.624 \cdot 10^{-3}$$

delta

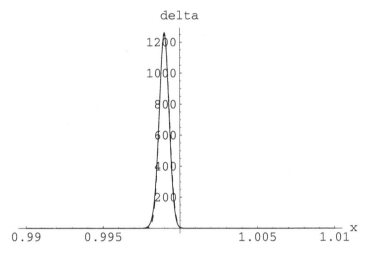

Fig. 4.3. (d) Solid line: Numerical MOL delta at $t = .001$ after 20 time steps. Broken line: Black Scholes delta at $t = .001$.

gamma

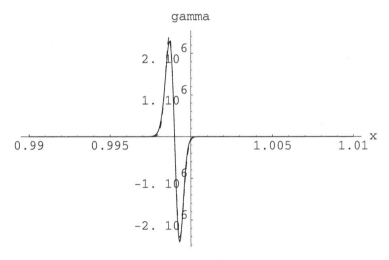

Fig. 4.3. (e) Solid line: Numerical MOL gamma at $t = .001$ after 20 time steps. Broken line: Black Scholes gamma at $t = .001$.

which amounts to a relative error of 1.3% in the price of the option. Smaller time steps again fail to reduce the error further. Such fine grids require long run times per time step and may well be impractical.

It is apparent from this example that convection dominated diffusion is a serious complication for the numerical calculation of Black Scholes prices which demands special numerical methods (as in [68]) or very fine grid spacings.

Mispricing diminishes with increasing volatility and decreasing interest rate. For $\sigma \geq .05$ we again have the situation of Example 4.2 where the spatial errors can be entirely suppressed for acceptably small Δx.

Example 4.4. The Black Scholes Barenblatt equation for a CEV process.

The final example of this chapter illustrates the iterative solution of a non-linear generalization of the Black Scholes equation, the so-called Black Scholes Barenblatt equation, with the method of lines.

The general problem is to find attainable upper and lower bounds on the price of a European option modeled with the Black Scholes equation

$$\frac{1}{2}\sigma(x,t)^2 x^2 u_{xx} + (r - q)x u_x - ru - u_t = 0$$

when the volatility function $\sigma(x,t)$ is an arbitrary piecewise continuous function which satisfies

$$\sigma_0(x,t) \leq \sigma(x,t) \leq \sigma_1(x,t)$$

for given continuous functions σ_0 and σ_1.

It is known that upper and lower bounds on all prices for the option with volatility in the given range are given by the so-called Black Scholes Barenblatt equation ([56], see also Example 1.9)

$$\frac{1}{2}\bar{\sigma}(x,t)^2 x^2 u_{xx} + (r - q)x u_x - ru - u_t = \pm F(x,t,|u_{xx}|) \qquad (4.9)$$

where

$$\bar{\sigma}(x,t)^2 = \frac{\sigma_1(x,t)^2 + \sigma_0(x,t)^2}{2}$$

and

$$F(x,t,|u_{xx}|) = \frac{1}{2}\frac{\sigma_1(x,t)^2 - \sigma_0(x,t)^2}{2}x^2|u_{xx}|$$

subject to the payoff and boundary conditions of the option under consideration. The upper bound is found from (4.9) with right hand side $+F$, the lower bound corresponds to right hand side $-F$.

We point out that equation (4.9) can be rewritten in several ways. For example, if we write $a^+ = \max\{a, 0\}$, $a^- = \min\{a, 0\}$, substitute

$$u_{xx} = u_{xx}^+ + u_{xx}^-, \qquad |u_{xx}| = u_{xx}^+ - u_{xx}^-$$

into (4.9) and cancel common terms then the more familiar version of the Black Scholes Barenblatt equation results where the volatility is a function of the convexity of u. Moreover, if σ_0 and σ_1 are constant then equation (4.9) with positive right hand side is identical to an option model incorporating transaction costs [56].

Here we shall assume that σ_0 and σ_1 are bounding functions determined from a CEV model with different exponents. We shall set

$$\sigma_0(x) = \min\{c_0 x^{-\alpha}, c_1 x^{-\beta}\}$$

$$\sigma_1(x) = \max\{c_0 x^{-\alpha}, c_1 x^{-\beta}\}$$

where

$$0 < \alpha < \beta.$$

The curves $c_0 x^{-\alpha}$ and $c_1 x^{-\beta}$ cross at a point $\hat{x}^{\beta-\alpha}$ given by

$$\hat{x}^{\beta-\alpha} = c_1/c_0.$$

The unknown volatility could be, for example, any other CEV volatility $c x^{-\gamma}$ for

$$\alpha \leq \gamma \leq \beta$$

with the same value as $\sigma_0(x)$ at $x = \hat{x}$.

To illustrate the influence of the exponent we shall solve for the price of a double barrier European straddle satisfying

$$u(.8, t) = u(1.2, t) = 0$$

$$u(x, 0) = \max\{1 - x, 0\} + \max\{0, x - 1\}.$$

This option will have several sign changes in its gamma.

The method of lines approximation of (4.9) obtained after discretizing time is a nonlinear problem due to $|u_{xx}|$ in the source term F. Its solution is found by simple iteration. Let $u^0(x)$ denote our initial guess for the solution of (4.9) at time level n. The choice of this guess is not critical. We can set

$$u^0(x) = 0$$

at the first time level, and

$$u^0(x) = u_{n-1}(x)$$

at all other time levels, where u_{n-1} is the solution at t_{n-1}. We then generate a sequence $\{u^k(x)\}$, $k = 1, 2, \ldots$ where $u^k(x)$ is the solution of (4.4), (4.5) with known source terms

$$\pm F\left(x, t, |u_{xx}^{k-1}(x)|\right).$$

The two point boundary value problem for u^k is solved with the Riccati method. Note that the Riccati equation does not depend on k and usually not on n. We accept as MOL solution at $t = t_n$ the last iterate $u^k(x)$ when

$$\max_x |u^k(x) - u^{k-1}(x)| \leq tol$$

for some preset convergence tolerance *"tol"*. Thus the solution method for the Black Scholes Barenblatt equation is not any more difficult than for the Black Scholes equation, except that at each time level we need to solve the sweep equations for several source terms. Numerical experiments and a mathematical convergence analysis of a related problem [53] show that this iteration is robust and fast.

Figure 4.4 shows the Black Scholes Barenblatt solutions for the following (exaggerated) volatility data:

$$\sigma_0(x) = \min\{.3x^{-.5}, .3x^{-3}\}$$
$$\sigma_1(x) = \max\{.3x^{-.5}, .3x^{-3}\}$$

The volatility curves cross at $S = K$, i.e. at $x = 1$ where

$$\sigma_0(1) = .3.$$

We also compute the Black Scholes price of a straddle when

$$\sigma(x) = .3x^{-4}$$

so that $\sigma_0(x) \leq \sigma(x) \leq \sigma_1(x)$.

Figure 4.4(a) shows the price of the CEV process over $[.8, 1.2]$ and its upper and lower bound when $r = 0.05$, $q = 0$, $T = .01$ for $\Delta t = .01/10$ and $\Delta x = 1/4000$. Fig. 4.4(b) and Fig. 4.4(c) show the first and second derivatives of these curves. The convergence tolerance was set to $tol = 10^{-5}$. The number of iterations decreases monotonically from $k = 15$ at the first time level to $k = 3$ at $t = .01$ as the solution decays with time.

For a more challenging uncertain parameter problem we refer to Example 1.9 and Example 7.10 where the derivation and numerical solution of a Black Scholes Barenblatt equation associated with an uncertain correlation factor of options on two assets is discussed. The simple substitution iteration of the current example will again be applied. For most of these problems no analysis is available, but numerical calculations are easy to implement and reveal quickly enough whether they will converge.

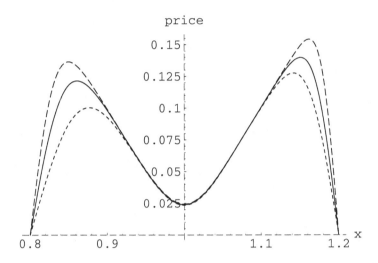

Fig. 4.4. (a) Broken lines: Upper and lower bounds on the option price. Solid line: Price for a CEV process with intermediate volatility.

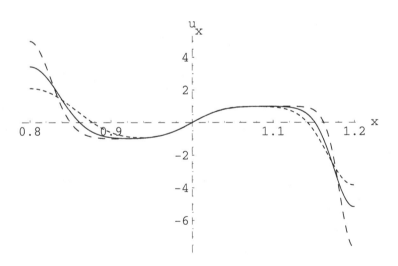

Fig. 4.4. (b) Broken lines: u_x for the Black Scholes Barenblatt solutions. Solid line: Delta of the CEV process.

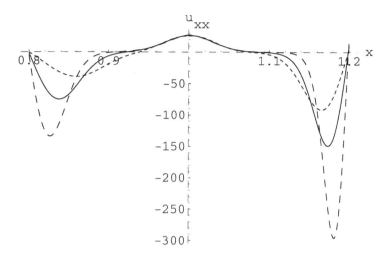

Fig. 4.4. (c) Broken lines: u_{xx} for the Black Scholes Barenblatt solutions. Solid line: Gamma of the CEV process.

Chapter 5

American Puts and Calls

As outlined in Chapter 3 the method of lines approximation and the sweep method for its solution are only marginally affected by the early exercise feature of American options. We shall solve some representative American option problems to illustrate the application of the method of lines and its numerical performance.

Example 5.1. An American put.

We begin with a standard American put where the scaled Black Scholes equation

$$\frac{1}{2}\sigma^2 x^2 u_{xx} + (r - q)x u_x - ru - u_t = 0 \qquad (5.1)$$

must be solved subject to the boundary conditions

$$u(s(t), t) = 1 - s(t) \qquad (5.2)$$

$$u_x(s(t), t) = -1$$

$$\lim_{x \to \infty} u(x, t) = 0 \qquad (5.3)$$

and the initial condition

$$u(x, 0) = \max\{0, 1 - x\}$$

$$s(0) = 1. \qquad (5.4)$$

$s(t)$ denotes the scaled early exercise boundary which must be determined together with $u(x, t)$. Once $s(t)$ is found the value of the put is continued over $[0, s(t)]$ as

$$u(x, t) = 1 - x.$$

It is known that the solutions u and s are continuous for all $x > 0$ and $t \in (0, T]$, smooth for $t > 0$, that

$$u_t(s(t), t) = 0$$

and that

$$\lim_{t \to 0} s(t) = \min\{1, r/q\}.$$

$s(t)$ is continuous at $t = 0$ for $r \geq q$, but even then

$$\lim_{t \to 0} s'(t) = -\infty.$$

We may infer from Chapter 4 that the option price can be computed without difficulty once $s(t)$ is known. Hence the question here is how well does the sweep method pin down the early exercise boundary. Since any discontinuity of the solution will occur at $t = 0$ we shall again consider the worst case scenario of the solution at the first time level.

The time discrete method of lines approximation of (5.1) based on an implicit Euler or a three level method is identical to that of Chapter 4, and as for a European option, the method of lines approximation at the first time level has a computable analytic solution. The representation of the MOL solution for a put at $t = \Delta t$ on (s, ∞) is

$$u(x) = \begin{cases} c_1 x^{\gamma_1} + c_2 x^{\gamma_2} + \frac{1}{1+r\Delta t} - \frac{x}{1+q\Delta t}, & x < 1 \\ d_2 x^{\gamma_2}, & x \geq 1 \end{cases} \tag{5.5}$$

where γ_1 and γ_2 are the positive and negative roots of

$$\frac{1}{2}\sigma^2 \gamma(\gamma - 1) + (r - q)\gamma - \left(r + \frac{1}{\Delta t}\right) = 0. \tag{5.6}$$

The two boundary conditions at $x = s$ and the continuity of u and u' at $x = 1$ allow us to determine algebraically that the analytic MOL early exercise boundary at $t = \Delta t$ is a root of the nonlinear equation

$$\left[\gamma_2 \frac{(q - r)\Delta t}{(1 + r\Delta t)(1 + q\Delta t)} + \frac{1}{(1 + q\Delta t)}\right] s^{\gamma_1} - (\gamma_2 - 1)\frac{q\Delta t}{(1 + q\Delta t)} s$$

$$+ \gamma_2 \frac{r\Delta t}{(1 + r\Delta t)} = 0. \tag{5.7}$$

For $q = 0$ this equation has the solution

$$s = \left[\frac{-\gamma_2 r\Delta t}{1 + r\Delta t - \gamma_2 r\Delta t}\right]^{1/\gamma_1}. \tag{5.8}$$

For $q \neq 0$ it can be solved numerically. Once s is known the coefficients $c_{1,2}$ and d_2 can be found as functions of s. For the record, we obtain

$$c_1 = \frac{s^{-\gamma_1}}{\gamma_2 - \gamma_1}\left[\gamma_2\left(\frac{r\Delta t}{1 + r\Delta t}\right) - (\gamma_2 - 1)\frac{sq\Delta t}{1 + q\Delta t}\right]$$

$$c_2 = \frac{s^{-\gamma_2}}{\gamma_2 - \gamma_1}\left[-\gamma_1\left(\frac{r\Delta t}{1 + r\Delta t}\right) + (\gamma_1 - 1)\frac{sq\Delta t}{1 + q\Delta t}\right]$$

$$d_2 = c_1 + c_2 + \frac{1}{1 + r\Delta t} - \frac{1}{1 + q\Delta t}.$$

u is continued over $[0, s]$ as

$$u(x) = 1 - x.$$

We shall compare this analytic solution of the MOL approximation at the first time level with the numerical solution obtained with the Riccati transformation in order to gain some insight into the quality of the numerical solution.

As in Example 4.4 we introduce an artificial barrier at $x = x_J$ and replace the asymptotic condition

$$\lim_{x \to \infty} u(x, t) = 0$$

with the boundary condition

$$u(x_J, t) = 0.$$

We shall again use $x_J = 3$, i.e. the barrier is at three times the strike price. The forward sweep for the MOL equations (4.4), (4.5) is carried out over the grid

$$0 < x_0 < x_1 < \cdots < x_J$$

and proceeds from x_J with initial conditions

$$R(x_J) = 0$$
$$w(x_J) = 0$$

toward x_0 where $0 < x_0 \ll 1$ is a lower limit on the early exercise boundary $s(t)$. Since $x_0 > 0$ we do not have to contend with the vanishing coefficient of u_{xx} at $x = 0$. If there is no numerical free boundary on $[x_0, 3]$ then x_0 was chosen too large. For most applications we can set x_0 equal to the early exercise boundary of a perpetual put given by

$$x_0 = \frac{\gamma_2}{\gamma_2 - 1}$$

where γ_2 is the negative root of (5.6) as $\Delta t \to \infty$.

Let $\{u, s\}$ ($\equiv \{u_n, s_n\}$) denote the numerical solution of the MOL approximation of (5.1)–(5.4) at time level t_n. Then the early exercise condition (5.2) and the Riccati transformation require that at $x = s$

$$u = 1 - s$$

$$u' = v = -1$$
$$u = R(s)v + w(s),$$

i.e. that

$$\phi(s) \equiv R(s)(-1) + w(s) - (1 - s) = 0.$$

Hence the additional step in the forward sweep compared to the European put is a check of the algebraic sign of the function

$$\phi(x_j) \equiv R(x_j)(-1) + w(x_j) - (1 - x_j) \tag{5.9}$$

at each meshpoint x_j. If for some k, $\phi(x_k)\phi(x_{k+1}) \leq 0$ then the early exercise boundary s is taken to be the zero of the cubic interpolant to ϕ at the points $\{x_{k-1}, x_k, x_{k+1}, x_{k+2}\}$ as described in Chapter 3. For American puts and calls we have not observed multiple zeros of $\phi(x)$. In other applications, where multiple zeros can occur, it is generally simple to pick the correct zero because $s(t)$ is continuous in t, usually monotone increasing or decreasing with time, and already known numerically at the preceding time level.

The reverse sweep calls for the integration of (3.6) from s to x_J. In general the root s of the cubic interpolant of ϕ does not coincide with any of the a priori chosen mesh points $\{x_j\}$. To get back to the regular mesh the first step for the trapezoidal rule is carried out over the interval $[s, x_{k+1}]$. Data not available at s, such as $R(s)$, $w(s)$, $g(s)$ are approximated by linear interpolation of the values at x_k and x_{k+1}. Thus at every time level we find the numerical solution $u(x)$ on the fixed mesh $\{x_j\}$ augmented by the time dependent early exercise boundary s.

For a numerical example we shall consider an American put with

$$\sigma = .3, \quad r = .05 \quad \text{and} \quad q = .02$$

after one time step with $t = \Delta t = .001$. A numerical solution of (5.7) yields the analytic MOL early exercise boundary

$$s_{an} = .964488.$$

An application of the sweep method to the MOL approximation on $[.2, 3]$ with

$$\Delta x = \begin{cases} .7/5600 = 1.25 \times 10^{-4} & \text{on } [.2, .9] \\ .2/1600 = 1.25 \times 10^{-4} & \text{on } [.9, 1.1] \\ 1.9/475 = 4 \times 10^{-3} & \text{on } [1.1, 3], \end{cases}$$

i.e. with 7675 mesh points on $[.2, 3]$, yields the numerical free boundary

$$s = .964487.$$

We note that since $s > .9$ the mesh on $[.2, .9]$ does not influence the calculation. In fact, an efficient implementation of the sweep method provides the Riccati transformation at time t_n only on an interval $[x_k, x_J]$ where x_k is a lower bound on the expected location of s_n. Furthermore, an efficient implementation requires some experimentation with the number of grid points needed for the accurate numerical solution of the MOL equations. The above grid is unecessarily fine and too costly if hundreds of time steps must be computed.

We also note that formally the expression (5.5) is not the MOL solution on the finite interval $[s, x_J]$ since $u(x_J) \neq 0$. However, for the parameters of this example we find that $u(3) \cong 10^{-73}$ so that the barrier condition is appropriate and the comparison of the numerical and analytic MOL solution at $t = \Delta t$ is valid.

It should be pointed out that the analytic (and numerical) MOL early exercise boundary for a put after one time step is in general not the correct Black Scholes free boundary just before expiry [54]. To illustrate this point suppose the asset pays no distributed dividend so that $s(0) = 1$ and the MOL free boundary s is given analytically by (5.8). Since $|\gamma_1|$ and $|\gamma_2|$ behave like $1/\sqrt{\Delta t}$ as $\Delta t \to 0$ it is straightforward to verify that

$$1 - s = o\left(\sqrt{\Delta t}|\ln\left(\sqrt{\Delta t}\right)|\right)$$

as $\Delta t \to 0$. On the other hand, it is known from an analysis of the Black Scholes equation that the time continuous early exercise boundary $s(t)$ has the asymptotic behavior

$$1 - s(\Delta t) = o\left(\sqrt{\Delta t}|\ln(\Delta t)|\right)$$

as $\Delta t \to 0$ (for a detailed discussion see [7]). It follows that

$$\frac{1 - s}{1 - s(\Delta t)} \to \infty$$

as $\Delta t \to 0$. Hence the MOL free boundary converges to $s(0) = 1$ at the wrong rate.

If an accurate early exercise boundary for the put near expiry is desired then it is suggested to compute instead the premium

$$u(x, t) = p_{Am}(x, t) - p_{Eu}(x, t)$$

where p_{Am} and p_{Eu} are the American and European put prices. $u(x,t)$ now satisfies the Black Scholes equation subject to

$$u(x,0) = 0$$

and the boundary conditions

$$u(s,t) = 1 - s(t) - p_{Eu}(s(t),t)$$
$$u_x(s(t),t) = -1 - \partial p_{Eu}(s(t),t)/\partial x.$$

Here $p_{Eu}(x,t)$ is given by the Black Scholes formula for a European put. It is plausible (but not proven) that $u(x,t)$ is much smoother than $p_{Am}(x,t)$ and therefore easier to compute accurately than $p_{Am}(x,t)$.

The numerical solution of the premium $u(x,t)$ with the method of lines is as straightforward as the solution of the American put described above. The differential equations for $R(x)$ and $w(x)$ remain unchanged while the early exercise boundary is found from a root of the following analog of (5.9)

$$\phi(x) = R(x)\left[-1 - \partial p_{Eu}(x,\Delta t)/\partial x\right] + w(x) - \left[1 - x - p_{Eu}(x,\Delta t)\right].$$

Once s is known the reverse sweep starts with the initial condition

$$v(s) = -1 - \partial p_{Eu}(s,\Delta t)/\partial x.$$

For $r = .05$, $q = .02$ and $\sigma = .3$ the numerical MOL early exercise boundary obtained for $u(x,t)$ after one time step at $t = \Delta t = .001$ on the mesh given above is now

$$s = .974440.$$

Numerical experiments with $\Delta t = .001/N$ for $N > 0$ suggest that this value of s is a stable approximation to the Black Scholes value $s(.001)$. However, for a calculation over hundreds of time steps the MOL approach for the premium $u(x,t)$ becomes time consuming because of the need to find the values of the European put and its delta at every mesh point and time. Fortunately, the initial error in the early exercise boundary obtained from the MOL approximation of the put does not persist at later times as is indicated by the numerical results of Table 5.1 for the free boundary at expiration $T = .01$.

As a check on the computation we compare in the last two columns of Table 5.1 the numerical (scaled) gamma $u''(s)$ at the free boundary with the gamma u_{xx} predicted by the Black Scholes equation which is given by

$$u_{xx}(s,t) = \frac{2(r - qs)}{\sigma^2 s^2}.$$

Table 5.1. MOL free boundary $s(.01)$ after N time steps with $\Delta t = .01/N$ obtained from the MOL approximation of $u(x,t) = p_{Am}(x,t) - \theta p_{Eu}(x,t)$.

	$\theta = 1$	$\theta = 0$		
N	$s(.01)$	$s(.01)$	$u''(s)^*$	$u_{xx}(s, .01)$
1	.93247	.91441	.843	.843
10	.92768	.92772	.812	.812
20	.92785	.92793	.811	.812
40	.92789	.92793	.812	.811
100	.92790	.92792	.812	.812

*Since in general s is not a regular mesh point we set $u''(s) = v'(x_j)$ where x_j is the first mesh point to the right of the computed free boundary s.

A mismatch between these two columns would indicate that the computed early exercise boundary or the gamma are questionable.

A similar calculation is carried out for the parameters

$$\sigma = .3, \quad r = .02 \quad \text{and} \quad q = .05.$$

Here the early exercise boundary is discontinuous at $t = 0$ and qualitatively reflects the behavior of the free boundary for a dividend paying American call. (5.7) yields the analytic MOL free boundary at $\Delta t = .001$

$$s_{an} = .397332.$$

The numerical MOL early exercise boundary found with the sweep method is

$$s = .397332.$$

We conclude that finding the free boundary with the Riccati transformation is simple, accurate and basically non-iterative, except for finding the zero of the cubic interpolant.

In summary, unless the put is to be priced very close to the time of expiry, it is more efficient to compute

$$u(x,t) = p_{Am}(x,t) - \theta p_{Eu}(x,t)$$

for $\theta = 0$ than for $\theta = 1$. For $q \geq r$ both approaches yield comparable free boundaries at $t = \Delta t$ so that $\theta = 0$ is preferable at all times.

Example 5.2. An American put with sub-optimal early exercise.

In a recent study [37] a detailed analysis of the cost is presented when American options are hedged according to a penalty solution of the complementarity formulation of the option instead of the (unavailable) analytic solution. The results of Example 5.1 suggest that the numerical MOL results for the free boundary formulation can be found with sufficiently high accuracy that hedging according to them is close to optimal. The discussion of [37] also suggests a reverse problem. What is the cost of exercising early at a given non-optimal delta to get, so to speak, a jump on the market? For example, let $\{u_0(x,t), s_0(t)\}$ be the correct price and exercise boundary of an American put following (5.1), and let $\{u(x,t), s(t)\}$ denote the price of the option when exercised according to

$$u(s(t),t) = 1 - s(t) \tag{5.10}$$

$$u_x(s(t),t) = \Delta, \quad -1 \le \Delta < 0.$$

We note that (5.1) with the free boundary condition (5.10) is not an obstacle problem and does not allow a complementarity formulation when $\Delta \ne -1$. The loss in value of the option is

$$V(x,t) = u_o(x,t) - u(x,t). \tag{5.11}$$

For the MOL front tracking method the value of Δ is immaterial and it is straightforward to compute $V(x,t)$ and $V_x(x,t)$. For an illustration we show in Figs. 5.1 and 5.2 the functions $V(x,T)$ and $V_x(x,T)$ for an American put exercised optimally when

$$u_{ox}(s_o(T),T) = -1$$

and suboptimally when

$$u_x(s(T),T) = -.9.$$

For the data chosen the exercise boundaries are found with the method lines. For $T = 1$ they are to five significant figures

$$s_o(1) = .585248, \quad s(1) = .640147.$$

$V(x,T)$ assumes its maximum at $s(1)$, while the difference in the deltas is most pronounced at $x = .846$. The numerical values are

$$V(s(1),1) = 0.00270$$

$$V_x(.846,1) = -.03700.$$

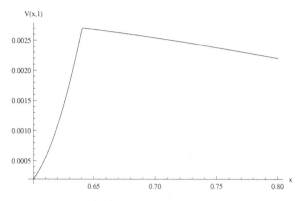

Fig. 5.1. Loss of put-value V(x,t) due to sub-optimal early exercise at $\Delta = -.9$. $r = 0.05$, $q = 0$, $\sigma = .4$, $K = 1$. $T = 1$, $\Delta t = T/1000$. $X = 4$, uniform x-grid on $[0, X]$ with up to 8000 mesh points.

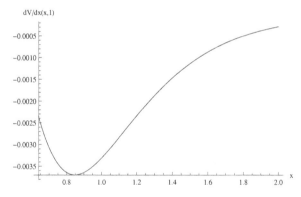

Fig. 5.2. Comparison of deltas for the two puts of Fig. 5.1.

Example 5.3. A put on an asset with a fixed dividend.

Suppose an American put with maturity T is written on a stock paying a fixed dividend $D(S) = D_0 + \alpha S$ at time $\tau_d < T$ consisting of a known amount $D_0 \geq 0$ and a proportional amount αS where $\alpha \geq 0$.

With the usual scaling $x = S/K$, $u = P/K$ and time reversal $t = T - \tau$ the problem is:

$$\frac{1}{2}\sigma^2 x^2 u_{xx} + r u_x - r u - u_t = 0$$

$$\lim_{x \to \infty} u(x, t) = 0.$$

The Black Scholes equation is to be solved over $(0, t_d]$ and $(t_d, T]$ where $t_d = T - \tau_d$. The pay-off at maturity yields the usual initial condition

$$u(x, 0) = \max\{1 - x, 0\}.$$

For $t \in (0, t_d]$ we have a standard American put with early exercise at $x = s(t)$ where

$$u(s(t), t) = 1 - s(t)$$

$$u_x(s(t), t) = -1.$$

There is an early exercise boundary $s(t_d-) > 0$ and to its left the put assumes its intrinsic value

$$u(x, t_d-) = 1 - x, \qquad 0 \le x \le s(t_d-).$$

At the ex-dividend date the value of the asset decreases by the amount of the dividend $D(S)$ (more generally, by some function of $D(S)$ if tax considerations apply). Continuity of the option price then imposes the interface condition

$$u(x, t_d+) = u((1 - \alpha)x - D_0/K, t_d-). \tag{5.12}$$

We note that $u(x, t_d+)$ is not defined over $[0, x_0)$, where $x_0 = \frac{D_0}{K(1-\alpha)}$, because $u(x, t_d-)$ is not defined for negative x. We see from (5.12) that the American put price $u(x, t_d-)$ is shifted to the right by the known amount $D_0/K + \alpha x$. It follows that for $D_0 > 0$, $u(x, t_d+)$ lies strictly above the intrinsic value $\max\{1 - x, 0\}$. Since the option price is continuous in time there will be an interval $[t_d, t^*]$ where it will remain strictly above $\max\{1 - x, 0\}$ so that there is no early exercise to the right of x_0. After some time t^* early exercise may again become advantageous, i.e. the boundary condition (5.2) applies to a solution $\{u(x, t), s(t)\}$ with $s(t) \ge x_0$. To find the option price $u(x, t)$ for $t \in (t_d, t^*]$ we need the boundary condition $u(x_0, t)$. For this purpose we consider the initial value problem

$$rxu_x - ru - u_t = 0 \tag{5.13}$$

$$u(x, t_d) = 1 - \left(x - \alpha x - \frac{D_0}{K}\right).$$

(5.13) is thought to be a reasonable approximation of the Black Scholes equation near the continuation region where $x \ll 1$ and $u_{xx}(x, t_d-) = 0$. The solution of (5.13) is

$$u(x, t) = \left(1 + \frac{D_0}{K}\right) e^{-r(t-t_d)} - (1 - \alpha)x \tag{5.14}$$

$u(x_0, t)$ serves as a boundary condition for the Black Scholes equation over $[x_0, \infty)$ as long there is no early exercise. We observe that the solution (5.14) will decay to $1 - x$ at a given point x in the time interval $\Delta t(x)$ determined by

$$u(x, t_d + \Delta t) = 1 - x.$$

We find

$$\Delta t(x) = \frac{1}{r} \left[\ln\left(1 + \frac{D_0}{K}\right) - \ln(1 - \alpha x) \right] \tag{5.15}$$

which for $\alpha x < 1$ can be rewritten in the form

$$\Delta t(x) = \frac{1}{r} \ln\left[\left(1 + \frac{D_0}{K}\right)(1 + \alpha x + (\alpha x)^2 + (\alpha x)^3 \ldots) \right].$$

We see from (5.15) that for $\alpha = 0$

$$\Delta t = \frac{1}{r} \ln\left(1 + \frac{D_0}{K}\right)$$

while for $D_0 = 0$ it follows that $x(0) = 0$ and

$$\lim_{\Delta t \to 0} \frac{x(\Delta t) - x(0)}{\Delta t} = s'(t) = \frac{r}{\alpha}.$$

Such estimates are usually derived by balancing the risk free interest $K(e^{r\Delta t} - 1)$ against the jump $D_0 + \alpha S$ in the value of the put at the ex-dividend date. Note that for $D_0, \alpha \neq 0$ the balance

$$e^{r\Delta t} - 1 = \frac{D_0}{K} + \alpha x$$

is an approximation of, but not the same as, (5.15). Unfortunately, the approximate solution does not provide information about the location of the early exercise boundary as it reappears at t^*.

For the numerical solution of the discrete dividend problem we use the program of the preceding example. At each time level $t_n < t_d$ we find $R(x)$ and $w(x)$ by integrating the forward sweep equations (3.4) corresponding to (4.4) from $x_J = 3$ to $x = 0$. We then check the algebraic sign of $\phi(x)$ given by (5.9). If a sign change occurs then the early exercise boundary is determined as above from the cubic interpolant to $\phi(x)$ through the four neighboring points. The initial value for the reverse sweep is in this case

$$v(s) = -1.$$

To the left of s the option value is

$$u(x) = 1 - x.$$

At t_d we restart the calculation with the initial condition $u(x, t_d+)$ given by (5.12). If no sign change of ϕ is detected on $[x_0, 3]$ then there is no early exercise and we carry out the reverse sweep over $[x_0, 3]$ subject to the initial value

$$v(x_0) = -(1 - \alpha)$$

obtained from (5.14).

Figure 5.3 shows the early exercise boundaries for three American puts. Expiration is $T = .5$ and the dividend $D(S) = D_0 + \alpha S$ is paid at $\tau_d = .3$ years, i.e. at $t_d = T - \tau_d = .2$. The dividend payments are

   i) $D(S) = .02K$,   i.e. $D(x) = .02$
   ii) $D(S) = .02K + .01S$,   i.e. $D(x) = .02 + .01x$
   iii) $D(S) = .02K + .02S$,   i.e. $D(x) = .02 + .02x$.

The remaining data are: $\sigma = .4$, $r = .08$, $q = 0$, $x_0 = .01$ and

$$\Delta x = \begin{cases} 2.5\ 10^{-4} & \text{on } [.01, .5] \\ 5\ 10^{-4} & \text{on } [.5, 1] \\ 4\ 10^{-3} & \text{on } [1, 3]. \end{cases}$$

Results are shown for $\Delta t = 5\ 10^{-4}$. As demonstrated in [55], the numerical results change little on further mesh refinements.

The numerical results for this time step yield the following values for the time t^* of reappearance of the free boundary:

   i) $t^* \sim [.4475, .448]$
   ii) $t^* \sim [.4485, .449]$
   iii) $t^* \sim [.450, .4505]$.

The numerical values also suggest that in cases ii) and iii) the speed of the free boundary is

   ii) $s'(t) \sim 8$ for $t > t_d$
   iii) $s'(t) \sim 4$ for $t > t_d$

so that the estimate $s'(t) \sim r/\alpha$ obtained earlier appears to be independent of D_0 if the dividend contains a component proportional to S.

Finally, we point out that the boundary condition at x_0 based on (5.14) replaces the boundary condition used in [55] over the time interval $[t_d, t^*]$. That boundary condition does not enforce continuity of the option price at (x_0, t_d) and is incorrect. Yet numerically, both boundary conditions

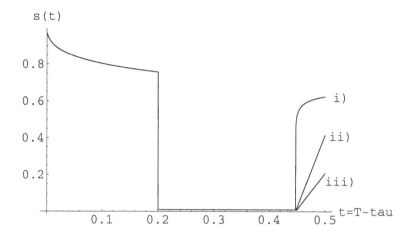

Fig. 5.3. Early exercise boundary for a put with discrete dividend $D(x)$ at $t_d = .2$.
i) $D(x) = .02$
ii) $D(x) = .02 + .01x$
iii) $D(x) = .02 + .02x$.

yield the same numerical results. In fact, for numerical methods one may continue the intrinsic value $u(x, t_d-) = 1 - x$ over $-\infty < x < s(t_d-)$ and solve the Black Scholes equation for $t > t_d$ over $(0, \infty)$ without boundary condition at $x = 0$. The numerical results appear to be the same in all cases.

Example 5.4. An American lookback call.

Algorithmically, the solution of a continuously monitored American lookback call is simply the repeated solution of plain American calls. To illustrate the application of the method of lines in this setting let us price a capped floating strike fractional lookback call $C(S, \tilde{m}, t)$ with pay-off

$$C(S, \tilde{m}, 0) = \max\{0, S - \alpha \max\{Km_T, \tilde{m}\}\}$$

where S is the price of the asset, t is time to expiry and $\tilde{m} \in [0, m_T]$ denotes the minimum asset price in the time interval $[0, t]$ for today's spot price m_T. Km_T for $K \in [0, 1]$ defines a cap on the strike price and $\alpha \geq 1$ is a parameter. If we set $x = S/m_T$, $m = \tilde{m}/m_T$ and $u(x, m, t) = C(xm_T, mm_T, t)/m_T$ then the capped call satisfies the pricing equation

$$\frac{1}{2} \sigma^2 x^2 u_{xx} + (r - q)x u_x - ru - u_t = 0, \quad m < x < s(t, m), \quad t \in (0, T]$$

$$u(x, m, 0) = \max\{0, x - \alpha m\}$$
$$u_m(m, m, t) = 0$$
$$u(s(t, m), m, t) = s(t, m) - \alpha m$$
$$u_x(s(t, m), m, t) = 1,$$

where $s(t, m)$ denotes the early exercise boundary for the call. All financial parameters may be functions of x, t and m.

The computational domain in the x–m plane is

$$D = \{(x, m) : m \leq x \leq X, K \leq m \leq 1\}$$

where X is chosen sufficiently large to lie to the right of the early exercise boundary $s(t, m)$ for all t and m.

On the line $m = K$ the solution $u(x, K, t)$ is the price of a standard American call with given strike price αK. If $K = 0$ then $u(x, 0, t) = x$.

A recent discussion of this and other fractional lookback options for $K = 0$ may be found in [43] and [67].

A numerical approximation can be obtained by solving a call for a sequence of increasing discrete values of m. For $I \geq 1$ let

$$\Delta m = (1 - K)/I \quad \text{and} \quad m_i = K + i\Delta m.$$

Then for $i = 0, \ldots, I$ we solve the standard American calls

$$\frac{1}{2}\sigma^2 x^2 u_{xx}(x, m_i, t) - (r - q)x u_x(x, m_i, t) - r u(x, m_i, t) - u_t(x, m_i, t) = 0$$

$$u(x, m_i, 0) = \max\{0, x - \alpha m_i\}$$

$$u(m_i, m_i, t) = \begin{cases} U(m_0, t) & \text{if } i = 0 \\ u(m_1, m_0, t) & \text{if } i = 1 \\ (4u(m_i, m_{i-1}, t) - u(m_i, m_{i-2}, t))/3 & \text{if } i \geq 2 \end{cases}$$

$$u(s(t, m_i), m_i, t) = s(t, m_i) - \alpha m_i, \quad u_x(s(t, m_i), m_i, t) = 1$$

where $U(x, t)$ is an American call defined on $x > 0$ with strike price αK.

The above boundary value $u(m_i, m_i, t)$ is obtained from a three-level backward difference approximation of $u_m(m_i, m_i, t) = 0$ for $i > 2$ and from a first order approximation at $i = 1$ (see eqs. (2.4), (2.5)).

After a time discretization the forward sweep equations (4.4), (4.5) apply. For given i the forward sweep at $t = t_n$ proceeds from $x = m_i$ toward X. The function

$$\phi(x) \equiv x - \alpha m_i - \{R(x)(1) + w(x)\}$$

Table 5.2. Values $V(S, m_T, t)$ of the floating strike fractional lookback call at $S = 100$ for $m_T = 80$.

σ	cap Km_T	α	MOL solution	[43]
.2	0	1	21.0932	20.7353
	40	1	21.0932	
	80	1	20.1970	20.7424
	0	1.3	5.4587	5.3885
	40	1.3	5.4587	
	80	1.3	5.4134	5.4695
.4	0	1	29.9082	29.6306
	40	1	29.8195	
	80	1	24.8519	24.897
	0	1.3	14.8419	14.7776
	40	1.3	14.8298	
	80	1.3	13.0569	13.0622

$r = .03$, $q = .05$, $T = 1$, $\Delta t = 1/200$, $\Delta m = 1/200$.

is monitored, and its root, which is observed to be unique, is chosen as the free boundary $s(t_n, m_i)$.

For representative financial parameters the numerical solution of each such call is straightforward. Moreover, numerical results are quite insensitive to the discretization of time and the lookback minimum, at least for $m \gg 0$. The calculated prices and early exercise boundaries obtained with the Riccati transformation solve the time- and m-discrete MOL equations accurately.

For illustration we show some plots for the option prices $u(m, m, T)$ and the corresponding deltas $u_x(m, m, T)$ on the computational boundary $x = m$ where $u_m(m, m, T) = 0$ has to be enforced, and for the early exercise boundary $s(T, m)$ near $m = 0$ for an uncapped lookback call.

For all cases: $\sigma = .2$, $T = 1$, $\Delta t = 1/200$, $\Delta m = 1/200$; 3300 meshpoints in $[0, X]$ with $X = 3$ are used for the Riccati transformation. Lookback fractional parameter $\alpha = 1.3$.

For reference we list in Table 5.2 some values for capped and uncapped lookback calls and, where available, the equivalent values reported in [43].

Most of the MOL values are close to those in [43], but the discrepancy rises to 2.6% for the value of the plain American call ($\sigma = .2$, $\alpha = 1$, cap = 80). A comparison with results obtained from some web-based calculators and with results for the test problem in [67, p. 357] suggest that the MOL values are reliable.

The irregular behavior of the price, the delta and of the early exercise boundary near $m = 0$ for the uncapped call appears to be a consequence of the discontinuity of $u_m(x, m, t)$ as $(x, m) \to (0, 0)$ inherent in the PDE formulation. The commonly accepted boundary condition

$$u_m(m, m, t) = 0, \quad m > 0$$

is in conflict with the early exercise boundary condition

$$u(s(t, m), m, t) = s(t, m) - \alpha m,$$

$$u_x(s(t, m), m, t) = 1.$$

If we assume smoothness of the solution for $t > 0$ and $m > 0$, then the free boundary conditions imply that

$$\frac{d}{dm} u(s(t, m), m, t) = u_x(s(t, m), m, t)\frac{ds}{dm} + u_m(s(t, m), m, t)$$

$$= \frac{ds}{dm}(t, m) - \alpha,$$

so that

$$u_m(s(t, m), m, t) = -\alpha.$$

Since $s(t, m) \to 0$ as $m \to 0$ it follows that

$$-\alpha = \lim_{m \to 0} u_m(s(t, m), m), t) \neq \lim_{m \to 0} u_m(m, m, t) = 0.$$

Unlike the lack of smoothness introduced by the pay-off function at $t = 0$, this singularity does not disappear with time.

The discontinuity of $u_m(x, m, t)$ at $x = m = 0$ makes the approximation of $u_m(\Delta m_1, \Delta m_1, t) = 0$ with a backward Euler formula of doubtful value. We do not know what better boundary condition to impose near $m = 0$ but note that the problem disappears when the call is capped (e.g. $K \geq .1$). Moreover, as Table 5.2 suggests and the following discussion shows, this cap has no discernible influence on the option price and the early exercise boundary if $m \gg Km_T$.

It is well known that the uncapped lookback call with constant parameters can be priced with a 1-dimensional problem. If we set

$$V(y, t) = \frac{u(x, t)}{x} \qquad y = \frac{\alpha m}{x}$$

then one can show (see, e.g. [67, p. 131]) that $\{V(y,t), Y(t)\}$ satisfies the free boundary problem

$$\frac{1}{2}\sigma^2 y^2 V_{yy} + (q-r)yV_y - qV - V_t = 0$$
$$V(y,0) = \max\{0, 1-y\}$$
$$V_y(\alpha, t) = 0$$
$$V(Y(t), t) = 1 - Y(t)$$
$$V_y(Y(t), t) = -1. \tag{5.16}$$

It follows that for each t the free boundary $s(t,m)$ in the x–m plane should be the straight line

$$s(t,m) = \frac{\alpha}{Y(t)}\, m.$$

Similarly, the curves for the uncapped lookback calls in Figs. 5.4 and 5.5 along the line $m = x$ are related to $V(y,t)$ through

$$u(m,m,T) = mV(\alpha, T)$$
$$u_x(m,m,T) = V(\alpha, T).$$

The numerical solution of this put-like problem with the method of lines and the Riccati transformation is straightforward and instantaneous. Note

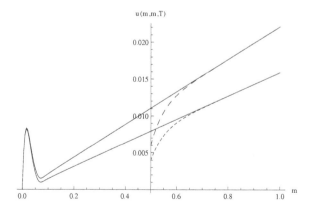

Fig. 5.4. Call prices $u(m,m,T)$ along the line $x = m$ at $T = 1$.
long-dash curve: $r = .05$, $q = .03$, capped $m \in [.5, 1]$
upper solid curve: $r = .05$, $q = .03$, $m \in [0, 1]$.
short-dash curve: $r = .03$, $q = .05$, capped $m \in [.5, 1]$
lower solid curve: $r = .03$, $q = .05$, $m \in [0, 1]$.

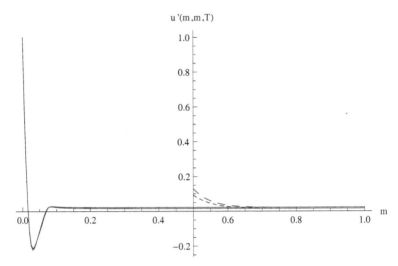

Fig. 5.5. Corresponding deltas $u_x(m, m, T)$ along the line $x = m$ at $T = 1$.

that because of the boundary condition

$$V_y(\alpha, t) = 0$$

the inverse transformation of Section 3.1

$$v(y) = RI(y)u(y) + wi(y)$$

must be employed at each time level $t = t_n$ where $u(y)$ and $v(y)$ approximate $V(y, t_n)$ and $V_y(y, t_n)$. The free boundary $Y(t_n)$ is found as a root of the equation

$$\phi(y) \equiv -1 - [RI(y)(1 - y) + wi(y)] = 0.$$

We observe that $V_y(y, 0)$ is discontinuous at $y = 1$ so that for $\alpha > 1$ we expect $Y(t)$ to behave much like the early exercise boundary of a put near expiration. For $\alpha = 1$ the solution V is subject to the boundary condition $V_y(1, t) = 0$. We have not found any information on the asymptotic behavior of $Y(t)$ as $t \to 0$ for this case.

Figure 5.7 shows two representative plots of the free boundary $Y(t)$.

The lack of convexity for the free boundary of an American put with $q/r > 1$ is proven in [11] and therefore expected for $Y(t)$ when $q/r < 1$.

Finally, we note that the free boundaries in Fig. 5.6 continue as straight lines for $m > .1$ with exactly the numerical slopes predicted by $V(y, 1)$. Some representative values are listed in Table 5.3.

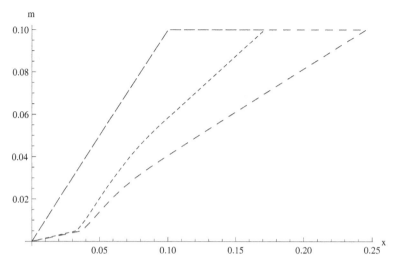

Fig. 5.6. Free boundaries $s(T, m)$ near $m = 0$ for $K = 0$.
left curve: boundary $x = m$
middle curve: $s(T, m)$ for $r = .03$, $q = .05$
right curve: $s(T, m)$ for $r = .05$, $q = .03$.

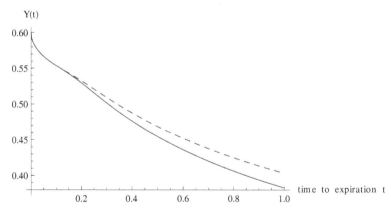

Fig. 5.7. Early exercise boundary $Y(t)$ for (5.16).
Solid line: $r = .05$, $q = .03$, $\sigma = .4$, $\alpha = 1.0$, $T = 1$, $\Delta t = T/400$.
Broken line: $r = .05$, $q = .03$, $\sigma = .4$, $\alpha = 1.3$, $T = 1$, $\Delta t = T/400$.

Example 5.5. An American strangle for power options.

An American strangle is similar to a combination of an American put
and call but where the early exercise of one option knocks out the other

Table 5.3. Numerical values obtained from the two- and one-dimensional equations for an uncapped American lookback option.

alfa	r	q	sigma	$u(1,1,1)$	$u_x(1,1,1)$	$s(1,1)$	$V(\alpha,1)$	$\alpha/Y(1)$
1	.03	.05	.4	0.26543	0.26544	2.0555	.26543	2.0554
1	.05	.03	.4	0.28033	0.28033	2.6116	.28032	2.6115
1.3	.03	.05	.2	0.01587	0.01592	1.7123	.01588	1.7123
1.3	.05	.03	.2	0.02209	0.02211	2.4550	.02210	2.4551

For all calculations: $\Delta t = 1/200$, $\Delta m = 1/200$.

option. A detailed study of such an option based on an integral equation is described in [13], where the American strangle is compared with a combination of a plain long American put and call.

The MOL approach to pricing a strangle uses the familiar Black Scholes equation and will be presented here in a slightly more general setting by combining power options instead of plain puts and calls. A strangle for power options may not have financial significance but does serve to ilustrate how readily the MOL/Riccati approach can cope with new nonlinearities in the boundary conditions for the Black Scholes equation.

The Black Scholes formulation of the strangle (in unscaled variables) is

$$\frac{1}{2}\sigma^2 S^2 V_{SS} + (r-q)SV_S - rV - V_t = 0$$

where t measures time to expiry. The pay-off is assumed to be

$$V(S,0) = \max\{0, K_1 - S^{\alpha_1}\} + \max\{0, S^{\alpha_2} - K_2\}$$

where K_1 and K_2 are the strikes for the put and call sides of the strangle and $\alpha_1, \alpha_2 > 0$ are given exponents. Early exercise occurs at $S_1(t)$ and $S_2(t)$ when

$$V(S_1(t),t) = K_1 - S_1^{\alpha_1}(t), \quad V_S(S_1(t),t) = -\alpha_1 S_1(t)^{\alpha_1-1}$$

$$V(S_2(t),t) = S_2^{\alpha_2}(t) - K_2, \quad V_S(S_2(t),t) = \alpha_2 S_2(t)^{\alpha_2-1}.$$

In mathematical terms we have a double obstacle problem where the solution $V(S,t)$, if it exists, attaches itself to the left and right obstacles $o_1(S)$ and $o_2(S)$ described by

$$o_1(S) = K_1 - S^{\alpha_1}, \quad o_2(S) = S^{\alpha_2} - K_2.$$

In analogy to the terminology for a standard strangle ($\alpha_1 = \alpha_2 = 1$) we say the strangle is in the money if $K_2^{1/\alpha_2} < S(T) < K_1^{1/\alpha_1}$, out of the money if $K_1^{1/\alpha_1} < S(T) < K_2^{1/\alpha_2}$, or a straddle if $K_1^{1/\alpha_1} = K_2^{1/\alpha_2} = S(T)$. At all times we expect that

$$S_1(t) \leq \min\left\{K_1^{1/\alpha_1}, K_2^{1/\alpha_2}\right\} \leq \max\left\{K_1^{1/\alpha_1}, K_2^{1/\alpha_2}\right\} \leq S_2(t).$$

Note that $V(S,t)$ can lift off the obstacles at S_1 and S_2 only if the functions $V(S,t) - o_1(S)$ and $V(S,t) - o_2(S)$ have a local minimum at S_1 and S_2 so that

$$V_{SS}(S,t) - o_1''(S) \geq 0 \quad \text{and} \quad V_{SS}(S,t) - o_2''(S) \geq 0$$

at the contact points.

Since there are two strike prices we cannot scale both of them out of the problem. To non-dimensionalize the problem shall define

$$C = \frac{K_1^{1/\alpha_1} + K_2^{1/\alpha_2}}{2}, \qquad x = \frac{S}{C}$$

where C is chosen such that $V(C,0) \leq V(S,0)$. $x = 1$ is expected to lie at all times between the two early exercise boundaries. We shall also set

$$u(x,t) = \frac{V(Cx,t)}{C}.$$

The strangle is then modeled with the usual Black Scholes equation

$$\frac{1}{2}\sigma^2 x^2 u_{xx} + (r - q)x u_x - r u - u_t = 0$$

subject to

$$u(x,0) = \frac{1}{C}\left[\max\{0, K_1 - (Cx)^{\alpha_1}\} + \max\{0, (Cx)^{\alpha_2} - K_2\}\right]$$

and

$$u(s_1(t),t) = ufb_1(s_1(t))$$
$$u_x(s_1(t),t) = vfb_1(s_1(t))$$
$$u(s_2(t),t) = ufb_2(s_2(t))$$
$$u_x(s_2(t),t) = vfb_2(s_2(t))$$

where

$$ufb_1(x) = \frac{1}{C}\left[K_1 - (Cx)\right)^{\alpha_1}]$$
$$vfb_1(x) = -\alpha_1(Cx))^{\alpha_1-1}$$

and

$$ufb_2(x) = \frac{1}{C}\left[(Cx))^{\alpha_2} - K_2\right]$$
$$vfb_2(x) = \alpha_2(Cx))^{\alpha_2-1}.$$

We shall solve this problem as a put on the interval $[s_1, 1]$ and as a call on the interval $[1, s_2]$ where $x = 1$ serves as an upper barrier for the put and a lower barrier for the call. The value $u(1, t)$ acts like a rebate for both barrier options. It is not known a priori but will be found iteratively by enforcing continuity of the delta $u_x(x, t)$ at $x = 1$. The method of lines approximation of this problem is the same as for an American put and call. As before, let $u(x)$ and s_1 and s_2 denote the MOL solutions at time level t_n and assume that u^* is our guess for the unknown value $u(1)$. Then for this guess the solution $u(x)$ is found over $[s_1, 1]$ with the forward sweep for $\{R(x), w(x, u^*)\}$ which integrates equations (3.4) from $x = 1$ toward $x = 0$ subject to the initial conditions

$$R(1) = 0, \qquad w(1, u^*) = u^*.$$

Once $R(x)$ and $w(x, u^*)$ are known the early exercise boundary s_1 is found as a root of the equation

$$\phi_1(x) \equiv R(x)vfb_1(x) + w(x) - ufb_1(x) = 0.$$

Given s_1 we can then carry out the reverse sweep (3.6) subject to

$$v(s_1, u^*) = vfb_1(s_1)$$

to obtain $v_1(x, u^*)$ over $[s_1, 1]$. Here the notation $w(x, u^*)$ and $v_1(x, u^*)$ is meant to indicate that v on $[s_1, 1]$ depends on u^* through the value of w.

Similarly, $u(x)$ is found over $[1, s_2]$ by carrying out the forward sweep (3.4) from $x = 1$ toward $x = X$ subject to

$$R(1) = 0, \qquad w(1, u^*) = u^*.$$

The free boundary s_2 is found as a root of

$$\phi_2(x) \equiv R(x)vfb_2(x) + w(x) - ufb_2(x) = 0.$$

$v_2(x, u)$ is the solution of the reverse sweep from s_2 toward $x = 1$ with the initial value

$$v_2(s_2, u) = vfb_2(s_2).$$

To enforce continuity of $u'(x)$ at $x = 1$ we are looking for a solution u^* of the equation

$$F(u) \equiv v_1(1, u) - v_2(1, u) = 0.$$

The strangle is more restrictive than a long put and call so that

$$0 \le u(1, t) \le \frac{1}{C} \left[V_p(C, t) + V_c(C, t) \right]$$

where V_p and V_c are the unscaled put and call prices of the combination. Hence we may assume that u^* belongs to a bounded interval. u^* can always be found with a bisection search, but a more efficient approach is to employ a secant method. At time level t_n we choose for u^* the initial guess

$$u^0 = u_{n-1}(1)$$

i.e. the value of the option at $x = 1$ at the preceding time level. The initial guess is updated according to

$$u^{k+1} = u^k - \frac{F(u^k)(u^k - u^{k-1})}{F(u^k) - F(u^{k-1})}.$$

The iteration is said to have converged if

$$|F(u^{k+1})| \leq 10^{-6}.$$

While convergence is not guaranteed it has been observed in our numerical experiments after at most 3 iterations. $F(u)$ is almost linear in u. Alternatively, a discrete Newton's method could be used which typically is more robust than a secant method.

To illustrate that this iterative approach can solve the American strangle we show in Table 5.4 some representative numerical results. Included in this table is a comparison with some numerical values from the study of [13].

Table 5.4. Price of the American strangle and early exercise boundary for the put and call side at $T - t = 0$.

(α_1, α_2)	$(.5, 2)$	$(1, 1)$		$(2, .5)$
S	MOL	MOL	[13]*	MOL
0.75	0.153733	0.275647	0.275647	0.455736
1.00	0.081152	0.100332	0.100332	0.175782
1.25	0.238578	0.038559	0.038561	0.040542
1.50	0.754494	0.092338	0.092340	0.006843
1.75	1.562501	0.255634	0.255633	0.004434
$S_1(1)$	0.349880	0.446835		0.593227
$S_2(1)$	1.547784	1.833344		2.715095

$r = .05$, $q = .10$, $\sigma = .2$, $K_1 = 1$, $K_2 = 1.5$, $T = 1$.
*Numerical option prices listed in Table 1 of [13].
MOL solution with $\Delta t = T/500$ and 3200 spatial mesh points.
MOL run time is of the order of 5 secs per column on a two-processor 2.13 GHz desktop work station.

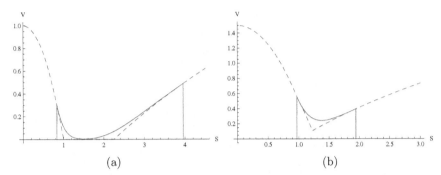

(a)   (b)

Fig. 5.8. (a): Strangle price at $T - t = 0$, $K_1 = 1$, $K_2 = 1.5$.
(b): Strangle price at $T - t = 0$, $K_1 = 1.5$, $K_2 = 1$.
$r = .10$, $q = .05$, $\sigma = .2$, $\alpha_1 = 2$, $\alpha_2 = .5$, $T = 1$, $\Delta t = T/500$.
Broken line: pay-off at $t = 0$.

Table 5.5. Early exercise boundary one time step
before expiration for the strangles of Figs. 5.8(a)
and (b) for different time steps.

| | $K_1 = 1$, $K_2 = 1.5$ | | $K_1 = 1.5$, $K_2 = 1$ | |
Δt	$S_1(\Delta t)$	$S_2(\Delta t)$	$S_1(\Delta t)$	$S_2(\Delta t)$
.001	.98146	3.53132	.98898	1.56948
.0005	.98582	3.52674	.99113	1.56744
.0001	.99262	3.52062	.99497	1.56472

Graphs of two strangle prices are shown in Figs. 5.8.

The early exercise boundaries corresponding to the prices of Figs. 5.8 look qualitatively like those of [13] and are not shown. However, some numerical values near expiry are given in Table 5.5.

We remark that the contact conditions and the Black Scholes equation yield the following estimate for the call side free boundary S_2

$$rV(S_2, t) - (r - q)S_2 V_S(S_2, t) = \frac{1}{2}\sigma^2 S_2^2 V_{SS}(S_2, t) \geq \frac{1}{2}\sigma^2 \alpha_2 (\alpha_2 - 1) S^{\alpha_2}$$

so that a necessary condition for the location of the early exercise boundary is

$$S_2^{\alpha_2}(t) \geq \frac{rK_2}{(1 - \alpha_2)r + \alpha_2 q - \frac{1}{2}\sigma^2 \alpha_2 (\alpha_2 - 1)}.$$

For the parameters of Table 5.5 and $K_2 = 1.5$ we obtain the estimate

$$S_2(\Delta t) \geq 3.515625.$$

In analogy with a plain American call we expect that

$$\lim_{t \to 0} S_2^{\alpha_2}(t) = \frac{rK_2}{(1 - \alpha_2)r + \alpha_2 q - \frac{1}{2}\sigma^2\alpha_2(\alpha_2 - 1)} = 3.515625$$

which is consistent with the numerical results of Table 5.5.

Example 5.6. Jump diffusion with uncertain volatility.

The last example of this chapter is similar to Example 4.4. It is chosen to show how various approximations and iterations can be cobbled together to solve a fairly nonlinear problem for a partial-integro-differential-equation (PIDE) of Black Scholes Barenblatt type with the method of lines.

The price V of an option in the jump diffusion model of Merton requires the solution of the linear PIDE

$$\frac{1}{2}\sigma^2(S,t)S^2V_{SS} + (r - q - \lambda k)SV_S - (r + \lambda)V$$
$$+ \lambda \int_0^\infty V(JS,t)g(J)dJ - V_t = 0 \qquad (5.17)$$

subject to a pay-off condition at $t = 0$ and boundary conditions which are specific to the option under consideration. The λ terms in (5.17) account for random Poisson jumps in the value S of the underlying asset. λ is the intensity of the jumps, g is the distribution of the jumps and k denotes the expected jump size given by

$$k = \int_0^\infty (J - 1)g(J)dJ.$$

For a detailed description of this jump diffusion model we refer to [64].

The integral in (5.17) is a non-local term and complicates the numerical valuation of options compared to the Black Scholes case of $\lambda = 0$. Since even for the linear equation (5.17) an iterative solution method will be suggested here, we shall consider the application of the MOL approach to the more general Black Scholes Barenblatt equation associated with (5.17) which includes (5.17) as a special case and which is no more complicated to solve numerically than (5.17).

As in Example 4.4 we shall assume that the volatility $\sigma(S,t)$ in (5.17) is uncertain but bounded. Specifically, we assume that we know continuous functions $\sigma_0(S,t)$ and $\sigma_1(S,t)$ such that

$$0 < \sigma_0(S,t) \le \sigma(S,t) \le \sigma_1(S,t) \qquad (5.18)$$

We shall find functions $V_0(S, t)$ and $V_1(S, t)$ such that

$$V_0(S, t) \leq V(S, t) \leq V_1(S, t)$$

for all volatilities satisfying (5.18). Moreover, these bounds are sharp, i.e. there is a (usually discontinuous) volatility $\sigma^*(S, t)$ such that the corresponding option price $V^*(S, t)$ given by (5.17) satisfies

$$V^*(S, t) = V_0(S, t),$$

and another volatility $\sigma^{**}(S, t)$ such that option price $V^{**}(S, t)$ satisfies

$$V^{**}(S, t) = V_1(S, t).$$

It has been shown [57] that for European and some American options the function $V_0(S, t)$ is the solution of the Black Scholes Barenblatt PIDE

$$\frac{1}{2}\bar{\sigma}^2(S, t)S^2 V_{SS} + (r - q - \lambda k)SV_S - (r + \lambda)V$$

$$+ \lambda \int_0^\infty V(JS, t)g(J)dJ - V_t = F(|V_{SS}|, S, \underline{\sigma}) \quad (5.19)$$

where

$$\bar{\sigma}^2 = \frac{\sigma_1^2 + \sigma_0^2}{2}, \quad \underline{\sigma}^2 = \frac{\sigma_1^2 - \sigma_0^2}{2}$$

and

$$F(|V_{SS}|, S, \sigma) = \frac{1}{2}\sigma^2 S^2 |V_{SS}|.$$

Note that the unknown volatility $\sigma(S, t)$ does not occur in (5.19). Similarly, the upper bound $V_1(S, t)$ is the solution of (5.19) provided the source term $F(|V_{SS}|, S, \underline{\sigma})$ is replaced by $-F(|V_{SS}|, S, \underline{\sigma})$. V_0 and V_1 are subject to the same inital and boundary conditions which apply to the option price V.

We remark that (5.19) is one version of three equivalent BSB formulations derived in [57] for the PIDE (5.17). Formulation (5.19) consists of a non-degenerate linear PIDE operator with a nonlinear source term. It is convenient for the MOL/Riccati numerical approach and, possibly, for proving existence and uniqueness of its solution. Here we shall assume that the initial/boundary value problem for (5.19) considered below has a unique solution.

The MOL approximation of (5.19) at time level t_n is the following ordinary-integro-differential equation (OIDE) analog of equation (4.3):

$$\frac{1}{2}\bar{\sigma}^2(S,t)S^2V''(S) + (r - q - \lambda k)SV'(S) - (r+\lambda)V(S) - D_nV(S)$$

$$= -\lambda \int_0^\infty V(JS)g(J)dJ + F(|V''(S)|, S, \underline{\sigma}) \quad (5.20)$$

which is augmented by the boundary conditions imposed on $V(S,t)$ at time t_n. We shall rewrite this OIDE in the form

$$\mathcal{L}_n(\bar{\sigma})V = G_n(|V''|, V, S, \underline{\sigma}) \quad (5.21)$$

where $\mathcal{L}_n(\bar{\sigma})$ is the usual linear MOL differential operator for the Black Scholes equation, and where G_n collects the integral, the nonlinear term and the data from the preceding time levels. For example, for $n = 1, 2$ we obtain from the implicit Euler approximation

$$\mathcal{L}_n(\bar{\sigma})V \equiv \frac{1}{2}\bar{\sigma}^2(S,t)S^2V''(S) + (r - q - \lambda k)SV'(S) - \left(r + \lambda + \frac{1}{\Delta t}\right)V(S)$$

and

$$G_n(|V''|, V, S, \underline{\sigma}) = -\lambda \int_0^\infty V(JS)g(J)dJ + F(|V''(S)|, S, \underline{\sigma}) - \frac{V_{n-1}(S)}{\Delta t}.$$

For $n \geq 3$ the three level time differencing scheme changes $\mathcal{L}_n$ and G_n slightly.

The nonlinear MOL approximation (5.21) will be solved iteratively. Let $V^0(S)$ denote our initial guess for the solution of (5.21) at time level t_n. Typically we set

$$V^0(S) = V_{n-1}(S).$$

Then for $k = 1, 2, \ldots$ the function $V^k(S)$ is the solution of

$$\mathcal{L}_n(\bar{\sigma})V^k = G_n(|V''^{k-1}(S)|, V^{k-1}(S), S, \underline{\sigma}). \quad (5.22)$$

Hence we have a sequence of linear problems with a known source term which we can solve with the sweep method. For $\lambda = 0$ this iteration solves the usual Black Scholes Barenblatt equation, for $\sigma_0(S,t) = \sigma_1(S,t)$ it solves the standard jump diffusion PIDE with known volatility σ_0.

The numerical difficulties in solving (5.22) are due primarily to the integral term in G_n. It will usually require a numerical quadrature. However, the integrand $V^{k-1}(JS)$ will be available only at the mesh points used for the integration of the sweep equations with the trapezoidal rule. Of course, interpolation can be used to provide V^{k-1} as a function of S so that the quadrature points can be chosen independently of the mesh points for the trapezoidal rule (see, e.g. [14]). To avoid interpolation we shall choose here a mesh which can be used simultaneously for the numerical approximation of the integral in G_n and for the solution of the sweep equations with the trapezoidal rule.

To illustrate this approach, and to point out the problem dependent choices which have to be made along the way, let us solve a very specific problem.

The problem statement is as follows: Let S^* be the spot price of the asset at $t = T$. We wish to find bounds V_0 and V_1 on the price $P(S^*, T, \sigma)$ of an American put for (5.17) with strike price K and expiration T written on an asset S whose volatility σ is not given explicitly but known to satisfy (5.18). We assume further that the price $E(S^*, T, \sigma)$ of another option written on S is available from market data.

We know from the above discussion that we can find bounds $V_0(S, t)$ and $V_1(S, t)$ from the Black Scholes Barenblatt equation (5.19) such that for all S and t

$$V_0(S, t) \leq P(S, t, \sigma) \leq V_1(S, t).$$

However, these bounds may be too coarse at S^* and T to be financially significant. We shall attempt to tighten these bounds through a so-called static hedge with the option $E(S, t, \sigma)$.

To be specific, and to generate a challenging numerical environment, let us assume that $E(S, t, \sigma)$ is the price of a European digital call on S with expiration T and payoff

$$E(S, 0, \sigma) = H(S - K_2)$$

where $K_1 < K_2$ and $H(x)$ is the Heaviside step function. Let $c \in (-\infty, \infty)$ be a constant and let V be the value of the combination

$$V(S, t, \sigma, c) = P(S, t, \sigma) + cE(S, t, \sigma).$$

It is a solution of the linear PIDE (5.17). Moreover, on the early exercise boundary $S(t)$ of the put, $V(S, t, \sigma, c)$ satisfies the free boundary conditions

$$V(S(t), t, \sigma, c) = K - S(t) + cE(S(t), t, \sigma)$$
$$V_S(S(t), t, \sigma, c) = -1 + cE_S(S(t), t, \sigma).$$

However, $E(S, t, \sigma)$ cannot be found because σ is not known with certainty. Only the payoff, the boundary values

$$E(0, t, \sigma) = 0$$

$$\lim_{S\to\infty} E(S,t,\sigma) = e^{-rt}$$

and the price $E(S^*,T,\sigma)$ are known with certainty.

To obtain a solvable problem we shall assume that $E(S,t,\sigma)$ is negligible for $S < K_1$ (which can be expected to hold for suffciently small t). Then the free boundary condition can be approximated by

$$V(S(t),t,\sigma,c) = K_1 - S(t)), \quad S(t) \leq K_1, \qquad (5.23\text{a})$$
$$V_S(S(t),t,\sigma,c) = -1. \qquad (5.23\text{b})$$

We also know the barrier like condition

$$\lim_{S\to\infty} V(S,t,\sigma,c) = ce^{-rt} \qquad (5.23\text{c})$$

and the pay-off value

$$V(S,0,\sigma,c) = P(S,0,\sigma) + cE(S,0,\sigma). \qquad (5.23\text{d})$$

The Black Scholes Barenblatt formalism discussed above applies to $V(S,t,\sigma,c)$ and yields computable bounds V_0 and V_1 such that

$$V_0(S,t,c) \leq V(S,t,\sigma,c) \leq V_1(S,t,c).$$

In particular, since $E(S^*,T,\sigma)$ is known, we have

$$V_0(S^*,T,c) - cE(S^*,T,\sigma) \leq P(S^*,T,\sigma) \leq V_1(S^*,T,c) - cE(S^*,T,\sigma).$$

The interval enclosing the unknown value $P(S^*,T,\sigma)$ is smallest for c^* found such that

$$f(c^*) \leq f(c)$$

where

$$f(c) = V_1(S^*,T,c) - V_0(S^*,T,c). \qquad (5.24)$$

For any given c the value $f(c)$ is computable and c^*, if it exists, can be read off the graph of f.

For the discussion of the numerical aspects we shall introduce the change of variables

$$x = S/K_1, \quad u(x,t,\sigma,c) = \frac{V(K_1 x, t, \sigma(K_1 x, t), c)}{K_1}$$

and the notation

$$s(t) = \frac{S(t)}{K_1}.$$

The PIDE for V can be rewritten as

$$\frac{1}{2}\sigma^2 x^2 u_{xx} + (r - q - \lambda k)xu_x - (r + \lambda)u - u_t$$

$$= -\lambda \int_0^\infty u(Jx, t, \sigma, c)g(J)dJ. \tag{5.25}$$

The boundary conditions become

$$u(s(t), t, \sigma, c) = 1 - s(t), \quad u_x(s(t), t, \sigma, c) = -1$$

$$\lim_{x \to \infty} u(x, t, \sigma, c) = \frac{c}{K_1} e^{-rt}.$$

The initial condition is

$$u(x, 0, \sigma, c) = \max\{0, 1 - x\} + \frac{c}{K_1} H\left(\frac{K_2}{K_1} - x\right).$$

To simplify the notation we shall rewrite (5.18) in the new variables as

$$0 < \sigma_0(x, t) \le \sigma(x, t) \le \sigma_1(x, t). \tag{5.26}$$

Let $\{u_0(x, t, c), s_0(t)\}$ and $\{u_1(x, t, c), s_1(t)\}$ denote the solution of the nonlinear Black Scholes Barenblatt PIDEs corresponding to (5.25) with the same initial and boundary conditions which apply to $\{u(x, t, \sigma, c), s(t)\}$. Then it follows from the discussion in [57] that

$$u_0(x, t, c) \le u(x, t, \sigma, c) \le u_1(x, t, c)$$

and

$$s_1(t) \le s(t) \le s_0(t).$$

Moreover, (5.24) is equivalent to

$$f(c) = u_1(x^*, T, c) - u_0(x^*, T, c)$$

where $x^* = S^*/K_1$. $f(c)$ is independent of the uncertain volatility $\sigma(x, t)$.

For $c < 0$ the solution $\{u_0(x, t, c), s_0(t)\}$ can be expected to exist for t sufficiently small (i.e. near expiry) because $u_0(x, 0, c) \equiv 0$ for $1 \le x \le K_2/K_1$. We say that the solution fails to exist at time t_c whenever

$$u_0(x, t_c, c) < 1 - x \quad \text{for some } x \in [0, 1].$$

When c is fixed then we can compute $f(c)$ with the MOL/Riccati approach. We shall obtain $\{u_0(x, t_n, c), s_0(t_n)\}$ (denoted below by $\{u(x), s_0\}$) iteratively as outlined above. In the new variables the equation (5.22) becomes

$$\mathcal{L}_n(\bar{\sigma})u^k = G_n(|u''^{k-1}(x)|, u^{k-1}(x), x, \underline{\sigma})$$

were G_n requires the evaluation of

$$\int_0^\infty u^{k-1}(Jx)g(J)dJ.$$

Let $[y_0, Y]$ denote the interval chosen for the numerical integration of the MOL approximation with the sweep method. We assume that y_0 is to the left of the early exercise boundary $s(t)$ so that at all times

$$u(x) = 1 - x, \quad 0 < x < y_0.$$

Y denotes an artificial barrier. It is chosen large enough so that we can set

$$u(x) = \frac{c}{K_1} e^{-rt} \quad \text{for } x > Y.$$

For the integral we introduce the change of variable

$$y = Jx$$

and write for $x > 0$

$$\int_0^\infty u^{k-1}(Jx)g(J)dJ = \frac{1}{x}\int_0^\infty u^{k-1}(y)g\left(\frac{y}{x}\right)dy$$

$$= I_{(0,y_0)}(x) + I_{(y_0,Y)}(x) + I_{(Y,\infty)}(x)$$

where

$$I_{(a,b)}(x) = \frac{1}{x}\int_a^b u^{k-1}(y)g\left(\frac{y}{x}\right)dy.$$

Since u is given analytically outside the interval $[y_0, Y]$ the integrals $I_{(0,y_0)}(x)$ and $I_{(Y,\infty)}(x)$ are assumed to be known analytically or numerically for all $x \in [y_0, Y]$. For the approximation of $I_{(y_0,Y)}(x)$ we shall choose a composite two point Gaussian quadrature. Let $y_0 < y_1 < \cdots < y_M = Y$ be a partition of $[y_0, Y]$ into M auxiliary subintervals. We shall assure that the points $\{y_m\}$ are distributed such that they would be suitable for the integration of the sweep equations with the trapezoidal rule and for the composite Gaussian rule. For example, they will cluster around $x = 1$ and around $x = K_2/K_1$ where the solution and the delta of the PIDE will be discontinuous at expiration. The points $\{y_m\}$ are used to generate the actual computational mesh. We set

$$x_0 = y_0, \quad x_{2M+1} = Y$$

and for $m = 1, \ldots, M$

$$x_{2m-1} = \frac{\left[y_m + y_{m-1} - \frac{y_m - y_{m-1}}{\sqrt{3}}\right]}{2}$$

$$x_{2m} = \frac{\left[y_m + y_{m-1} + \frac{y_m - y_{m-1}}{\sqrt{3}} \right]}{2}.$$

Then $\{x_j\}_{j=0}^{2M+1}$ is the computational grid for the equations (3.4), (3.6) while the integral $I_{(y_0, Y)}(x_j)$ is approximated with the composite two-point Gaussian formula

$$I_{(y_0, Y)}(x_j) = \frac{1}{x_j} \sum_{m=1}^{M} I_{(y_{m-1}, y_m)}(x_j)$$

$$\approx \frac{1}{x_j} \sum_{m=1}^{M} \frac{(y_m - y_{m-1}))}{2} \left[u^{k-1}(x_{2m-1}) g\left(\frac{x_{2m-1}}{x_j} \right) + u^{k-1}(x_{2m}) g\left(\frac{x_{2m}}{x_j} \right) \right].$$

The probability densities $g(x_i/x_j)$ can be computed once and stored and the values $u^{k-1}(x_j)$ are available from the trapezoidal integration of the sweep equations. We point out that applying the trapezoidal rule on the mesh coinciding with the Gaussian quadrature points eliminates the need for an interpolation of u which becomes necessary when the integration of the jump integral is decoupled from the PDE solver as in [17].

Quadrature methods for the remaining two integrals

$$I_{(a,b)}(x) = \frac{1}{x} \int_a^b u^{k-1}(y) g(y/x) dy \quad \text{for } (a,b) = (0, y_0), \quad (Y, \infty)$$

usually will depend on the asymptotic behavior of the density g as $y \to 0, \infty$.

Since $u''^{k-1} = v'^{k-1}(x)$ the complete source term in (5.22) is now available at the mesh points $\{x_j\}$. We integrate the equations (3.4) of the forward sweep from $x = Y$ to $x = y_0$ subject to

$$R(Y) = 0$$

$$w(Y) = \frac{c}{K_1} e^{-rt_n}.$$

Going from $x = 1$ toward $x = 0$, we determine the first two adjacent mesh points between which

$$\phi(x) \equiv R(x)(-1) + w(x) - (1 - x)$$

changes its sign and find the early exercise boundary $s^k(t_n)$ as the root of the cubic interpolant to ϕ through the four nearest points. The reverse sweep requires the integration of (3.6) from s^k to Y. The Riccati transformation furnishes $u^k(x)$. The iteration is terminated when

$$\max_x |u^k(x) - u^{k-1}(x)| + |s^k - s^{k-1}| < 10^{-6}.$$

For a numerical example let us choose

$$r = .05, \quad q = 0, \quad \sigma_0(S,t) = .2, \quad \sigma_1(S,t) = .4$$

$$K_1 = 1, \quad K_2 = 1.1$$

and

$$\lambda = .1, \quad g(J) = \frac{e^{-\frac{1}{2}\left(\frac{\ln J - \mu}{\gamma}\right)^2}}{\sqrt{2\pi}\gamma J}$$

where

$$\mu = -.9, \quad \gamma = .35.$$

We remark that the choice of density is not restricted in any way. For the Gaussian density it follows that

$$k = e^{(\mu + \gamma^2/2)} - 1.$$

For the interval of computation $[y_0, Y]$ we use

$$y_0 = .5, \quad Y = 3K_2 = 3.3$$

and an auxiliary mesh consisting of 800 unevenly spaced points $\{y_m\}$. The integrals

$$I_{(0,y_0)}(x_j) = \int_0^{y_0} (1 - Jx_j)g(J)dJ$$

and

$$I_{(Y,\infty)}(x_j) = K_2/K_1 e^{-rt_n} \int_Y^{\infty} g(J)dJ$$

could have been evaluated analytically but are here approximated with a composite two point Gaussian formula with 100 and 500 intervals in order not to tie the program to a Gaussian distribution for the jumps.

Figure 5.9 shows a plot of $f(c)$ given by (5.24). It is based on a linear interpolation of f for eleven values of c evenly distributed over $[-.05, 0]$ when

$$S^* = 1, \quad T = .25 \quad \text{and} \quad \Delta t = T/180.$$

The numerical minimum occurs at $c = -.03$ where

$$u_0(1, T, -.03) = .0312417$$
$$u_1(1, T, -.03) = .0690583$$

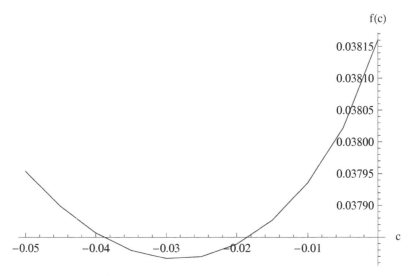

Fig. 5.9. Plot of $f(c) = u_1(1, .25, c) - u_0(1, .25, c)$ vs. c when the uncertain volatility satisfies $.2 \le \sigma \le .4$.

and

$$f(-.03) = .0378166.$$

This compares with

$$u_0(1, T, 0) = .0394856$$
$$u_1(1, T, 0) = .0776458$$

and

$$f(0) = 0.0381602$$

for the unhedged put.

These numerical values appear to change little when the number of spatial mesh points is doubled or halved. This again suggests that the time discrete method of lines equations are solved accurately. Similarly, halving the time step has little influence on the answers at $T = .25$.

The effect of hedging a long American put with a short European binary option for the parameters of this jump diffusion model happens to be insignificant. However, the algorithm is not tied to this model and remains applicable to a variety of options with or without jump diffusion and/or uncertain volatility.

We conclude our discussion by showing in Fig. 5.10 the graphs for $u_0(x, .424, -1)$ and $u_1(x, .424, -1)$, of the solution $u(x, .424, .3, -1)$ of (5.25)

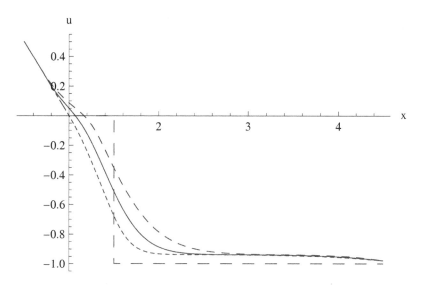

Fig. 5.10. Plot of the pay-off $u(x, 0, \sigma, -1)$, of the Black Scholes Barenblatt functions $u_0(x, .424, -1)$, $u_1(x, .424, -1)$ and of the solution $u(x, .424, .3, -1)$ of (5.25) for $K_1 = 1$, $K_2 = 1.5$.

and of the pay-off $u(x, 0, .3, -1)$. The above parameter holds except that now

$$K_1 = 1, \quad K_2 = 1.5.$$

$$\Delta t = .001.$$

The solution u_0 fails to exist at $t = .425$ because it falls below zero at $x = 1$. The solution $u(x, t, .3, -1)$ fails to exist at $t = 1.047$ while the upper bound u_1 appears to remain above the pay-off at all times.

Chapter 6

Bonds and Options for One-Factor Interest Rate Models

Interest rate derivatives based on one-factor interest rate models can be priced with a diffusion equation which has much the same structure as the Black Scholes equation. For some interest rate models the corresponding diffusion equation has an analytic solution, for others one again has to rely on numerical approximations. This chapter explores the application of the method of lines/Riccati method for bonds and bond options based on one-factor interest rate models.

Given a stochastic interest rate model for the spot rate $r(\tau)$ of the form

$$dr = \hat{u}(r, \tau)d\tau + \hat{w}(r, \tau)dW, \tag{6.1}$$

where $\hat{u}$ and $\hat{w}$ are deterministic functions of r and real time τ and $W(\tau)$ is a Wiener process, then the price $V(r, \tau)$ of a zero coupon bond maturing at time T can be determined from the bond equation

$$\frac{1}{2}\hat{w}^2 V_{rr} + (\hat{u} - \lambda(r, \tau)\hat{w})V_r - rV + V_\tau = 0 \tag{6.2}$$

where the so-called market price of risk $\lambda(r, \tau)$ is assumed to be specified.

The bond equation is subject to the final condition

$$V(r, T) = 1$$

and the boundary condition

$$\lim_{r \to \infty} V(r, \tau) = 0, \quad 0 \le \tau < T.$$

As in Chapters 4 and 5 we shall rewrite this problem as a standard initial value problem in the variable $t = T - \tau$, and impose a limiting boundary condition at some finite interest rate R_1. In the new variable the bond price $u(r, t) = V(r, T - t)$ will be determined from

$$a(r, t)u_{rr} + b(r, t)u_r - ru - u_t = 0 \tag{6.3a}$$

where

$$a(r,t) = \frac{1}{2}\hat{w}^2(r, T-t) \quad \text{and}$$

$$b(r,t) = \hat{u}(r, T-t) - \lambda(r, T-t)\hat{w}(r, T-t),$$

and

$$u(r, 0) = 1 \tag{6.3b}$$

$$u(R_1, t) = e^{-R_1 t}. \tag{6.3c}$$

A second boundary condition for (6.3a) may or may not be needed which requires some discussion.

If equation (6.3a) is to be solved for $r_0(t) \leq r \leq R_1$, where $r_0(t)$ is given, and if there is a constant $a_0 > 0$ such that

$$a(r,t) \geq a_0 > 0 \quad \text{for } r_0(t) \leq r \leq R_1, \quad t > 0,$$

then the equation (6.3a) is said to be uniformly parabolic and needs a second boundary condition for u at $r_0(t)$. This boundary condition may not be available from financial considerations. The situation is even more complicated when

$$\lim_{r \to r_0(t)} a(r,t) = 0.$$

The coefficient matrix in the $x - t$ plane associated with (6.3a) is

$$A = \begin{pmatrix} a(r,t) & 0 \\ 0 & 0 \end{pmatrix}.$$

At any time t the inward unit normal at the point $(r_0(t), t)$ in the $r - t$ plane is the vector

$$\vec{n} = (n_1, n_2) = (1, -r_0'(t))/\sqrt{1 + r_0'(t)^2}.$$

If $a(r_0(t), t) = 0$ for $t \in I$ for some open set I, then the Fichera theory of Chapter 1 applies on $(r_0(t), t)$. The Fichera function of Section 1.2.1

$$h(r,t) = [b(r,t) - a_r(r,t)]n_1 + [-1]n_2$$

is now a positive multiple of

$$h(t) = [b(r_0(t), t) - (a_r(r_0(t), t)] + r_0'(t).$$

If it satisfies $h(t) \geq 0$ for $t \in I$ then the differential equation (6.3a) has to hold on $(r_0(t), t)$.

On the other hand, when

$$h(t) < 0$$

then a second boundary condition must be provided on $r_0(t)$. For example, in the Cox-Ingersoll-Ross (CIR) one factor interest rate model where

$$a(r,t) = \frac{1}{2}\sigma^2 r$$

$$b(r,t) = (\eta - \mu r)$$

we find that at $r_0(t) \equiv 0$

$$h(t) = \eta - \frac{1}{2}\sigma^2$$

so that a boundary condition at $r = 0$ is required whenever $\eta < \sigma^2/2$.

Fortunately, it has already been observed [21] that the choice of boundary condition is not critical. The bond equation with the perturbed coefficient

$$a_\epsilon(r,t) = \frac{1}{2}\sigma^2 r^{1+\epsilon}, \quad \epsilon > 0$$

yields $h(t) = \eta > 0$ and can be solved without boundary condition at $r_0 = 0$. The numerical bond prices $u_\epsilon(r,t)$ change little as $\epsilon \to 0$ regardless of the algebraic sign of $\eta - \frac{1}{2}\sigma^2$ and can be taken as a good approximation of the bond prices for the CIR model. Alternatively, we can interpret the CIR bond equation at $r = 0$ as an admissible oblique boundary condition for the equation on $r > 0$ (see Section 1.2.3) and infer that (6.3a) with boundary condition

$$\eta u_r - ru - u_t = 0 \quad \text{on } r = 0 \tag{6.4}$$

is a well-posed problem regardless of the algebraic sign of the Fichera function, i.e. of the Feller expression

$$h(t) = \eta - \frac{\sigma^2}{2}.$$

We recall from Example 1.13 that if $h(t) < 0$ then a Dirichlet condition can be imposed on $r = 0$ which need not be consistent with (6.4) or with the limit of $u(0,t)$ as $t \to 0$.

Here we shall completely bypass the issue of degeneracy. We modify (6.3a) such that it always is uniformly parabolic, and provide a second boundary condition. The validity of our approach rests on the demonstration that we compute numerically correct results for those one factor models which have analytic bond prices, and stable answers in cases where we do not have an analytic solution.

We shall make the following assumptions:

i) $\hat{u}$, $\hat{w}$ and λ are continuous in t and differentiable in r.

ii) There is an interval $[r_0(t), r_1(t)]$ such that the solution $u(r, t)$ is required only for interest rates $r \in [r_0(t), r_1(t)]$.

iii) Equation (6.3a) is uniformly parabolic (i.e. $a(r, t) \geq a_0 > 0$) for $r \geq r_0(t)$.

These assumptions hold for each one-factor interest rate model discussed in [23, p. 132].

For example, for the CIR model we might set $r_0(t) = 10^{-3}$, $r_1(t) = 1$, so that $a(r, t) \geq a_0 = \frac{1}{2}\sigma^2 r_0 > 0$. To generate a second boundary condition at some point $R_0 < r_0(t)$ we shall imbed (6.3a) into the uniformly parabolic equation

$$\tilde{a}(r, t)u_{rr} + \tilde{b}(r, t)u_r - ru - u_t = 0 \tag{6.5a}$$

on the ficticious domain $R_0 < r < R_1$, $t > 0$, where the coefficients of (6.5a) coincide with those of (6.3a) for $r > r_0$ and are extended linearly below $r_0(t)$ so that

$$\tilde{a}(r, t) = \begin{cases} a(r, t), & r > r_0(t) \\ a(r_0(t), t), & r \leq r_0(t) \end{cases}$$

$$\tilde{b}(r, t) = \begin{cases} b(r, t), & r > r_0(t) \\ b(r_0(t), t) + b_r(r_0(t), t)(r - r_0(t)), & r \leq r_0(t). \end{cases}$$

We note that b and $\tilde{b}$ coincide for interest rate models with linear mean reversion. We impose the initial condition

$$u(r, 0) = 1, \quad R_0 < r < R_1 \tag{6.5b}$$

and the boundary condition

$$u(R_1, t) = e^{-R_1 t}. \tag{6.5c}$$

Since $\tilde{a}(r, t) \geq a_0 > 0$ the equation (6.5a) is a standard diffusion equation and needs a boundary condition at $r = R_0$. Because the coefficients $\tilde{a}$ and $\tilde{b}$ are linear in r to the left of r_0 we can verify that the function

$$u(r, t) = e^{A(t) + B(t)r} \tag{6.6}$$

is a formal solution of (6.5a) on $[R_0, r_0(t)]$. Indeed, substituting into (6.5a) for $r < r_0(t)$ we see that $A(t)$ and $B(t)$ satisfy the initial value problem

$$B' = -1 + \tilde{b}_r(r_0(t), t)B(t) \tag{6.7}$$

$$B(0) = 0$$

$$A' = \tilde{a}(r_0(t), t)B^2(t) + [\tilde{b}(r_0(t), t) - \tilde{b}_r(r_0(t), t)r_0(t)]B(t)$$
$$A(0) = 0.$$

It follows that

$$B(t) = -\int_0^t \left[\exp\left(\int_s^t b_r(r_0(y), y) \right) dy \right] ds.$$

Note that if $b_r \equiv 0$ then $B(t) = -t$ and $b_r = -\mu$ then $B(t) = \frac{e^{-\mu t} - 1}{\mu}$. For some models, like the Black Karazinski model, $B(t)$ may require numerical integration. If $B(t)$ is available then the solution (6.6) suggests the boundary condition

$$u_r(R_0, t) = B(t)u(R_0, t). \tag{6.8}$$

In summary, instead of the original bond equation with possibly an unspecified boundary condition we solve instead the well defined boundary value problem (6.5a,b,c), (6.8). We hasten to add that the ficticious domain approach adopted here is not a legitimate mathematical trick for solving a diffusion equation. Its justification rests on the assumption that the one-factor interest rate model can be extended as a Vasicek like equation for interest rates below $r_0(t)$, and that the bond price at R_0 shows the functional relationship (6.8) which holds for Vasicek like models. This approximation is deemed acceptable if the computed bond prices over $[r_0(t), r_1(t)]$ can be shown to be insensitive to R_0 and R_1 and the boundary conditions imposed there. In subsequent applications problem (6.5a,b,c) with (6.8) will be solved with the method of lines approximation/Riccati transformation detailed in Chapter 3.

We shall use the notation of Chapters 3 and 4 and let $u(r)$ and $v(r)$ denote the approximations to $u(r, t_n)$ and $u_r(r, t_n)$. Then the MOL approximation $u(r)$ at time t_n solves

$$\tilde{a}(r, t_n)u''(r) + \tilde{b}(r, t_n)u'(r) - ru(r) - D_n u(r) = 0.$$

The forward sweep proceeds from $r = R_1$ toward R_0 and requires the integration of (3.4) where the coefficients are read off from the equations analogous to (4.4) and (4.5), i.e. for $n = 1, 2$

$$u'(r) = v$$
$$v'(r) = \frac{1}{\tilde{a}(r, t)} \left[\left(r + \frac{1}{\Delta t} \right) u - \tilde{b}(r, t_n)v - \frac{1}{\Delta t} u_{n-1}(r) \right]$$

and for $n \geq 3$

$$u'(r) = v$$

$$v'(r) = \frac{1}{\tilde{a}(r,t_n)} \left[\left(r + \frac{3}{2\Delta t} \right) u - \tilde{b}(r,t_n)v - \frac{3}{2\Delta t} u_{n-1}(r) \right.$$

$$\left. - \frac{1}{2\Delta t} \left(u_{n-1}(r) - u_{n-2}(r) \right) \right].$$

The boundary condition

$$v(R_0) = B(t_n)u(R_0)$$

and the Riccati transformation

$$u(r) = R(r)v(r) + w(r)$$

yield the initial value

$$v(R_0) = \frac{B(t_n)w(R_0)}{1 - B(t_n)R(R_0)}$$

for the reverse sweep (3.6) from R_0 toward R_1. Note that the coefficients of the Riccati equation may be time dependent in which case $R(r)$ has to be recomputed at each time level.

In principle the algorithm, and in particular the boundary conditions, apply to all bond equations based on the interest rate model (6.1). The following examples will illustrate the validity of our ficticious domain approach.

Example 6.1. The Ho Lee model.

The Ho Lee model is based on the choice of

$$\hat{u}(r,\tau) - \lambda(r,\tau)\hat{w}(r,\tau) = \theta(\tau)$$

$$\hat{w}(r,\tau) = \sigma > 0$$

so that

$$\tilde{a}(r,t) = \frac{1}{2}\sigma^2,$$

$$\tilde{b}(r,t) = \theta(T-t).$$

Integration of (6.7) yields

$$A(t) = \frac{1}{6}\sigma^2 t^3 - \int_{T-t}^{T} (T-s)\theta(s)ds, \quad B(t) = -t.$$

We note that the analytic solution

$$u_{an}(r,t) = e^{A(t)-rt}$$

satisfies (6.8) everywhere but not (6.5c) for any finite R_1. The model allows negative interest rates but we assume that the relevant interest rate range is $r \in [0,1]$. We choose

$$R_0 < r_0(t) \equiv 0 \quad \text{and} \quad R_1 > 1$$

and impose the boundary conditions (6.5c) and (6.8). We have a standard diffusion problem and expect the MOL approximation to yield accurate solutions over $(R_0, R_1) \times (0,T]$. For our numerical simulation we shall choose the drift

$$\theta(\tau) = \sigma^2\tau + .05\,\omega\cos\omega\tau$$

obtained from a hypothetical short term rate of

$$r(\tau) = .1 + .05\sin\omega\tau \tag{6.9}$$

with corresponding bond price

$$Z(T-t,T) = \exp\left(-\int_{T-t}^{T} r(s)ds\right)$$

(see [64, p. 439]). It follows that

$$A(t) = -\sigma^2 t^2 \frac{T-t}{2} + \frac{0.05}{\omega}[\cos(\omega T) - \cos(\omega(T-t)) + \omega t\sin(\omega(T-t))].$$

For the numerical simulation we shall price a ten year bond for the following data:

$$\sigma = .05, \quad \omega = 1$$
$$R_0 = -.1, \quad R_1 = 3$$
$$T = 10, \quad \Delta t = T/10000 = .001.$$

The MOL equations are solved numerically with the trapezoidal rule on a grid with 3201 meshpoints distributed unevenly over $[R_0, R_1]$. Execution of 10000 time steps with the Riccati transformation sweep method takes about one minute.

Figure 6.1 shows a graph of the bond prices $u(r,T)$ today over the interval $[0,.2]$.

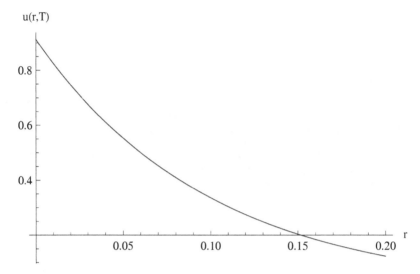

Fig. 6.1. Numerical Ho Lee bond prices $u(r,T)$ for $0 < r < .2$ and $T = 10$ years.

Figure 6.2 shows the difference between the numerical and analytical solution for $0 < r < 1$. The maximum error for $(r,t) \in [0,1] \times [0,10]$ is 1.26×10^{-6}.

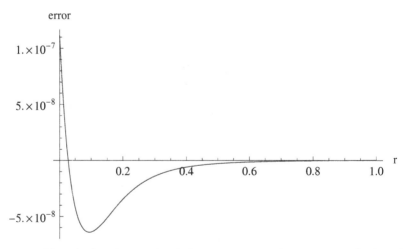

Fig. 6.2. Plot of $u(r,T) - u_{an}(r,T)$ for $0 < r < 1$ and $T = 10$. $u_{an}(r,t)$ is the analytic Ho Lee solution implied by (6.9).

u(r(t),t)

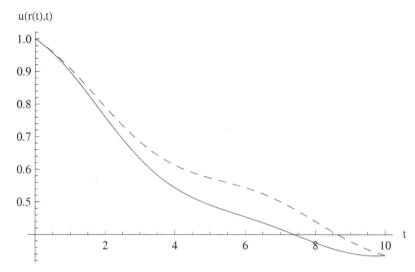

Fig. 6.3. Ho Lee solution $u(r(t), t)$ (solid line) and bond price $Z(T-t, T)$ (dashed line) implied by the hypothetical short rate $r(t)$ for $0 < t < T$ and $\sigma = .05$.

Above, Fig. 6.3 compares the Ho Lee bond price $u(r(t), t)$ with the deterministic bond price $Z(T - t, T)$ for $t \in [0, T]$ along the short rate curve $r(t)$ given by (6.9).

We see that the numerical solution of the bond equation for the Ho Lee model accurately reproduces the analytic solution for $(r, t) \in [0, 1] \times [0, 10]$. The choice of $R_1 = 3$ is unncessarily large for $\sigma = .05$ since $R_1 = 1.4$ yielded the same results. On the other hand, a large volatility of $\sigma = .5$ required $R_1 = 12$ for a maximum error of less than 6.4×10^{-4}. For even larger volatilities long term numerical solutions appear difficult to compute for the Ho Lee model, as might be inferred from the analog to Fig. 6.3 shown below for $\sigma = 1.00$.

Example 6.2. A one-factor CEV model.

We shall assume that for $t = T - \tau$, where τ is calendar time, we have

$$\hat{u}(r, t) - \lambda(r, t)\hat{w}(r, t) = (\eta - \mu r) \qquad (6.10)$$

$$\hat{w}(r, t) = \sigma r^\gamma,$$

where $\eta, \mu, \gamma \geq 0$ and $\sigma > 0$. Several named one-factor interest rate models, such as Vasicek, Cox-Ingersoll-Ross, and Courtadon are special cases of the

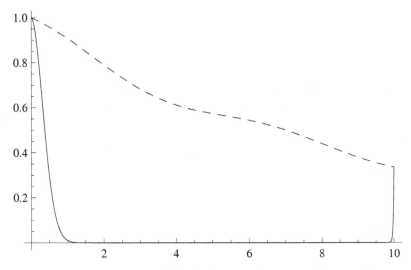

Fig. 6.4. Ho Lee solution $u_{an}(r(t), t)$ (solid line) and bond price $Z(T - t, T)$ (dashed line) implied by the hypothetical short rate $r(t)$ (6.9) for $0 < t < T$ and $\sigma = 1.00$.

above choice. For $\gamma > 0$ the bond equation (6.3a) becomes degenerate at $r = 0$, leads to uncertainty about the correct boundary condition at $r = 0$ but fits the framework postulated for our ficticious domain approach. We note that

$$\tilde{a}(r, t) = \begin{cases} \frac{1}{2} \sigma^2 r^{2\gamma}, & r \geq r_0 \\ \frac{1}{2} \sigma^2 r_0^{2\gamma}, & r < r_0 \end{cases}$$

and

$$\tilde{b}(r, t) \equiv b(r, t) = \eta - \mu r \quad \text{for all } r.$$

To illustrate the performance of the MOL/Riccati approach for the above one-factor CEV model we shall compute the ten year bond price $u(r, t)$ from (6.5a,b,c) and (6.8) with

$$B(t) = \frac{e^{-\mu t} - 1}{\mu}$$

for a range of γ with the following data:

$$\hat{u} - \lambda \hat{w} = \eta - \mu r = .15(.05 - r)$$

$$\hat{w} = \sigma r^\gamma = 0.05 r^\gamma, \quad 0 \leq \gamma \leq 1.$$

We recall from Chapter 1 that for all $\eta \geq 0$ and $\gamma > 0$ the restriction of equation (6.3a) to $r = 0$ will yield an acceptable oblique boundary condition which, moreover, can be expected to lead to solutions $u(r, t)$ which are continuous with respect to all financial parameters of (6.3a). If $\gamma = 0$ then the ficticious domain imbedding can be used to generate the reflection condition (6.8) We note that for $\gamma > .5$ no other boundary condition can be imposed on (6.3a) at $r = 0$. For $\gamma = .5$ we see that

$$\eta - \frac{1}{2}\sigma^2 = .0075 - .00125 < 0$$

so that a Dirichlet condition could be given at $r = 0$. For $\gamma < .5$ the Fichera function is undefined at $r = 0$ and gives no information, although we expect that a Dirichlet condition would lead to a well-posed problem. None of these issues arise for (6.5a). Moreover, from continuity considerations we would expect that for all $\gamma > 0$ the ficticious domain solution is "close" to the solution obtained with the oblique boundary condition.

For our numerical experiments we shall choose as relevant the interest interval $[r_0, r_1] = [.001, 1]$ and imbed the problem into the computational r-domain $[R_0, R_1] = [-.1, 4]$. The time step is

$$\Delta t = 10/10000 = .001.$$

The grid size in the computational r-domain is

$$\Delta r = [.001 + .1]/1000 \quad \text{on } [R_0, r_0]$$
$$\Delta r = [.01 - .001]/1000 \quad \text{on } [r_0, .01]$$
$$\Delta r = [1 - .01]/2000 \quad \text{on } [.01, 1]$$
$$\Delta r = [3 - 1]/1000 \quad \text{on } [1, R_1].$$

A run with the above grid and with 10000 time steps takes about 80 seconds to find all bond prices for $r \in [r_0, r_1]$ and $t \in [0, T]$. The above the mesh is not optimized. The critical point for the numerical method is $r_0 = .001$ since the sweep equations for w and, especially, for v become very stiff as $r \searrow r_0$. For some critical exponent $\gamma_c \geq 1.7$ the computation of $u(r, t)$ blows up on the above grid and would need further grid refinement.

For illustration we show in Fig. 6.5 today's prices $u(r, T)$ of a ten year bond at a short rate $r = .05$ as a function of the CEV exponent γ.

A comparison of the numerical bond prices with the analytic solutions for the Vasicek and CIR models yields the following global error bounds:

$$\max_{\substack{r_0 \leq r \leq r_1 \\ 0 \leq t \leq T}} |u(r, t) - u_{an}(r, t)| \leq 1.4210^{-6} \quad \text{for } \gamma = 0, .5.$$

u(.05,10)

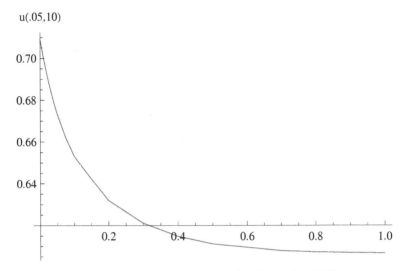

Fig. 6.5. Plot of the discount bond price $u(r,T)$ vs. the CEV exponent γ for $T = 10$ and $r(T) = .05$ for the one-factor CEV model (6.10).

Decreasing r_0 to $r_0 = .0001$ has no effect on $u(.05, T)$ for $\gamma \in [0,1]$ but is necessary to obtain comparable errors for $\gamma = 0, .5$ for a high volatility of $\sigma = .2$ (instead of the above $\sigma = .05$).

An application of the ficticious domain approach for a CEV model with jumps [24] and solution of the resulting PIDE appears possible in view of Example 5.6 but has not been implemented.

For a second illustration we shall consider an implied volatility problem. Suppose the price of a five year discount bond is quoted at a short rate of $\hat{r} = .06$ as

$$u(\hat{r}, 5, \sigma) = .757111.$$

If we accept the mean reversion CEV interest rate model

$$dr = .15(.05 - r)dt + \sigma r^\gamma dW$$

what is the volatility implied by this price for any $\gamma \in [0,1]$?

For a fixed $\gamma \in [0,1]$ we need to find σ such that

$$f(\sigma) \equiv u(.06, 5, \sigma) - .757111 = 0$$

where $u(r,t,\sigma)$ for given σ is found as described in the first part of this example. We shall use a discrete Newton method. Let σ^0 be an initial guess then successive $\{\sigma^k\}$ are obtained from the equation

$$\frac{f(\sigma^k + \Delta\sigma) - f(\sigma^k)}{\Delta\sigma}(\sigma^{k+1} - \sigma^k) + f(\sigma^k) = 0$$

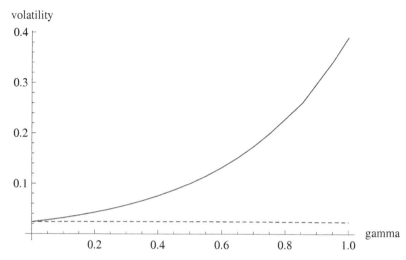

Fig. 6.6. Implied interest rate volatility for a five year CEV discount bond.
solid curve: volatility σ as a function of the CEV exponent γ
dashed curve: normalized volatility $\sigma \hat{r}^\gamma$ for a spot price $\hat{r}$
Bond price $u(\hat{r}, 5) = .757111$, $\hat{r} = .06$, $\Delta t = 5/2500$.

where $\Delta \sigma = .000001$. The iteration is terminated and σ^{k+1} is accepted as the implied volatility when

$$|f(\sigma^k)| \leq 10^{-6}.$$

Hence each step of the iteration requires two bond price calculations to find $f(\sigma^k)$ and $f(\sigma^k + \Delta \sigma)$. For $\gamma = 1$ the initial guess is not critical. Even $\sigma^0 = 1$ leads to convergence in six iterations and a final answer of $\sigma = .38964$. For smaller values of γ the computed volatility at the nearest γ served as an initial guess. We remark that the bond price $u(.06, 5) = .757111$ is actually the CIR bond price corresponding to $\sigma = .1$ which serves as a check on the numerical calculation.

Figure 6.6 shows a plot of the volatility σ and the normalized volatility $\sigma \hat{r}^\gamma$ as as a function of γ obtained by linearly interpolating the results for $\gamma_j = j/20$, $j = 0, \ldots, 20$. The normalized values fall roughly onto a parabola through $(0, .237)$, $(.4, .245)$ and $(1, .234)$ which looks flat on the scale of Fig. 6.6.

Example 6.3. An implied volatility for a call on a discount bond.

The ficticious domain approach in the preceding example remains useful for pricing bond options for one-factor interest rate models. Thus let us suppose that the one-factor model (6.10)

$$dr = (\eta - \mu r)dt + \sigma r^\gamma dW$$

is chosen for the short rate of a discount bond price $u(r, t, Tb)$, where Tb denotes the maturity of the bond and $t = Tb - \tau$ for calendar time τ is its time to maturity. Let $c(r, t, To)$ denote the price of a European call written on the bond which expires at some time $To < Tb$. Then $u(r, t, Tb)$ and $c(r, t, To)$ satisfy equation (6.3a) for $0 < t < Tb$ and $Tb - To < t < Tb$, resp.

As in Example 6.2, the interest rate model is extended for negative interest rates as a Vasicek like model and $u(r, t, Tb)$ and $c(r, t, To)$ are assumed to solve the non-degenerate equation (6.5a) for $r \in [R_0, R_1]$. As before the bond will satisfy the initial condition (6.5b) and the boundary conditions (6.5c), (6.8) with

$$B(t) = \frac{e^{-\mu t} - 1}{\mu}.$$

The initial condition for the call on $R_0 < r < R_1$ is

$$c(r, Tb - To, To) = \max\{u(r, Tb - To, Tb) - K, 0\} \qquad (6.11a)$$

where K is the strike price of the option. The boundary conditions are chosen as

$$c(R_0, t, To) = \max\{u(R_0, t, Tb) - K, 0\} \qquad (6.11b)$$

$$c(R_1, t, To) = \max\{u(R_1, t, Tb) - K, 0\} \qquad (6.11c)$$

for $t \in (Tb - To, Tb]$. In general, R_1 is sufficiently large so that $c(R_1, t, To) = 0$. The boundary condition (6.11b) is not dictated by financial considerations. As discussed in Example 6.2, for $\gamma > .5$ no negative interest rates occur in the CEV model, and no boundary condition should be imposed on u and c at $r = 0$, while for $\gamma < .5$ a second boundary condition is required but generally not available. With (6.11) both $u(r, t, Tb)$ and $c(r, t, To)$ satisfy well defined boundary value problems for all $\gamma \geq 0$. Their numerical values are acceptable if they are shown to be insensitive to R_0 and R_1 for r in the relevant interest range $[r_0, r_1]$.

The computation of the call is straightforward. We use the algorithm of Example 6.2 to find the bond price $u(r, t, Tb)$ for $t \in (0, Tb - To]$. Once $u(r, Tb - To, Tb)$ is found we know (6.11a) and solve at discrete times for $t \in (Tb - To, Tb]$ equation (6.5a) first for $u(r, t, Tb)$ and then for $c(r, t, To)$. Note that for the first three time levels after $t = 0$ and $t = Tb - To$ we will use a backward Euler method before switching back to a three level time differencing. The forward and backward sweep for $u(r, t, Tb)$ and $c(r, t, To)$ use the same Riccati equation and differ only in the source term $g(r)$.

As an illustration we shall price first a one year call on a five year discount bond depending on a Vasicek interest rate equation (i.e. $\gamma = 0$) for the parameters used in Example 6.2 so that

$$\mu = .15, \quad \eta = .0075, \quad \sigma = .05, \quad Tb = 5, \quad To = 1, \quad K = .67.$$

The ficticious domain $[R_0, R_1]$ and the relevant interest range $[r_0, r_1]$ are chosen to be $[-.1, 3]$ and $[.001, 1]$. The computational r-grid is the same as in the previous example. It is probably finer than it needs to be.

For $t \in (0, Tb - To]$ where only the bond needs to be priced we use

$$\Delta t = (Tb - To)/2000 = 2 \cdot 10^{-3}.$$

For $t \in (Tb - To, Tb]$ we use a smaller time step

$$\Delta t = 5 \cdot 10^{-4}$$

because the option has a discontinuous delta at $t = 4$ and $r = r^*$ where $u(r^*, Tb - To, Tb) = K$.

We already know from Example 6.2 that the MOL numerical bond price reproduces the analytic bond price for the Vasicek model. It is also well known that the European call on the bond is given analytically by a Black Scholes type formula [40]. A comparison of the MOL bond and call prices with the exact solutions at calendar time $\tau = 0$ (i.e. $t = Tb$) yields

$$\max_{r \in [r_0, r_1]} |u(r, 5, 5) - u_{an}(r, 5, 5)| = 6.7 \cdot 10^{-8}$$

$$\max_{r \in [r_0, r_1]} |c(r, 5, 1) - c_{an}(r, 5, 1)| = 4.03 \cdot 10^{-4}.$$

The maximum error in the call decreases to $1.36 \cdot 10^{-5}$ if $R_0 = -.2$. We infer that the ficticious domain apoproach can accurately price bonds and options on bonds.

The European call on a discount bond based on the CIR model is also known analytically but not as readily evaluated as the Vasicek call and not calculated here. We observe, however, that the numerical MOL call prices at $r = .001$, $r = .05$, $r = .1$ remain unchanged to six significant digits as R_0 is decreased from $R_0 = -.1$ to $R_0 = -.2$. Hence for all subsequent calculations with the CEV model with $\gamma \geq 0$ we shall choose $R_0 = -.1$.

Let us next turn again to an implied volatility problem. For the CIR model

$$dr = (\eta - \mu r)dt + \sigma \sqrt{r}\, dW$$

with

$$\mu = .15, \quad \eta = .15^*.05 \quad \text{and} \quad \sigma = .1$$

the MOL results for the bond and call at $r = .06$ are

$$u(.06, 0, 5) = 0.7571111$$
$$c(.06, 0, 1) = 0.1258467.$$

The analytic bond price is

$$u_{an}(.06, 0, 5) = 0.7571110 \tag{6.12}$$

so that the MOL bond price is correct to seven digits while the MOL call price is observed to be stable with respect to mesh refinements.

Assume now that the market bond and call prices are the rounded values

$$u(.06, 0, 5) = .7571$$
$$c(.06, 0, 1) = .1259.$$

We intend to answer the question. What is the volatility σ implied by these rounded bond and call prices?

This question is somewhat ambiguous. We can, of course, compute an implied volatility σ_b for the bond price such that

$$u(.06, 0, 5, \sigma_b) = .7571.$$

In fact, a calculation with the discrete Newton's method of Example 6.2 yields

$$\sigma_b = .0999, \quad u(.06, 0, 5, \sigma_b) = .7571, \quad c(.06, 0, 1, \sigma_b) = .125834.$$

Alternatively, we can compute an implied volatility σ_c for the call price such that

$$c(.06, 0, 1, \sigma_c) = .1259.$$

Numerical values in this case are found to be

$$\sigma_c = .10046, \quad c(.06, 0, 1, \sigma_c) = .1259, \quad u(.06, 0, 5, \sigma_c) = .757158.$$

However, because the bond equation (6.3a) is allowed to have variable co-efficients and there are two prices to match we can try to fit a variable volatility with two degrees of freedom. Here we shall assume, rather arbitrarily, a term structure for the volatility of the form

$$\sigma(t) = a + bt$$

and compute a and b such that the MOL solutions take on the given market prices exactly. Note that a time dependent volatility makes the coefficients of the sweep equations time dependent so that the Riccati equation has to be resolved at each time level.

As before we shall apply a discrete Newton's method to the nonlinear problem

$$f_1(a, b) \equiv u(.06, 0, 5, a, b) - .7571 = 0$$
$$f_2(a, b) \equiv c(.06, 0, 1, a, b) - .1259 = 0.$$

Given an initial guess (a^0, b^0) we solve for $k = 1, 2, \ldots$ the linear system

$$J(a^k, b^k) \left(\begin{pmatrix} a^{k+1} \\ b^{k+1} \end{pmatrix} - \begin{pmatrix} a^k \\ b^k \end{pmatrix} \right) + F(a^k, b^k) = 0$$

where

$$F(a, b) = \begin{pmatrix} f_1(a, b) \\ f_2(a, b) \end{pmatrix}$$

and, for given Δa and Δb,

$$J(a, b) = \begin{pmatrix} \dfrac{f_1(a + \Delta a, b) - f_1(a, b)}{\Delta a} & \dfrac{f_1(a, b + \Delta b) - f_1(a, b)}{\Delta b} \\ \dfrac{f_2(a + \Delta a, b) - f_2(a, b)}{\Delta a} & \dfrac{f_2(a, b + \Delta b) - f(a, b)}{\Delta b} \end{pmatrix}.$$

Thus for each k we solve three well defined bond/call problems.

For the above CIR model the initial guess

$$(a^0, b^0) = (.1, 0)$$

and

$$\Delta a = \Delta b = .000001$$

requires five iterations to yield

$$a^5 = 0.0831558$$
$$b^5 = 0.0045694$$

and

$$u(.06, 0, 5) = 0.7571000$$
$$c(.06, 0, 1) = 0.1259000.$$

Table 6.1. Implied volatility functions
implied by bond price (6.12) and four
different call prices.

call price	volatility function
.1258	$\sigma_1(t) = .1123 - .0037t$
.12584	$\sigma_2(t) = .1018 - .0005t$
.1258467	$\sigma = .1$
.12585	$\sigma_3(t) = .0991 + .00025t$
.1259	$\sigma_4(t) = .0864 + .00372t$

a^5 and b^5 are independent of the choice of R_0 and fairly insensitive to Δt in the call interval $[4, 5]$. For example, $\Delta t = 1/6000$ leads to

$$a^5 = 0.0839170$$
$$b^5 = 0.0043628.$$

We remark that for this particular example the slope of the affine volatility function appears to be a measure of whether the call is priced high or low compared to the theoretical call price. For example we show in Table 6.1 the implied volatility functions for several call prices when the bond price is given by (6.12).

A plot of the implied volatility functions is given in Fig. 6.7.

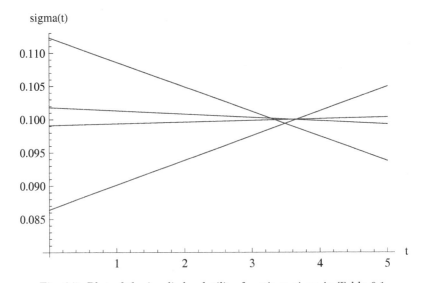

Fig. 6.7. Plot of the implied volatility functions given in Table 6.1.

Convergence of the discrete Newton iteration is not guaranteed. For the short rate $r = .06$ we find that

$$\det J(a^4, b^4) \cong .00155$$

so one knows (a posteriori) that the iteration will converge provided the initial guess is close enough to the final solution. An analogous calculation to determine the volatility implied by the rounded values

$$u(.05, 0, 5) = .7835$$
$$c(.05, 0, 1) = .1461$$

reported in [19, p. 199] for a spot rate equal to the mean reverting rate $r = .05$ consistently failed to converge because $\det J(a^k, b^k) \to 0$ as $k \to \infty$.

Example 6.4. An American put on a discount bond.

Suppose that the price of a discount bond is modeled with the exponential Vasicek interest rate equation

$$dr = \mu r (\ln(\bar{r}) - \ln(r)) dt + \sigma r \, dW \qquad (6.13)$$

where μ, $\bar{r}$ and σ are positive parameters. The solution of the corresponding bond equation (6.3a) is not known analytically and requires numerical methods. We note that the drift term

$$b(r, t) = \mu r (\ln(\bar{r}) - \ln r)$$

satisfies

$$b(r, t) > 0 \quad \text{for } r \in (0, \bar{r}) \text{ and } b(r, t) \leq 0 \text{ for } r \geq \bar{r}$$
$$b_r(r, t) = \mu \left(\ln \frac{\bar{r}}{r} - 1 \right)$$

so that the model behaves much like the CEV mean reversion model with $\gamma = 1$ in the neighborhood of $r = \bar{r}$ except that the mean reversion is not symmetric about $\bar{r}$.

For the exponential Vasicek model the solution of the bond equation at $r = 0$ can be found. The Fichera function for (6.3a) is

$$h(r, t) = [b(r, t) - a_r(r, t)]n_1 + [-1]n_2$$

so that on $r = 0$ we have

$$h(t) = \lim_{r \to 0} [b(r, t) - \sigma^2 r] = 0.$$

No boundary condition should be imposed at $r = 0$, instead (6.3a) should hold at $r = 0$, i.e.

$$u_t(0, t) = 0 \text{ so that } u(0, t) = 1.$$

This boundary condition will be enforced at $R_0 > 0$ to avoid the logarithm in (6.3a) at $r = 0$. As in previous examples, the relevant interest rate interval $[r_0, r_1]$ is the interval $[.001, 1]$.

We shall price an American put on a discount bond when the short rate is given by (6.13). The price of the bond expiring at Tb and the price of the put expiring at To will be denoted by $u(r, t, Tb)$ and $p(r, t, To)$, respectively, where t is the time to expiry of the bond. Both prices satisfy equation (6.3a) on $[R_0, R_1]$ which will include the relevant interval $[r_0, r_1]$.

$u(r, t, Tb)$ is subject to the initial and boundary conditions

$$u(r, 0, Tb) = 1$$

$$u(R_0, t, Tb) = 1$$

$$u(R_1, t, Tb) = e^{-R_1 t} \qquad \text{for } t \in (0, Tb].$$

The boundary condition for the bond at R_1 has no discernible influence on u over $[r_0, r_1]$ for sufficiently large R_1. For example, with $R_1 = 3$ the boundary conditions

$$u(R_1, t, Tb) = 0, \quad u(R_1, t, Tb) = e^{-R_1 t} \quad \text{and} \quad u_{rr}(R_1, t, Tb) = 0$$

all lead to the same bond prices over $[r_0, r_1]$.

The put satisfies (6.3a) for $Tb - To < t \leq Tb$ with the initial and boundary conditions [65]

$$p(r, Tb - To, To) = \max\{0, K - u(r, Tb - To, Tb)\}$$

$$p(R_0, t, To) = 0$$

$$p(s(t), t, To) = K - u(s(t), t, Tb)$$

$$p_r(s(t), t, To) = -u_r(s(t), t, Tb)$$

where $K < 1$ is the strike price and $s(t)$ denotes the early exercise boundary for the put.

The method of lines time discretization of the problems for $u(r, t, Tb)$ and $p(r, t, To)$ is straighforward. The time discrete approximations are solved with the Riccati transformation on a common grid. The bond price $u(r, t_n, Tb)$ is found by integrating the sweep equations (3.4) from $r = R_0$ to $r = R_1$ subject to

$$R(R_0) = 0, \quad w(R_0) = 1$$

and by integrating (3.6) in the reverse direction with initial condition

$$v(R_1) = \frac{u(R_1, t_n, Tb) - w(R_1)}{R(R_1)}.$$

For given $u(r, t_n, Tb)$ and $t_n > Tb - To$ the option $p(r, t_n, To)$ is found by integating the corresponding sweep equation (3.4) for w from R_0 toward R_1 subject to

$$w(R_0) = 0.$$

The early exercise boundary $s(t_n)$ is the root of equation (3.8) which in this case is

$$\phi(r) \equiv K - u(r, t_n, Tb) - [R(r)(-u_r(r, t_n, Tb) + w(r)] = 0.$$

Once $s(t_n)$ is known the backward sweep from $s(t_n)$ toward R_0 is carried out with initial condition

$$v(s(t_n)) = -u_r(s(t_n), t_n, Tb)$$

so that $p(r, t_n, To) = R(r)v(r) + w(r)$.

For a sample calculation the following parameters are chosen for the exponential Vasicek model (6.13):

$$\mu = .15, \quad \bar{r} = .05, \quad \sigma = .2.$$

The expiration of the bond is

$$Tb = 1.$$

The strike price and expiration of the put are taken to be

$$K = .9, \quad To = .25.$$

Figures 6.8–6.11 show bond and option prices and some of their derivatives at $t = 1$ (i.e. $\tau = 0$) as well as the early exercise boundary over the life of the put.

Results are shown for an MOL solution with

$$\Delta t = (Tb - To)/325 = .002, \quad t \in [0, .75]$$
$$\Delta t = To/250 = .001, \quad t \in [.75, 1],$$

on a computational interval $[R_0, R_1]$ with

$$R_0 = .0001, \quad R_0 = 3.$$

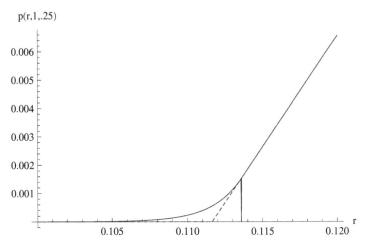

Fig. 6.8. Bond and option prices at $t = Tb - \tau = 1$ near the early exercise boundary.
solid line: $p(r, 1, .25)$
broken line: pay-off $\max\{0, K - u(r, 1, 1)\}$
vertical line: location of the early exercise boundary $s(1)$.

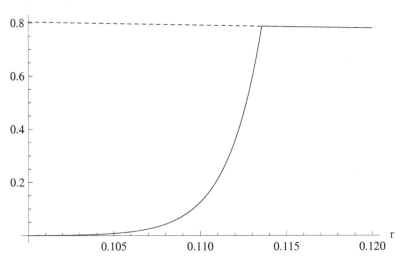

Fig. 6.9. Graphs of $p_r(r, 1, .25)$ and $-u_r(r, 1, 1)$ near the early exercise boundary.
solid line: $p_r(r, 1, .25)$
broken line: $-u_r(r, 1, 1)$.

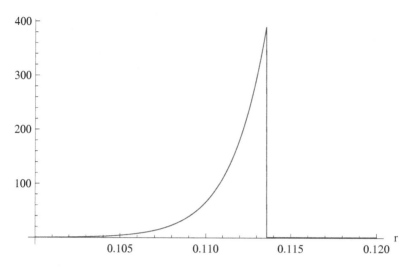

Fig. 6.10. Graph of $p_{rr}(r, 1, .25)$ near the early exercise boundary. $u_{rr}(r, 1, 1)$ decreases from 1.268 to 1.1319 over this interval and is not shown.

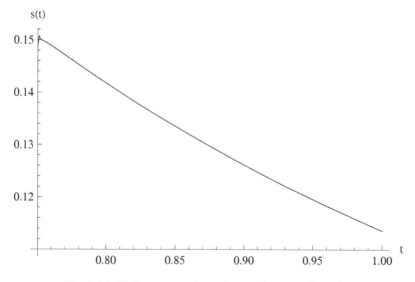

Fig. 6.11. Early exercise boundary $s(t)$ for $t \in [.75, 1]$.

They are obtained with 3050 mesh points distributed over $[R_0, R_1]$ with mesh sizes

$$\Delta y = (.001 - .0001)/50 \quad \text{on } [.0001, .001]$$
$$\Delta y = (.1 - .001)/1000 \quad \text{on } [.001, .1]$$
$$\Delta y = (.15 - .1)/1000 \quad \text{on } [.1, .15]$$
$$\Delta y = (1 - .15)/500 \quad \text{on } [.15, 1]$$
$$\Delta y = (3 - 1)/500 \quad \text{on } [1, 3].$$

This mesh may be finer than required for an accurate solution of the MOL sweep equations, but no attempt was made to optimize it. However, halving Δt and Δy gave essentially the same numerical results. Hence the given numerical results are deemed stable with respect to mesh refinements.

The early exercise boundary deserves further comment. The pay-off for the put at expiry is $\max\{0, K - u(r, .75, 1)\}$. The numerical results yield $p(r, .75, .25) > 0$ for $r > s(.75) = .148876$. $p_r(r, .75, .25)$ is discontinuous at $r = s(.75)$ which complicates the calculation of $s(t)$ at $t = .75 + \Delta t$. The problem at this time is entirely analogous to that of an American Black Scholes put just before expiry (see Example 5.1). In contrast to the extensive mathematical analysis of the early exercise boundary near expiration for a Black Scholes put [11], little appears to be known about the early exercise boundary of a bond option near expiry. It is not even clear from numerical results whether $s(t)$ is continuous at expiry. For example, Fig. 6.12 shows the early exercise boundaries of the above bondoption for $t \in [.75, .7502]$, i.e. just prior to expiration, for the sequence of decreasing Δt given by

$$\Delta t = .0002/2^k, \quad k = 1, 2, 3, 4, 5.$$

We cannot conclude from Fig. 6.12 that $s(t)$ is continuous at expiry, i.e. that

$$\lim_{\Delta t \to 0} s(.75 + \Delta t) = s(.75) = .148876.$$

As in Example 5.1 there is a check on whether the computed $s(t)$ is consistent with the bond equation near the early exercise boundary. Suppose that the American put has a smooth solution $\{p(r, t, To), s(t)\}$. Then it follows from

$$\frac{d}{dt} p(s(t), t, To) = \frac{d}{dt} [K - u(s(t), t, Tb])$$

and

$$p_r(s(t), t, To) = -u_r(s(t), t, Tb)$$

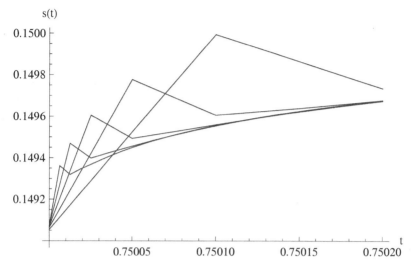

Fig. 6.12. Dependence of the numerical early exercise boundary near expiry on Δt. Shown are linear interpolants of the computed $s(t_n)$.

that

$$p_t(s(t), t, To) = -u_t(s(t), t, Tb).$$

Substitution into the option equation (6.3a) and using the fact that $u(r, t, Tb)$ also satisfies (6.3a) shows that

$$\lim_{r \to s(t)} \frac{a(r,t)}{K}[p_{rr}(r,t,To) - u_{rr}(r,t,Tb)] = s(t). \qquad (6.14)$$

Since p_{rr} and u_{rr} are automatically computed in the MOL/Riccati approach, one can check whether equation (6.14) holds at the computed $s(t)$.

For the above American put on a one-year discount bond the MOL computation yields the early exercise boundary in Fig. 6.11

$$s(1) = .11357.$$

Substituting the values for p_{rr} and u_{rr} at $r = s(1)$ (obtained by extrapolating the MOL values from the three nearest regular mesh points in $[R_0, s(1)]$) into the left side of (6.14) yields the prediction

$$s_p(1) = .11367.$$

Thus the numerical early exercise boundary is reasonably consistent with (6.14).

Some concluding comments: Numerical experiments show that if equation (6.5a) for (6.13) were solved with the ficticious domain approach on

$[R_0, R_1] = [-.1, 3]$ with $r_0 = .0001$ then the model is not mean reverting on $[R_0, r_0]$. The numerical bond price will monotonically drift away from $u(0, t, Tb) = 1$ with time. For example, for the above parameters we obtain $u(0, 1, 1) = .99991$, $u(0, 10, 10) = .96600$, $u(0, 20, 20) = .82468$ and $u(0, 30, 30) = .77798$. However, even at $Tb = 30$ the bond prices over the relevant interest interval $[.001, 1]$ are the same as those obtained with the boundary condition $u(r_0, t, Tb) = 1$. This is further proof that the price of a discount bond is not very sensitive to the boundary conditions imposed on the bond equation for a one-factor interest rate model.

Finally, if an interest rate model is used for which the ficticious domain approach provides a left boundary condition, such as in the CEV setting of Example 6.3, then a slight change of the algorithm is reqired. The forward sweep (3.4) for the bond should proceed from R_1 toward R_0 to insure that the Riccati solution is time independent. The forward sweep for the option should proceed from R_0 toward R_1 in order to find the right boundary point $s(t)$. While the bond and option can share the same spacial r-mesh they do not share the Riccati solution in this case. For an illustration suppose that the interest rate model is the CIR equation

$$dr = (\eta - \mu r)dt + \sigma\sqrt{r}\, dW.$$

The bond is computed on $[-.1, 3]$ subject to

$$u_r(R_0, t, Tb) = B(t)u(R_0, t, Tb)$$

as in Example 6.3. The option is computed on $[R_0, R_1]$ with boundary condition

$$p(R_0, t, To) = 0$$

and uses the sweep described earlier in this example. An application to the problem of [65] with the data

$$\eta = .032, \quad \mu = .4, \quad \sigma = .5, \quad Tb = 5$$

$$K = .7, \quad To = 1$$

yields the following graph for the early exercise boundary.

Numerical values are

$$s(4) = .138885, \quad s(4.0025) = .16492, \quad s(5) = .23398.$$

The free boundary predicted by (6.14) at $s(5)$ is

$$s_p(5) = .23354.$$

The free boundary of Fig. 6.13 appears to be in good quantitative agreement with the early exercise boundary shown in [36] for a finite element solution of the bond equation for the put when the bond price is given by the CIR formula.

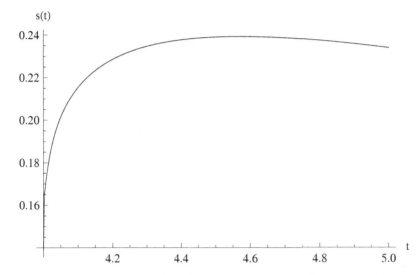

Fig. 6.13. Early exercise boundary for a one-year put on a five year CIR discount bond.

Chapter 7

Two-Dimensional Diffusion Problems in Finance

All the Black Scholes type problems treated in the preceding chapters have multi-dimensional analogs which, in principle, can be solved approximately with a variety of numerical methods. Not surprisingly, the numerical difficulties discussed above also have their multi-dimensional analogs which need to be resolved by whatever numerical technique is chosen for the problem at hand. The present chapter deals with two-dimensional problems for some partial differential equations in finance. It thus avoids the dominant difficulty brought on by the so-called "curse of dimensionality" which, for sufficiently high dimensionality, may make the PDE approach infeasible. But even in two space dimensions the lack of smoothness and nonlinear features cause complications which far exceed those encountered up to now. We shall again choose a variety of models to illustrate these complications. Our numerical results for these problems will be obtained with the line iterative approach outlined in Section 2.3. They may serve as a benchmark for readers developing or adapting their own codes for such problems.

All subsequent applications involve a diffusion equation of the form (2.7)

$$a_{11}(x, y, t)u_{xx} + a_{12}(x, y, t)u_{xy} + a_{22}(x, y, t)u_{yy} + b_1(x, y, t)u_x$$
$$+ b_2(x, y, t)u_y - c(x, y, t)u - d(x, y, t)u_t = f(x, y, t), \quad (7.1)$$

and its time discrete approximation (2.8). We now have to decide which spatial variable to discretize and which to retain as the independent variable for the system of ordinary differential equations, i.e. the MOL approximation. This choice is dictated by the behavior of u with respect to x and y, by the geometry of the computational domain and the nature of the boundary conditions. As in the one-dimensional case we go on the assumption that the MOL system can be solved to high accuracy in the direction of the continuous variable because we find its solution from a sequence of one-dimensional problems. Here we shall assume that y is the "difficult" direction and that the derivatives of u with respect to x can be approximated by difference quotients. Note that the role of x and y are reversed compared to Section 2.3 (for the author's convenience only).

Thus the time discrete approximation of equation (7.1), i.e.

$$a_{11}(x,y,t_n)u_{xx} + a_{12}(x,y,t_n)u_{xy} + a_{22}(x,y,t_n)u_{yy} + b_1(x,y,t_n)u_x$$
$$+ b_2(x,y,t_n)u_y - \hat{c}(x,y,t_n)u = \hat{f}(x,y,t_n), \qquad (7.2)$$

where $\hat{c}$ and $\hat{f}$ are defined on p. 65, is approximated by a system of ordinary differential equations in y similar to equation (2.9), but at a set of grid points $\{x_j\}$. In addition, the numerical work reported here is based on a slight generalization of the development of Section 2.3 because in general the points $\{x_j\}$ for $j = 0, \ldots, J$ need not be evenly spaced between the limits x_0 and $x_J = X$. Furthermore, upwinding may be employed at times. Thus instead of the central difference approximation of page 66, i.e.

$$u_x(x_j, y, t_n) = \frac{u_{j+1}(y) - u_{j-1}(y)}{x_{j+1} - x_{j-1}},$$

we may use at time level t_n

$$b_1(x_j,y,t_n)u_x(x_j,y,t_n) = b_j^+(y)(u_{j+1}(y) - u_j(y)) + b_j^-(y)(u_j(y) - u_{j-1}(y))$$

where

$$b_j^+(y) = \frac{\max\{b_1(x_j,y,t_n), 0\}}{x_{j+1} - x_j}, \quad b_j^-(y) = \frac{\min\{b_1(x_j,y,t_n), 0\}}{x_j - x_{j-1}}.$$

This upwinding formula is only first order accurate but tends to improve convergence of the line iterative method discussed below to solve the MOL equations. However, we usually prefer the higher order central difference approximation and enforce convergence of the MOL line Gauss-Seidel iteration by taking a sufficiently small time step Δt.

The central difference approximations on the line $x = x_j$ are

$$u_x(x_j, y, t_n) = \alpha_{j-1}u_{j-1}(y) - \alpha_j u_j(y) + \alpha_{j+1}u_{j+1}(y),$$

$$u_{xy}(x_j, y, t_n) = \alpha_{j-1}u'_{j-1}(y) - \alpha_j u'_j(y) + \alpha_{j+1}u'_{j+1}(y)$$

with

$$\alpha_{j-1} = -\frac{x_{j+1} - x_j}{x_j - x_{j-1}} \frac{1}{(x_{j+1} - x_{j-1})}$$

$$\alpha_{j+1} = \frac{x_j - x_{j-1}}{x_{j+1} - x_j} \frac{1}{(x_{j+1} - x_{j-1})}$$

$$\alpha_j = (\alpha_{j-1} + \alpha_{j+1}),$$

and

$$u_{xx}(x_j, y, t_n) = \beta_{j-1} u_{j-1}(y) - \beta_j u_j(y) + \beta_{j+1} u_{j+1}(y)$$

with

$$\beta_{j-1} = \frac{2}{(x_j - x_{j-1})(x_{j+1} - x_{j-1})}$$

$$\beta_{j+1} = \frac{2}{(x_{j+1} - x_j)(x_{j+1} - x_{j-1})}$$

and

$$\beta_j = (\beta_{j-1} + \beta_{j+1}).$$

For a uniform mesh $\{x_j\}$ these quotients reduce to expressions analogous to those on p. 66.

When difference approximations with upwinding replace the x-derivatives in equation (7.2) we obtain the MOL equations

$$\mathcal{L} u_j(y) \equiv a_{22}(x_j, y, t_n) u_j''(y) + \tilde{b}_2(x_j, y, t) n) u_j'(y) - \tilde{c}(x_j, y, t_n) u_j(y)$$

$$= F(x_j, y, t_n, u_{j-1}(y), u_{j+1}(y), u_{j-1}'(y), u_{j+1}'(y), u_{j,n-1}(y), u_{j,n-2}(y)) \tag{7.3}$$

where

$$\tilde{b}_2(x_j, y, t_n) = b_2(x_j, y, t_n) - a_{12}(x_j, y, t_n)\alpha_j$$

$$\tilde{c}(x_j, y, t_n) = \hat{c}(x_j, y, t_n) + a_{11}(x_j, y, t_n)\beta_j + b_j^+(y) - b_j^-(y)$$

and

$$F(x_j, y, t_n) = \hat{f}(x_j, y, t_n) - a_{11}(x_j, y, t_n)(\beta_{j-1} u_{j-1}(y) + \beta_{j+1} u_{j+1}(y))$$

$$- a_{12}(x_j, y, t_n)(\alpha_{j-1} u_{j-1}'(y) + \alpha_{j+1} u_{j+1}'(y))$$

$$+ b_j^-(y) u_{j-1}(y) - b_j^+(y) u_{j+1}(y).$$

The central difference approximation is given by (7.3) when we set

$$b_j^+(y) = b_1(x, y, t)\alpha_{j+1}, \quad b_j(y) = -b_1(x_j, y, t_n)\alpha_{j-1}.$$

(Recall the functions $\hat{f}$ and $\hat{c}$ are defined on p. 65.) We shall assume that $u_0(y)$, $u_0'(y)$ and $u_J(y)$, $y_J'(y)$ are known so that (7.3) is a system of $J - 1$ linear second order ordinary differential equations which are coupled through the source term F. We also assume that the equations (7.3) are subject to boundary conditions at the end of the lines $x = x_j$, $j = 1, \ldots,$ $J - 1$ which are problem specific.

The system (7.3) will be solved iteratively as a sequence of one-dimensional equations. If k is the iteration counter and $\{u_j^0(y)\}_{j=0}^{J}$ is chosen then we solve in iteration k for $j = 1, \ldots, J - 1$ the scalar differential equations

$$\mathcal{L}u_j^k(y) = F(x_j, y, t_n, u_{j-1}^k(y), u_{j+1}^{k-1}(y),$$
$$u_{j-1}'^k(y), u_{j+1}'^{k-1}(y), u_{j,n-1}(y), u_{j,n-2}(y)). \tag{7.4}$$

This iteration is known as a line Gauss Seidel iteration. It will be terminated when

$$\max_j \left[\max_y \left| u_j^k(y) - u_j^{k-1}(y) \right| + \theta \max_y \left| u_j'^k(y) - u_j'^{k-1}(y) \right| \right] \leq tol \tag{7.5}$$

where $tol = 10^{-6}$ is a commonly chosen convergence criterion and θ will be zero or one in specific applications. The last iterate is taken as the numerical approximation $\{u_{j,n}(y)\}$ of the exact solution

$$\{u(x_j, y, t_n)\}$$

and serves as $\{u_j^0(y)\}$ for the calculation at the next time level. Along every line $x = x_j$ the equation (7.4) will be solved with the Riccati transformation method discussed in Chapter 3.

To avoid a vanishing diffusion coefficient of the second order derivative $u_j''(y)$ in (7.4) we shall always regularize the equation with the substitution

$$a_{22}(x_j, y, t_n) \leftarrow \max\{\epsilon, a_{22}(x_j, y, t_n)\}.$$

Typically we choose $\epsilon \leq 10^3$. For multi-dimensional problems we find it more convenient to add a little diffusion than to restrict the computational domain to points where a_{22} is bounded away from zero.

For a computed MOL solution we can expect numerical errors due to

1) the discretization of the time derivative;
2) the discretization of the spatial derivatives orthogonal to the direction of the MOL lines;
3) the numerical integration of the MOL equations along a given line with the Riccati transformation method;
4) termination of the line iteration after finitely many cycles;
5) approximations of the geometry and the boundary conditions of the given pricing problem;
6) approximating $a_{22}(x, y, t)$ with a strictly positive function.

In the one-dimensional problems of the preceding chapters the effect of the time discretization was easy to identify from experiments with different time steps, while spatial errors due to the numerical integration of the initial value problems arising in the Riccati method could be suppressed by choosing a sufficiently fine mesh for the trapezoidal rule.

For multi-dimensional problems execution times and memory size of the computer may preclude controlling discretization errors with very small time steps, many lines and lots of points along a line. In addition, the lack of smoothness due the pay-off or to barrier conditions complicates the calculation along a line because the source term F in (7.3) can become large. We shall illustrate such problems for several option pricing models.

7.1 Front tracking in Cartesian coordinates

We begin with examples where the early exercise boundary at time t is expected to be of the form $y = s(x, t)$ and where s is smooth in x and computable at discrete $\{x_j\}$ with the Riccati transformation in the continuous variable y. In all examples y will be an asset price. x may stand for an asset price, a stochastic volatility v, a stochastic interest rate r, or any other independent financial variable leading to the diffusion model (7.1).

Example 7.1. An American call on an asset with stochastic volatility.

The intent is to examine the influence of the uncertain boundary condition on $v = v_{\max}$ discussed in Example 1.22 on the price of an American call and its early exercise boundary when the volatility of the asset follows the Heston square root model.

If $C(S, v, t)$ denotes the price of the call then we know from Example 1.22 that with

$$u(y, v, t) = C(S, v, t)/K, \quad y = S/K$$

the following problem needs to be solved on $[0, s(v, t)] \times [0, v_{\max}]$ for $t \in (0, T]$

$$\mathcal{L}u \equiv \frac{vy^2}{2} u_{yy} + \rho \sigma y v u_{yv} + \frac{\sigma^2 v}{2} u_{vv} + (r - q) y u_y$$
$$+ [\kappa(\theta - v) - \lambda v] u_v - ru - u_t = 0. \tag{7.6}$$

Although equation (7.6) depends on the two "spatial" variables y and v, it still has very much the flavor of a simple call because the pay-off depends only on y. We can expect that its solution u at fixed v behaves like a standard American call in the underlying asset y defined on $[0, s(v, t)]$ where $y = s(v, t)$ is the early exercise boundary. y is the continuous variable retained for the method of lines.

We already know from Example 1.15 that on $y = 0$ and on $v = 0$ the equation (7.6) is degenerate and will serve as a boundary condition. On $v = v_{\max}$ the time-discrete approximation of equation (7.6) is not degenerate so that we can impose Dirichlet, Neumann, oblique or Venttsel boundary conditions. Whatever boundary conditions we choose should be consistent with

$$u(0, v, t) = 0 \qquad (7.7)$$

implied by the volatility model for the call.

The method of lines will be applied to solve (7.6) along lines of constant v. Computational experience with the stochastic volatility model suggests that central difference quotients for derivatives with respect to v on a uniform grid work well enough to make upwinding unnecessary. This simplifies the method of lines approximation. Thus, for a given $v_{\max} > 0$ we define an equidistant grid $0 = v_0 < \cdots < v_J = v_{\max}$ and use the following method of lines approximation for (7.6) at time t_n along the line $v = v_j$

$$\mathcal{L}u_j(y) = a_{22}(v_j, y)u_j''(y) + b(y)u_j'(y) - c(v_j, y, t_n)u_j(y) = F_j(v_j, y, t_n) \quad (7.8)$$

where

$$a_{22}(v_j, y) = \max\left\{ \frac{v_j y^2}{2}, 10^{-4} \right\}$$

$$b(y) = (r - q)y$$

$$c(v_j, y, t_n) = \frac{\sigma^2 v_j}{2} \frac{2}{\Delta v^2} + r + \begin{cases} \frac{1}{\Delta t} & \text{for } n \leq 3 \\ \frac{3}{2\Delta t} & \text{for } n \geq 4 \end{cases}$$

and

$$F_j(v_j, y, t_n) = -\frac{\sigma^2 v_j}{2\Delta v^2}[u_{j+1}(y) + u_{j-1}(y)] - \frac{\rho \sigma v_j y}{2\Delta v}[u_{j+1}'(y) - u_{j-1}'(y)]$$

$$- \frac{[\kappa(\theta - v_j) - \lambda v_j]}{2\Delta v}[u_{j+1}(y) - u_{j-1}(y)]$$

$$- \begin{cases} \frac{1}{\Delta t} u_{j,n-1}(y) & \text{for } n \leq 3 \\ \frac{1}{2\Delta t}[4u_{j,n-1}(y) - u_{j,n-2}(y)] & \text{for } n \geq 4. \end{cases}$$

The equations (7.8) are solved iteratively as indicated in (7.4) for $j = 1, \ldots, J$ subject to

$$u_j(0) = 0$$
$$u_j(s(v_j, t_n)) = s(v_j, t_n) - 1$$
$$u'_j(s(v_j, t_n)) = 1$$

where $s(v_j, t_n)$ is the early exercise boundary for the call.

For the solution of (7.8) for $j = 1$ we need the solution of (7.6) with $v = 0$. However, no effort was made to solve the hyperbolic equation (7.6). Instead, we simply employ quadratic extrapolation and write for the kth iterate

$$u_0^k(y) = 3u_1^{k-1}(y) - 3u_2^{k-1}(y) + u_3^{k-1}(y)$$

$$u'_0^k(y) = 3u'_1^{k-1}(y) - 3u'_2^{k-1}(y) + u'_3^{k-1}(y).$$

Substitution of u_0 and u'_0 into (7.8) for $j = 1$ shows that (7.8) is a consistent approximation of (7.6) at $v = 0$ as $\Delta v \to 0$. For further comments we refer to the comparison of numerical methods for the American call with stochastic volatility and jump diffusion which also uses this quadratic extrapolation [17]. The line iteration converges reliably and terminates when

$$\max_j \left\{ \max_y \left| u_j^k(y) - u_j^{k-1}(y) \right| \le 10^{-6}, \, y \in [0, s^k(v_j, t_n)] \right\}.$$

On $v = v_{\max}$ three different boundary conditions will be tested. First we enforce the Venttsel boundary condition (1.56) for $(\kappa + \lambda)v_{\max} \ge \kappa\theta$, i.e.

$$a_{22}(v_{\max}, y)u_{yy} + (r - q)yu_y + [\kappa(\theta - v_{\max}) - \lambda v_{\max}]u_v - ru - u_t = 0 \quad (7.9)$$

simply by replacing the central difference quotient for u_v with a backward first order difference in (7.9) when $j = J$.

Next we check the influence of the commonly applied boundary condition of [18]

$$\frac{\partial u}{\partial v}(v_{\max}, y, t) = 0 \quad (7.10)$$

by setting $u_{J+1}(y) = u_J(y)$ and $u'_{J+1}(y) = u'_J(y)$ in (7.8). We note from

$$\frac{u_{J+1} + u_{J-1} - 2u_J}{\Delta v^2} = \frac{u_{J-1} - u_J}{\Delta v^2}$$

that equation (7.8) at $v = v_{\max}$ becomes an approximation of (7.10) as $\Delta v \to 0$ provided all other terms in the equation remain bounded.

The last boundary condition examined is the Venttsel boundary condition

$$a_{22}(v_{\max}, y)u_{yy} + (r - q)yu_y - ru - u_t = 0 \qquad (7.11)$$

which describes an American call with constant volatility $\sqrt{v_{\max}}$. It may be thought of as an analog of (1.54) for an American call. The boundary conditions for the Venttsel equations (7.9) and (7.11) are $u(0, v_{\max}, t) = 0$ and the early exercise conditions at $y = s(v_{\max}, t)$. All these boundary conditions are consistent with (7.7).

Figure 7.1 shows the early exercise boundary $s(v, T)$ at $T = 0.5$ for three different values of $v_{\max}$.

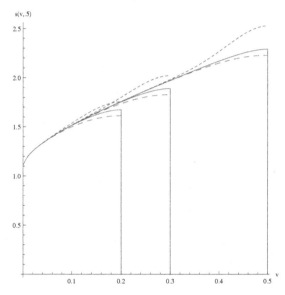

Fig. 7.1. Early exercise boundary $s(v, T)$ for the American call with stochastic volatility obtained with $v_{\max} = .2$, $.3$ and $.5$.
Solid curve: $s(v, T)$ for boundary condition (7.9).
Long dashes: $s(v, T)$ for boundary condition (7.10).
Short dashes: $s(v, T)$ for boundary condition (7.11).
Financial parameters (taken from [17]): $r = .03$, $q = .05$, $\kappa = 2$, $\theta = .04$, $\lambda = 0$, $\sigma = .4$, $\rho = -.5$.
Computing parameters: $T = .5$, $\Delta t = T/500$, $\Delta v = .005$, i.e.
40 evenly spaced lines on $[0, .2]$, 60 lines on $[0, .3]$ and 100 lines on $[0, .5]$.
5300 mesh points $\{y_k\}$ for the Riccati transformation, distributed over $[0, 5]$.

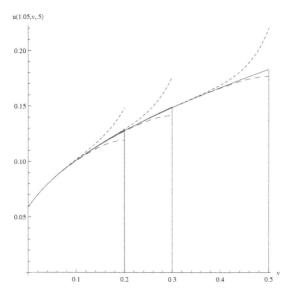

Fig. 7.2. Scaled price of the American call $u(y, v, T)$ at $y = S/K = 1.05$ over $[0, v_{\max}]$.
Solid curve: $u(1.05, v, .5)$ for boundary condition (7.9).
Long dashes: $u(1.05, v, .5)$ for boundary condition (7.10).
Short dashes: $u(1.05, v, .5)$ for boundary condition (7.11).

Figure 7.2 shows the scaled price of the call at $y = S/K = 1.05$ for $v \in [0, v_{\max}]$ for the same three boundary conditions and the parameters of Fig. 7.1.

These simulations show that the Venttsel tangential boundary condition (7.9) yields results which are the least sensitive to $v_{\max}$. In particular, $u(1.05, v, .5)$ appears to be a reliable solution of (7.7) for all $v \in [0, .1)$. Of course, these results are only a snapshot for a particular set of parameters and the conclusions may not hold in general. A calibration of the Heston model to market data likely will require repeated accurate solutions of (7.6). The efficiency of the method of lines for this task depends strongly on the number of lines and hence on the choice of the smallest $v_{\max}$ which guarantees reliable results for the relevant values of v.

Similar results appear obtainable for related CEV volatility models. Finally, we refer to Example 7.12 at the end of these notes where the effect of boundary conditions on options with stochastic volatility and interest rates is checked. The simulations reported in Example 7.12 suggest that the correlation term $\rho \sigma y v u_{yv}$ be included in the boundary equation (7.9) to further reduce the effect of $v_{\max}$ on the price and early exercise of the call.

Example 7.2. A European put on a combination of two assets.

The European put does not have an early exercise boundary and therefore does not require front tracking. For the line iterative MOL algorithm the free boundary feature of a put is a minor complication compared to the effect of the non-smooth pay-off on the price and the Greeks of the put near expiration. It makes the solution of the European put a more challenging numerical problem than the American call with stochastic volatility of Example 7.1.

The Black Scholes equation for the price $V(S_1, S_2, t)$ of an option depending on two assets with values S_1 and S_2 is

$$\frac{1}{2}\sigma_1^2 S_1^2 V_{S_1 S_1} + \rho\sigma_1\sigma_2 S_1 S_2 V_{S_1 S_2} + \frac{1}{2}\sigma_2^2 S_2^2 V_{S_2 S_2}$$

$$+ (r - q_1)S_1 V_{S_1} + (r - q_2)S_2 V_{S_2} - rV - V_t = 0, \qquad (7.12)$$

where the volatilities σ_1 and σ_2, the correlation coefficient ρ, the risk-free interest rate r and the dividend rates q_1 and q_2 are all assumed known, and where as before $t = T - \tau$ denotes the time to maturity. Suppose the option is a put $P(S_1, S_2, t)$ with strike price K written on the basket $a_1 S_1 + a_2 S_2$ so that the pay-off at maturity is

$$P(S_1, S_2, 0) = \max\{0, K - a_1 S_1 - a_2 S_2\}.$$

If we make the change of variables

$$x = \frac{a_1 S_1}{K}, \quad y = \frac{a_2 S_2}{K}, \quad u(x, y, t) = \frac{P\left(\frac{Kx}{a_1}, \frac{Ky}{a_2}, t\right)}{K}$$

then $u(x, y, t)$ satisfies

$$\frac{1}{2}\sigma_1^2 x^2 u_{xx} + \rho\sigma_1\sigma_2 xy u_{xy} + \frac{1}{2}\sigma_2^2 y^2 u_{yy} + (r - q_1)x u_x$$

$$+ (r - q_2)y u_y - ru - u_t = 0 \qquad (7.13)$$

and the initial condition

$$u(x, y, t) = \max\{0, 1 - x - y\}.$$

We would like to emphasize that the scaling applied to (7.12) leads to the convenient non-dimensional form (7.13) but may hide the posssibility that in specific applications x or y may dominate. For example, the option is at the money when $x + y = 1$, but the spot prices may place the point near

(.5, .5) (far away from the boundaries $x = 0$ and $y = 0$) where the effect of boundary data is slight, or near $(1, 0)$ or $(0, 1)$ where x or y dominate and the boundary data markedly affect the option value. This problem becomes pronounced when the boundary data are not known with certainty. In many of the examples discussed here an attempt will be made to assess the influence of the computational domain and of the boundary data on option values in a given region of interest. We shall assume that y describes the dominant asset of the put.

Equation (7.13) is defined for $x > 0$, $y > 0$ and $t \in (0, T]$. We know from Example 1.14 that on $x = 0$ and $y = 0$ the equation reduces to the one dimensional Black Scholes European put which can be solved by formula (or equally accurately with the sweep method of Chapter 4). The computational domain for equation (7.13) will be chosen as

$$(x, y, t) \in [0, X] \times [0, Y] \times [0, T]$$

for given X and Y (so that $0 < S_1 < KX/a_1$ and $0 < S_2 < KY/a_2$). X and Y serve as up-and-out barriers for the put. The boundary conditions for (7.13) will be:

$y = 0$: $u(x, 0, t)$ and $u_x(x, 0, t)$ obtained from the Black Scholes formula,

$x = X$: $u(X, y, t) = u_y(X, y, t) = 0$,

$y = Y$: $u(x, Y, t) = u_x(x, Y, t) = 0$,

$x = 0$: $u(0, y, t)$ and $u_y(0, y, t)$ obtained from the Black Scholes formula.

We shall use a grid of $J + 1$ points $\{x_j\}_{j=0}^{j=J}$ where $x_0 = 0$ and $x_J = X$. The MOL approximation of this problem at time t_n obtained from (7.13) is the the system (7.3) which is solved iteratively as given by (7.4). Thus, suppose that at time t_n in iteration k along line $x = x_j$ the source term F in (7.4) can be evaluated. Then the Riccati transformation

$$u_j^k(y) = R_j(y)v_j^k(y) + w_j^k(y)$$

requires a forward sweep for $R_j(y)$ and $w_j^k(y)$ and a reverse sweep for $v_j^k(y)$. Since we have boundary data

$$u^k(0) = u(x_j, 0, t_n)$$
$$u_j^k(Y) = 0$$

at both ends of the line, the forward sweep direction can be up or down the line.

We shall proceed from $y = Y$ toward $y = 0$ with initial conditions

$$R_j(Y) = 0$$

$$w_j^k(Y) = 0.$$

The reverse sweep goes from $y = 0$ toward $y = Y$, uses the initial condition

$$v_j^k(0) = \frac{u(x_j, 0, t_n) - w_j^k(0)}{R_j(0)}$$

and yields the solutions

$$u_j^k(y) = R_j(y)v_j^k(y) + w_j^k(y)$$

$$u_j'^k(y) = v_j^k(y)$$

which are needed for the computation along the line $x = x_{j+1}$. The solution of the sweep equations will again be found with the trapezoidal rule on a mesh $\{y_m\}$.

Note that the coefficients of the differential equations for the Riccati transformation blow up at $y = 0$ because

$$a_{22}(x_j, y, t_n) = \frac{1}{2}\sigma_2^2 y^2 \to 0 \quad \text{as } y \to 0.$$

We avoid this difficulty with the modification employed in (4.2). The numerical results shown here hold for

$$a_{22}(x_j, y, t_n) = \max\left\{\frac{1}{2}\sigma_2^2 y^2, 10^{-4}\right\}. \tag{7.14}$$

We note that the Riccati solution $R_j(y)$ depends on j, but not on the iteration k and the time level n, except when $n = 3$ where we switch from a backward Euler to a three level time approximation. w and v depend on j, k and n.

To give an indication of the performance of the MOL approach we shall solve the European put (7.13) for the following data:

$$\sigma_1 = \sigma_2 = .2, \quad \rho = .5, \quad r = .05, \quad q_1 = q_2 = .02$$

on the computational domain

$$X = Y = 3.$$

These data are chosen because they imply that the solution $u(x, y, t)$ of (7.13) satisfies for any point (a, b)

$$u(a, b, t) = u(b, a, t) \tag{7.15}$$

as well as

$$u_x(a, b, t) = u_y(b, a, t). \tag{7.16}$$

The symmetry conditions can be checked when assessing the quality of the MOL solution.

The MOL approximation is written for the $J + 1$ lines at $x = x_j$ for $j = 0, \ldots, J$ which are spaced evenly on

$$[0, 1.2] \text{ with } \Delta x = 1.2/J_1$$
$$[1.2, 2] \text{ with } \Delta x = .8/J_2$$
$$[2, 3] \text{ with } \Delta x = 1/J_3$$

so that $J = J_1 + J_2 + J_3$. For the finest grid we choose $J_1 = 1200$, $J_2 = 200$ and $J_3 = 200$. Fewer lines are obtained by dividing $\{J_1, J_2, J_3\}$ by a common integer factor J^*. The grid $\{y_m\}$ for the integration of the differential equations of the Riccati transformation along each line is obtained by setting $y_m = x_j$ for $m = j$, $j = 0, \ldots, 1600$. At $t = T$ the solution obtained for $J^* > 1$ is linearly interpolated between the lines so that the final results are always available and compared on the finest grid.

As in the one-dimensional case the lack of smoothness of the pay-off leads to delta functions for all second derivatives on $1 - x - y = 0$ as $t \to 0$ which cause severe numerical difficulties at the first time step. Let us therefore look at the solution of the put at

$$T = \Delta t = .001.$$

Note that much of the subsequent discussion concentrates on the numerical deltas of the put, which reflects the observation that prices are generally easy to compute compared to their derivatives and therefore do not say much about the quality of the numerical solution.

Table 7.1 shows the behavior of the numerical solution when the number of lines in each subinterval is determined by

$$J_1 = 1200/J^*, \quad J_2 = 200/J^* \quad \text{and} \quad J_3 = 200/J^*.$$

At each time step we compute first the Black Scholes solution along $x = 0$ and $y = 0$ on the finest grid and then cycle through the lines at $\{x_j\}$ for $j = 1, \ldots, J - 1$.

Column 3 shows the number of iterations required for convergence when (7.5) is enforced along the J lines at the 1601 points $\{y_m\}$. The fourth column of Table 7.1 shows the maximum departure from the symmetry condition (7.15) for the interpolated solution on the finest grid. The fifth column of the table shows the maximum change in the interpolated option price for a mesh refinement when one compares solutions for the nearest two J^* values. The last column shows the corresponding change in the delta $\{u'_j(y_m)\}$ for asset y.

Table 7.1. Results of the line Gauss Seidel iteration at $T = \Delta t = .001$.
Convergence criterion (7.5): $tol = 10^{-6}$, $\theta = 0$.

J^*	Number of lines	k	$\max\limits_{j,m} \|u_j(y_m) - u_m(x_j)\|$	$\max\limits_{j,m} \|\Delta u_j(y_m)\|$	$\max\limits_{j,m} \|\Delta u_j'(y_m)\|$
40	40	5	.001531		
				.009247	2.91
20	80	7	.001162		
				.003958	2.23
10	160	8	.000643		
				.001393	1.31
5	320	16	.000239		
				.000355	.81
2	800	58	.000034		
				.000053	.13
1	1600	190	.000012		

The iterative solution of the MOL equations is quite robust. The results of Table 7.1 are obtained with the initial guess

$$u^0(x_j, y_m) = \max\{0, 1 - x_j - y_m\},$$

but even for the initial guess

$$u_j^0(y_m) = (-1)^{(j+m)}$$

only a few more iterations are required to converge to the same answers.

It follows from Table 7.1 that the difference in option prices at $T = \Delta t = .001$ when going from 80 lines to 1600 lines is bounded by .005759. Seven iterations with 80 lines take less than five seconds, 190 iterations with 1600 lines take twenty-five minutes on the desktop computer used for this work.

Conspicuously absent from Table 7.1 is a check of the anti-symmetry condition (7.16). While it seems a simple matter to get put prices economically it is difficult to get good deltas at $T = \Delta t$. For example, approximating $u_x(x_j, y_m, \Delta t)$ with a second order difference quotient at each grid point and setting $u_y(x_j, y_m, \Delta t) = u_j'^k(y_m)$ we find that

$$\max_{j,m} |u_y(x_j, y_m, \Delta t) - u_x(y_m, x_j, \Delta t)| = .1184$$

which occurs at $x_j = 1$ and $y_m = 0$, i.e. at $j = 1000$ and $m = 0$.

The inaccuracy in the deltas at $T = \Delta t$ is due in part to a poor solution of the sweep equations near $y = 0$ and $x = 1$ caused by the source terms u_{xx} and u_{xy} which approach delta functions on $x + y - 1 = 0$ as $\Delta t \to 0$.

If we stay away from the singularities and maximize over all mesh points satisfying $|x + y - 1| \geq .01$ the error improves to .01832.

It is easy to demonstrate that the sweep equations are solved on too coarse a grid near $x = 1$ and $y = 0$ by comparing the MOL value $u'_j(0)$ with its approximation obtained from a difference quotient involving the calculated MOL values $\{u_j(y_m)\}$. Figure 7.3 shows (the linear interpolants of) the MOL values $\{u'_j(0)\}$ and of the corresponding difference quotients

$$u_y(x_j, 0, t) = (-3u_j(y_0) + 4u_j(y_1) - u_j(y_2))/2dy \qquad (7.17)$$

for $J^* = 5$ in a neighborhood of the critical point $x = 1$. The agreement is poor at $x = 1$ but can be shown to improve by refining the x- and y-mesh near $y = 0$. However, more mesh points will lead to even longer run times. Fortunately, the put price becomes smooth very quickly as time progresses. Figure 7.4 shows the analog of Fig. 7.3 after three time steps. The curves agree much better, and after a few more time steps they coincide so that the y-mesh is adequate for all times except immediately before expiration of the put.

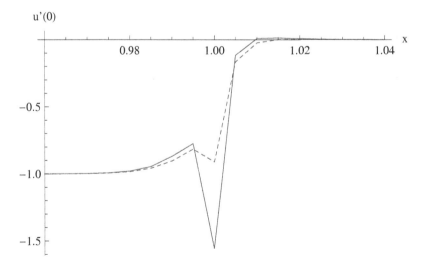

Fig. 7.3. Solid line: MOL values $\{u'_j(0)\}$ for $J^* = 5$ at $T = \Delta t = .001$ near $x = 1$ obtained with the Riccati method.
Broken line: Values of $\{u_y(x_j, 0, .001)\}$ obtained from (7.17).

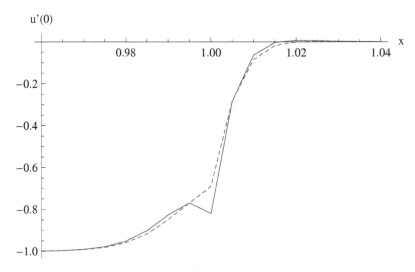

Fig. 7.4. Solid line: MOL values $\{u'_j(0)\}$ for $J^* = 5$ at $T = 3\Delta t$ near $x = 1$ obtained with the Riccati method.
Broken line: Values of $\{u_y(x_j, 0, .003)\}$ obtained from (7.17).

We conclude our discussion of the European put with some numerical results for an option with $T = .3$. We choose

$$\Delta t = T/300.$$

Results of our numerical experiments are shown in the following table.

Table 7.2. Results of the line Gauss Seidel iteration at $T = .3$.

Convergence criterion (7.5): $tol = 10^{-6}$, $\theta = 0$.

J^*	$\max\limits_{j,m} \|u_j(y_m) - u_m(x_j)\|$	$\max\limits_{j,m} \|u'_j(y_m) - u'_m(y_j)\|$	$\max\limits_{j,m} \|\Delta u_j(y_m)\|$	$\max\limits_{j,m} \|\Delta u'_j(y_m)\|$
40	.0003523	.141		
			.001038	.0799
20	.0003474	.061		
			.000305	.0400
10	.000241	.034		
			.000114	.0143
5	.000177	.029		
			.000056	.0094
2	.000133	.025		

We find that the MOL solution satisfies the symmetry condition (7.15) quite well, the anti-symmetry condition (7.16) tolerably well, and that $J^* \leq$

20 leads to prices which are stable with respect to space and time step refinements.

No results are given for $J^* = 1$ because of excessive run times with our research code. For a practical implementation of the MOL approach with 1600 lines a multigrid approach and parallelization would need to be explored.

Example 7.3. A perpetual American put – MOL with overrelaxation.

All of the numerical difficulties of the preceding example disappear when we consider a perpetual American put. In this case we have to find a time independent solution $\{u(x, y), s(x)\}$ which solves equation (7.13) subject to the free boundary conditions

$$u(x, s(x)) = 1 - x - s(x)$$
$$u_y(x, s(x)) = -1,$$

the usual boundary data

$$u(X, y) = u(x, Y) = 0$$

for sufficiently large X and Y, and given values

$$\{u(x, 0), s_\infty\}, \quad \{u(0, y), s(0)\}$$

known analytically for the one-dimensional perpetual American put or, alternatively, found with the sweep method of Example 5.1.

Since the problem is time independent we formally set $1/\Delta t = 0$ in the MOL equations and apply a line iterative method. Along each line $x = x_j$ the Riccati transformation is found as in Example 7.2. For $x_j < s_\infty$ the free boundary $s^k(x_j)$ in iteration k is a root of the equation

$$\phi_j^k(y) = R_j(y)(-1) + w_j^k(y) - (1 - x_j - y) = 0$$

and the reverse sweep proceeds from $s^k(x_j)$ to Y. For $x_j \geq s_\infty$ there cannot be early exercise because $u(x, 0)$ lies above the intrinsic value. In this case the reverse sweep proceeds from $y = 0$ to $y = Y$ subject to the initial condition

$$v'^k_j(0) = \frac{u(x_j, 0) - w_j^k(0)}{R_j(0)}.$$

It has been observed that for time independent problems (i.e. elliptic problems) the number of line Gauss Seidel iterations required for convergence can be large. Convergence can be accelerated through overrelaxation by setting

$$u_j^k(y) = u_j^{k-1}(y) + \omega(\tilde{u}_j(y) - u_j^{k-1}(y))$$

where $\tilde{u}_j(y)$ is the solution of (7.4) and ω is a relaxation factor. An analogous overrelaxation of the free boundaries $\{s_j^k\}$ is not recommended.

For a demonstration we show in Fig. 7.5 the early exercise boundary $y = s(x)$ for the data of Example 7.2

$$\sigma_1 = \sigma_2 = .2, \quad r = .05, \quad q_1 = q_2 = .02$$

$$X = Y = 3$$

and the three asset correlation factors

$$\rho = -.95, \quad \rho = 0, \quad \rho = .95$$

obtained on 120 evenly spaces lines in $[0, X]$ with 5000 mesh points on $[0, Y]$. Here again the answer should be symmetric with respect to the line $x = y$. The initial guess for the iteration is the pay-off

$$u^0(x, y) = \max\{0, 1 - x - y\}.$$

The convergence criterion for the line iteration is

$$\max_{j,y} |u_j^k(y) - u_j^{k-1}(y)| \le 10^{-6}.$$

At convergence the change in $\{u_j'^k(y)\}$ and in $\{s^k(x_j)\}$ with k was less than 10^{-5}. Overrelaxation for this elliptic problem is essential as the following table indicates:

Table 7.3. Number of iteration required for convergence.

ω	k
1	2908
1.85	314
1.9	199
1.95	227
2	no convergence

$\rho = 0$, 120 evenly spaced lines

The "optimum" relaxation factor will depend primarily on the number of lines and can be found by trial and error. $\omega = 1.9$ proved a good choice for all cases of Fig. 7.5. In principle, overrelaxtion can also be applied at each time level in a parabolic problem. It becomes relevant especially for large time steps.

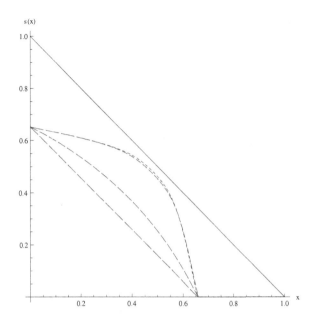

Fig. 7.5. Early exercise boundary for the perpetual American put on two assets
for different correlation factors.
Solid line: early exercise boundary at "expiry".
Short dashes: $\rho = -.95$.
  Note: The illustration shows two nearly coinciding early exercise
  boundaries obtained with 120 and 240 lines.
Medium dashes: $\rho = 0$.
Long dashes: $\rho = .95$.
Relaxation factor: $\omega = 1.9$.

Example 7.4. An American call, its deltas and a vega.

Suppose we wish to price an American call written on a small basket
containing a_1 shares of asset 1 and a_2 shares of asset 2 where the corresponding dividend rates may be assumed to satisfy $0 < q_1 \le q_2$.

The Black Scholes equation for the call is equation (7.12) defined on
$S_1, S_2 \ge 0$. At expiration the call pays

$$C(S_1, S_2, 0) = \max\{a_1 S_1 + a_2 S_2 - K, 0\}$$

The American feature of the call requires smooth pasting and the obstacle
condition

$$C(S_1, S_2, t) \ge \max\{a_1 S_1 + a_2 S_2 - K, 0\} \quad \text{for } t \in [0, T].$$

As in Example 7.2 we make the change of variables

$$x = \frac{a_1 S_1}{K}, \quad y = \frac{a_2 S_2}{K}, \quad u = \frac{C}{K}.$$

Then equation (7.13) results and is subject to the initial condition

$$u(x, y, 0) = \max\{x + y - 1, 0\}. \tag{7.18}$$

To set the boundary conditions we note that for $x = 0$ and $y = 0$ the problem turns into two uncoupled one-asset American calls. They are readily solvable with the MOL equations of Chapter 5. Thus we can impose the boundary conditions:

$$y = 0 : \{u(x, 0, t), u_x(x, 0, t), s_1(t)\} \quad \text{available numerically}$$

$$x = 0 : \{u(0, y, t), u_y(0, y, t), s_2(t)\} \quad \text{available numerically} \tag{7.19}$$

where $s_1(t)$ and $s_2(t)$ denote the early exercise boundaries of the scaled calls in assets x and y.

The call $u(x, y, t)$ for $x, y > 0$ will have a continuation region where $u(x, y, t) > x + y - 1$, and an early exercise region where $u(x, y, t) = x + y - 1$. It is known [9] that the early exercise region is convex in $x, y > 0$. Hence it is reasonable to assume that there is a smooth convex early exercise boundary

$$y = s(x, t)$$

linking the points $(0, s_2(t))$ and $(s_1(t), 0)$. We shall explicitly track this free boundary as we price the option with the method of lines.

On the early exercise boundary continuity of the price u and its deltas has to hold so that

$$u(x, s(x, t), t) = x + s(x, t) - 1$$

$$u_y(x, s(x, t), t) = 1 \tag{7.20a}$$

$$u_x(x, s(x, t), t) = 1. \tag{7.20b}$$

As we saw in Section 2.4, enforcement of (7.20a) implies (7.20b). To characterize the early exercise boundary we inject here a little bit of heuristic analysis based on the assumption that the call has a smooth (classical) solution.

If u and s are sufficiently differentiable then it follows from these boundary conditions and from

$$\frac{d}{dt} u(x, s(x, t), t) = \frac{d}{dt} [x + s(x, t) - 1]$$

that

$$u_y(x, s(x,t), t)s_t(x,t) + u_t(x, s(x,t), t)$$
$$\equiv s_t(x,t) + u_t(x, s(x,t), t) = s_t(x,t)$$

so that

$$u_t(x, s(x,t), t) = 0.$$

Moreover, the price surface $u(x, y, t)$ can lift off the obstacle surface, i.e. the plane, $z = x + y - 1$ only if $u(x, y, t)$ is convex in the continuation region near $y = s(x, t)$. It is known from calculus that a smooth function u is convex if and only if the matrix

$$U'' = \begin{pmatrix} u_{xx} & u_{xy} \\ u_{xy} & u_{yy} \end{pmatrix}$$

is positive semi-definite. If the point (x, y) belongs to the continuation region and (x_0, y_0) is a point on the early exercise boundary then it can be shown that convexity of u implies that

$$\lim_{(x,y) \to (x_0, y_0)} \left[\frac{1}{2}\sigma_1^2 x^2 u_{xx}(x, y, t) + \rho\sigma_1\sigma_2 xy u_{xy} + \frac{1}{2}\sigma_2^2 y^2 u_{yy} \right] \geq 0.$$

The Black Scholes equation (7.13) and $u_t(x_0, y_0, t) = 0$ yield

$$\lim_{(x,y) \to (x_0, y_0)} \left[\frac{1}{2}\sigma_1^2 x^2 u_{xx}(x, y, t) + \rho\sigma_1\sigma_2 xy u_{xy} + \frac{1}{2}\sigma_2^2 y^2 u_{yy} \right]$$
$$= (r - q_1)x_0 + (r - q_2)y_0 - r(x_0 + y_0 - 1)$$
$$\equiv -r + q_1 x_0 + q_2 y_0. \tag{7.21}$$

Convexity now assures that any point (x_0, y_0) on the exercise boundary has to satisfy

$$q_1 x_0 + q_2 y_0 \geq r.$$

Moreover, for $q_1, q_2 < r$ and any point (x, y) above the line $x + y - 1 = 0$ it follows that

$$\lim_{t \to 0} \left[\frac{1}{2}\sigma_1^2 x^2 u_{xx}(x, y, t) + \rho\sigma_1\sigma_2 xy u_{xy} + \frac{1}{2}\sigma_2^2 y^2 u_{yy} \right] = 0$$

because $u(x, y, t) \to x + y - 1$. Hence we conclude that the early exercise boundary $y = s(x, t)$ approaches the line

$$q_1 x + q_2 y = r$$

as we approach expiration. We conjecture that if $q_1 > r$ or $q_2 > r$ then

$$\lim_{t \to 0} s(x, t) = \max\left\{ 1 - x, \frac{r - q_1 x}{q_2} \right\}.$$

We note that equation (7.21) is the two-dimensional analog of the consistency condition of p. 122 for the gamma of a one-asset option. The numerical values for u_{xx}, u_{xy} and u_{yy} on the numerical early exercise boundary should approximately satisfy equation (7.21). The MOL with continuous y computes u_{yy} only in the continuation region and usually yields accurate values for u_{yy} on the free boundary. u_{xx} and u_{xy} have to be found from finite difference approximations but care has to be taken to avoid differencing across the early exercise boundary when checking for consistence because u_{xx} and u_{xy} are discontinuous on $y = s(x,t)$.

We now turn to the numerical solution of the American call with the method of lines. As in Example 7.1 we shall retain y as the continuous variable and use the computational domain

$$\{(x,y,t) \in [0,X] \times [0,Y] \times [0,T]\}$$

where X and Y are chosen large enough so that the early exercise boundary is contained in $[0,X] \times [0,Y]$ for all t. The MOL equations on a grid of lines at $\{x_j\}$ are again given by (7.3). The approximation of the discontinuous terms u_{xx} and u_{yy} with central difference quotients near the free boundary does not appear to cause difficulties on a sufficiently fine grid. Smooth extrapolations of the difference quotients for u_{xx} and u_{yy} into the exercise region appear unnecessary.

As in Example 7.2 the MOL equations are solved iteratively with the line Gauss-Seidel method. For the call the solution of equation (7.4), i.e. of

$$\mathcal{L}u_j^k(y) = F(x_j, y, t_n, u_{j-1}^k(y), u_{j+1}^{k-1}(y), u'^{k}_{j-1}(y),$$
$$u'^{k-1}_{j+1}(y), u_{j,n-1}(y), u_{j,n-2}(y))$$

begins with a forward sweep for $R_j(y)$ and $w_j^k(y)$ subject to

$$R_j(0) = 0$$

$$w_j^k(0) = u(x_j, 0, t_n).$$

As always, R_j and w_j^k are found on a set of discrete points $\{y_m\}$ with the trapezoidal rule. At each mesh point y_m we evaluate the function

$$\phi(y) \equiv R_j(y)(1) + w_j^k(y) - (x_j + y - 1).$$

If $\phi(y)$ changes its sign between mesh points $\{y_{m-1}, y_m\}$ then the zero of the cubic interpolant of the values of $\{\phi(y_{m-2}), \phi(y_{m-1}), \phi(y_m), \phi(y_{m-1})\}$ is taken as the free boundary $s^k(x_j, t_n) \equiv s_j^k$.

The reverse sweep for $v_j^k(y)$ then proceeds from s_j^k toward $y = 0$ subject to

$$v_j^k(s_j^k) = 1.$$

The solution is extended into the exercise region by setting

$$u_j^k(y_m) = x_j + y_m - 1, \quad v_j^k(y_m) = 1, \quad y_m \geq s_j^k.$$

To illustrate the performance of the MOL for an American call we choose the following data:

Number of shares: $a_1 = 3$, $a_2 = 2$.

Strike price: $K = 260$. The option is considered at the money when $S_1 = 60$, $S_2 = 40$.

Financial parameters: $\sigma_1 = .4$, $\sigma_2 = .1$, $\rho = -.5$.

(The large difference in volatility was chosen to accentuate the curvature of the early exercise boundary.)

$$r = .05, \quad q_1 = .025, \quad q_2 = .04.$$

Expiration: $T = .01$ and $T = .3$.

Our goal is to find the price $C(S_1, S_2, t)$ of the call at $t = T - \tau$ for calendar time $\tau = 0$, give the corresponding deltas $(\partial C/\partial S_1, \partial C/\partial S_2)$, and find the vegas $(\partial C(S_1, S_2, t)/\partial \sigma_1, \partial C(S_1, S_2, t)/\partial \sigma_2)$ at $(\sigma_1, \sigma_2) = (.4, .1)$.

An application of the MOL for a one-asset call described by (7.13) when $x = 0$ and $y = 0$ yields

$$\lim_{t \to 0} s_1(t) = 2.0, \quad s_1(.3) = 2.29899,$$

$$\lim_{t \to 0} s_2(t) = 1.25, \quad s_2(.3) = 1.29326.$$

Hence for our computational domain we shall choose

$$X = 2.4, \quad Y = 1.5,$$

so that $0 < S_1 < 208$, $0 < S_2 < 195$. In view of the experience with Example 7.2 we expect numerical problems near the line $x + y = 1$, and in particular at the point $(x, y) = (1, 0)$, near expiration. As before we smooth the problem with the replacement

$$\frac{1}{2}\sigma_2^2 y^2 \leftarrow \max\left\{\frac{1}{2}\sigma_2^2 y^2, 10^{-4}\right\}$$

in Eq. (7.13) so that the trapezoidal rule does not have to cope with unbounded coefficients near $y = 0$. We shall compute along lines $\{x_j\}$ which are evenly spaced on $[0, 2.4]$. The meshpoints $\{y_m\}$ are evenly spaced on the subintervals

$$[0, .1] \text{ with } \Delta y = .1/1000$$
$$[.1, .2] \text{ with } \Delta y = .1/1000$$
$$[.2, 1] \text{ with } \Delta y = .8/2000$$
$$[1, 1.5] \text{ with } \Delta y = .5/1000$$

for 5000 mesh points $\{y_m\}$. The number of mesh points along each line is excessive for long term calculations but no attempt was made to optimize the grid.

As always, the solution near expiration is the most difficult to find and requires a fine grid to yield reliable deltas. For example, Fig. 7.6 show the delta $\partial C/\partial S_2$ at $T = .01$ over the the restricted domain

$$D = \{(S_1, S_2) : 50 \leq S_1 \leq 70, 30 \leq S_1 \leq 50\}$$

which brackets the at-the-money values $(60, 40)$.

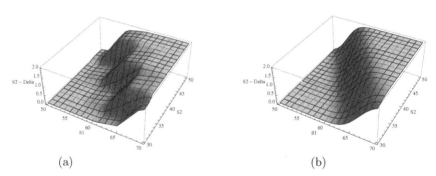

(a)   (b)

Fig. 7.6. Delta $\partial C/\partial S_2$ of the American call at $T = .01$, plotted over $50 \leq S_1 \leq 70$, $30 \leq S_2 \leq 50$.
(a) Results with 48 lines, $\Delta x = .05$.
(b) Results with 240 lines, $\Delta x = .01$.

For reference we show in Tables 7.4–7.6 some numerical values for the call $C(S_1, S_2, T) = 260 * u(x, y, t)$ and its deltas $\partial C(S_1, S_1, T)/\partial S_1 = a1 * \partial u(x, y, T)/\partial x$, $\partial C(S_1, S_2, T)/\partial S_2 = a2 * \partial u(x, y, T)/\partial y$, where $x = a_1 S_1/260$ and $y = a_2 S_2/260$.

Table 7.4. Call prices $C(S_1, S_2, .3)$.

$S_1 \backslash S_2$	30	40	50
50	1.5835	3.8326	8.7013
60	8.3548	15.5512	26.8887
70	23.4812	36.2835	52.5277

$$\Delta x = 2.4/240, \quad \Delta t = 0.3/300$$

Table 7.5. Delta $\partial C(S_1, S_2, .3)/\partial S_1$.

$S_1 \backslash S_2$	30	40	50
50	.3356	.6941	1.2892
60	1.0780	1.6608	2.2780
70	1.9241	2.4181	2.7700

Table 7.6. Delta $\partial C(S_1, S_2, .3)/\partial S_2$.

$S_1 \backslash S_2$	30	40	50
50	.1437	.3282	.6769
60	.5448	.9136	1.3574
70	1.0926	1.4643	1.7648

The early exercise boundary of the call at $T = .3$ in the (S_1, S_2) plane is shown in Fig. 7.7. A comparison with the straight line connecting the endpoints $(0, K s_2(T)/a_2)$ and $(K s_1(T)/a_1, 0)$ demonstrates the convexity of the early exercise boundary. A representative numerical value: If $S_1(T) = 60$, then early exercise is indicated for

$$S_2(T) \geq 112.6.$$

These numerical values were obtained with $\Delta t = T/300$. Little change is observed if we use instead $\Delta t = T/150$. Halving the number of lines changes the data of the above tables by less than one percent.

S2(S1,T)

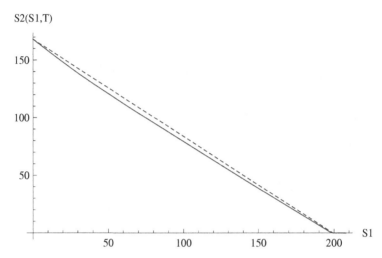

Fig. 7.7. Early exercise boundary for the American call at $T = .3$.
$\Delta t = T/300$, $\Delta x = .02$.
Solid curve: MOL free boundary.
Broken line: Straight line between $(Ks_1(T)/a_1, 0)$ and $(0, Ks_2(T)/a_2)$.

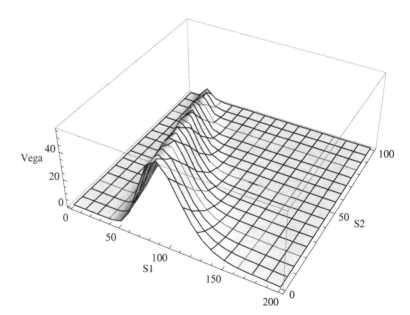

Fig. 7.8. Vega $\partial C/\partial \sigma_1$ over D at $T = .3$ for $(\sigma_1, \sigma_2) = (.4, .1)$.

Finally, we show in Fig. 7.8 the vega $\partial C(S_1, S_2, T)/\partial\sigma_1$ for $T = .3$ and $(\sigma_1, \sigma_2) = (.4, .1)$ over D obtained from a central finite difference of the call prices for $\sigma_1 = .401$ and $\sigma_1 = .399$. A representative change in the early exercise boundary is

$$\frac{\partial S_2(60.06, T)}{\partial\sigma_1} = -11.22.$$

Example 7.5. American spread and exchange options.

The MOL program for a two component basket call can be used for American spread and exchange options simply by changing the pay-off and the boundary conditions on the boundary of the computational domain.

Suppose the pay-off for the American spread call at maturity in reverse time is

$$V(S_1, S_2, 0) = \max\{a_2 S_2 - a_1 S_1 - K, 0\}$$

where $K \geq 0$ is the strike price. $V(S_1, S_2, t)$ is a solution of equation (7.13). Then with the change of variable

$$x = a_1 S_1, \quad y = a_2 S_2, \quad u(x, y, t) = V\left(\frac{x}{a_1}, \frac{y}{a_2}, t\right)$$

we see that $u(x, y, t)$ is a solution of (7.14) with the initial condition

$$u(x, y, t) = \max\{y - x - K, 0\}. \tag{7.22}$$

u is defined on $x, y > 0$, but in order to solve (7.14) we need to restrict ourselves to a computational domain

$$D = [0, X] \times [0, Y]$$

and impose boundary conditions on its sides.

It is reasonable to impose

$$y = 0 : u(x, 0, t) = 0 \tag{7.23}$$

$$x = X : u(X, y, t) = 0 \text{ for sufficiently large } X \tag{7.24}$$

$$\text{because } \lim_{x \to \infty} u(x, y, t) = 0.$$

$x = 0$: Both the Fichera and the Venttsel theory imply

that the pricing equation should hold at $x = 0$

which describes a simple American call.

Since the coefficients of all derivatives with respect to

x vanish at $x = 0$, the MOL solution along the line $x = 0$ needs to be computed only once per time step.

A difficulty arises at the upper boundary $y = Y$. It is known from [9] that the early exercise region is convex so that there is an early exercise boundary

$$y = s(x, t)$$

where

$$u(x, s(x, t), t) = s(x, t) - x - K \qquad (7.25)$$
$$u_y(x, s(x, t), t) = 1.$$

However, it is also known from [9] that $s(x, t) < x + K$. Hence for any choice of $Y > s(0, t)$ (i.e. the exercise boundary for the call $u(0, y, t)$) the curve $y = s(x, t)$ will cut the line $y = Y$ at some point $x(t) < Y - K$. Over the interval $[0, x(t)]$ the boundary condition (7.25) will hold, but no condition is known on $[x(t), X]$. Here we shall assume that

$$X > Y$$

and set

$$u(x, Y, t) = \max\{Y - x - K, 0\} \quad \text{for } x \in [x(t), X]. \qquad (7.26)$$

In other words, the early exercise boundary is taken to be

$$\min\{s(x, t), Y\}$$

which is not optimal for $x > x(t)$ because smooth pasting does not hold there. Hence the computed option price is only a lower bound on the actual American spread option price. The numerical example discussed below shows that if X and Y are sufficiently large then the influence of the boundary condition (7.26) on the option price far enough away from the boundary point (X, Y) is negligible.

We remark that the condition (7.26) is not needed if $X < x(t)$ for all t. However, in this case the boundary condition (7.24) is inconsistent with the free boundary condition (7.25) at $x = X$. In the application of the method of lines to American spread calls with a stochastic volatility discussed in [16] a boundary condition implied by the pricing equation is imposed as discussed in Chapter 2. While the resulting problem is not known to be well posed, the numerical results seem to be quite insensitive to the conditions on these computational boundaries.

The MOL price of the spread is found like the price of the American call. With y continuous the forward sweep along the lines $x = x_j$ proceeds from $y = 0$ with the initial conditions

$$R_j(0) = 0$$

$$w_j^k(0) = 0.$$

As we integrate the Riccati equation for R_j and the linear equation for w_j^k with the trapezoidal rule on the mesh $\{y_m\}$ we monitor the function

$$\phi(y) \equiv R_j(y)(1) + w_j^k(y) - (y - x_j - K).$$

If it changes its sign between meshpoints y_{m-1} and y_m then s_m^k is the root of the cubic interpolant of $\phi(y)$ through the four nearest neighbors. It is the early exercise boundary on the line $x = x_j$ in iteration k. The reverse sweep proceeds from $y = s_j^k$ to $y = 0$ with the initial condition

$$v_j^k(s_j^k) = 1.$$

If ϕ does not change its sign on $[0, Y]$ we have hit the barrier at Y where $u_j^k(y) = Y - x_j - K$ and

$$v_j^k(Y) = \frac{(Y - x_j - K - w_j^k(Y))}{R_j(Y)}.$$

For a numerical example we have chosen the parameters $\sigma_1 = .2$, $\sigma_2 = .3$, $\rho = -.9$, $r = .08$, $q_1 = .01$, $q_2 = .04$, $K = 1$, $T = .3$. The interest and dividend rates were chosen because convexity arguments and the pay-off dictate that

$$\lim_{t \to 0} s(x, t) = \max \left\{ x + K, \frac{Kr + q_1 x}{q_2} \right\}$$

so that the limiting curve is continuous and piecewise linear. In analogy to the simple American call the speed of the free boundary can be expected to be unbounded wherever it approaches the line $y = x + K$ because $u(x, y, 0)$ has discontinuous partial derivatives along $y = x + K$.

To illustrate this behavior we show in Fig. 7.9 the limiting curve and the computed free boundary after one time step at $T = .0001$ found with the method of lines. Figure 7.10 shows the early exercise boundary at $T = .3$ obtained over two nested computational domains after 150 time steps.

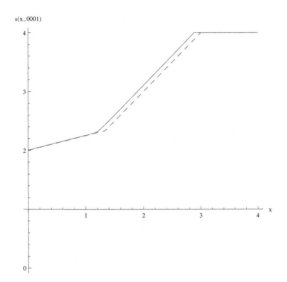

Fig. 7.9. Early exercise boundary for an American spread call one time step before expiration.
Broken curve: $\lim_{t\to 0} s(x,t)$.
Solid curve: MOL $s(x,.0001)$ found on $[0,4] \times [0,4]$.

To examine the influence of the computational domain on prices and their deltas at $T = .3$ we shall compare the two solutions of Fig. 7.10 on the square

$$D = \{(x,y) : 0 \le x \le 3, \ 0 \le y \le 3\}.$$

If u_4 denotes the price computed on $[0,4] \times [0,4]$ and u_5 is the solution on $[0,5] \times [0,5]$ we observe the following changes in the price u and its deltas:

$$\max_D |u_4(x,y,T) - u_5(x,y,T)| < 3.75\ 10^{-3}$$

$$\max_D |u_{4y}(x,y,T) - u_{5y}(x,y,T)| < .028$$

$$\max_D |u_{4x}(x,y,T) - u_{5x}(x,y,T)| < .012.$$

These differences increase markedly as one leaves the subdomain D. For example, at $x = 3$, $y = 4$ we have

$$u_4(3,4,T) = 0, \quad u_5(3,4,T) = .3741, \quad u_6(3,4,T) = .3746.$$

On the other hand, the above changes for the price and its deltas decrease to about 10^{-6} if the computational results obtained for (x,y) in $[0,5] \times [0,5]$ and $[0,6] \times [0,6]$ are compared over $D = [0,3] \times [0,3]$.

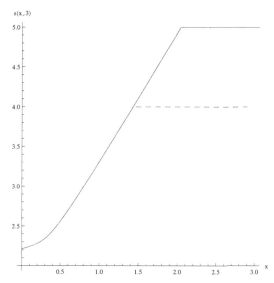

Fig. 7.10. Early exercise boundary for an American spread call at $T = .3$.
Broken curve: MOL $s(x, T)$ at $T = .3$ found on $[0, 4] \times [0, 4]$.
Solid curve: MOL $s(x, T)$ at $T = .3$ found on $[0, 5] \times [0, 5]$.
$\Delta x = 1/50$, $\quad \Delta y = 1/1000$, $\quad \Delta t = .3/150$.

Option prices and the early exercise boundary change little when the number of lines and time steps is doubled.

The MOL approach yields comparable results for an American exchange option. When we set $K = 0$ in $((7.25), (7.26))$ then the two dimensional free boundary problem with the same incorrect boundary conditions on $[x(t), X]$ and at $x = X$ yields

$$u_4(3, 4, T) = 1, \quad u_5(3, 4, T) = 1.0447, \quad u_6(3, 4, T) = 1.0447.$$

The corresponding value of a European option given by Margrabe's formula is

$$u_{Eu}(3, 4, T) = 1.0314.$$

The MOL free boundary for the exchange option computed in the $x - y$ plane is observed to be the straight line

$$s(x, t) = 1.66x.$$

It is known that the exchange problem can be reformulated as a one-dimensional American call (see, e.g. [67]). The numerical solution of this call with the 1-D MOL method of Chapter 5 yields the free boundary

$$s(x, t) = 1.664x.$$

Once again we can conclude that the uncertain far boundary conditions have little influence on the option sufficiently far away from those boundaries.

Example 7.6. An American call option on the maximum of two assets.

An American max call option written on two assets with spot prices S_1 and S_2 satisfies equation (7.12) and the pay-off condition

$$V(S_1, S_2, 0) = \max\{\max(a_1 S_1, a_2 S_2) - K, 0\}$$

where K is the strike price and $a_1, a_2 > 0$. Early exercise is initiated at time t when the surface $V(S_1, S_2, t)$ attaches itself smoothly to the two-dimensional pay-off (i.e. obstacle)

$$\phi(S_1, S_2) = \max(a_1 S_1, a_2 S_2) - K.$$

As in Example 7.2 we find that for $x = a_1 S_1 / K$ and $y = a_2 S_2 / K$ the scaled price

$$u(x, y, t) = V(Kx/a_1, Ky/a_2)/K$$

satisfies equation (7.13) in the continuation region and

$$u(x, y, t) = \max(x, y) - 1$$

in the exercise region.

It is known from the analysis of [9] that there are two non-overlapping early exercise regions $B_1(t)$ and $B_2(t)$ in the cones $x > y$ and $x < y$. u assumes its intrinsic value in $B_1(t)$ and $B_2(t)$ so that

$$u(x, y, t) = \begin{cases} x - 1, & (x, y) \in B_1(t) \\ y - 1, & (x, y) \in B_2(t). \end{cases}$$

This implies that $u(x, y, t)$ satisfies the inhomogeneous equation

$$\mathcal{L}u = st(x, y, t) \equiv \begin{cases} r - q_1 x & (x, y) \in B_1(t) \\ r - q_2 y & (x, y) \in B_2(t) \\ 0 & \text{otherwise} \end{cases} \tag{7.27}$$

where $\mathcal{L}$ is defined by equation (7.13) and $B_1(t)$ and $B_2(t)$ are to be determined together with $u(x, y, t)$.

It is hypothesized, and consistent with numerical simulations, that $B_1(t)$ lies to the right of a smooth early exercise boundary

$$x = s_1(y, t)$$

while $B_2(t)$ lies above an exercise boundary

$$y = s_2(x, t).$$

On $s_1(y, t)$ the free boundary condition

$$u(s_1(y, t), y, t) = s_1(y, t) - 1$$
$$u_x(s_1(y, t), y, t) = 1 \qquad (7.28)$$

applies. On $s_2(x, t)$ the condition

$$u(x, s_2(x, t), t) = s_2(x, t) - 1$$
$$u_y(s, s_2(x, t), t) = 1 \qquad (7.29)$$

has to hold.

In order to solve (7.27) numerically we introduce the square computational domain

$$D = [0, Z] \times [0, Z], \quad Z > 1$$

and impose boundary data on those parts of ∂D which do not lie in the exercise regions. On $x = y = 0$ the theory of Chapter 1 requires that the differential equation hold. For $x = 0$ and $y = 0$ the max option reduces to a standard American call which is readily solvable. Hence in view of Chapter 5 we may assume that

$$\{u(x, 0, t), s_1(0, t)\} \text{ and } \{u(0, y, t), s_2(0, t)\}$$

are known to a high degree of accuracy. For the far boundaries at $x = Z$ and $y = Z$ we impose, rather arbitrarily, the intrinsic value

$$u(x, y, t) = \max(x, y) - 1 \qquad (7.30)$$

on those parts of ∂D which belong to the continuation region. The actual option price would lie above its intrinsic value so that (7.30) will yield a lower bound on the option price. However, the influence of (7.30) on prices near the strike price appears to be slight provided Z is sufficiently large. As shown below, the choice of Z may depend strongly on the data of the problem.

For a numerical computation of the max option price at a given time level we shall use the method of lines in alternating directions. Let k be an iteration counter and let us suppose that at time t_n we have an estimate $B_2^{k-1}(t_n)$ for the exercise region above the line $x = y$ inside $[0, Z] \times [0, Z]$. Then (7.27), (7.28) and (7.30) define a standard two-dimensional free boundary problem which we solve by applying the method of lines along the horizontal lines $y = y_m$ for $0 = y_0 < y_1 < \cdots < y_M < y_{M+1} = Z$. We denote this horizontal MOL solution by

$$\left\{ uh_m^k(y), s_1^k(y_m) \right\}, \quad m = 0, 1, \ldots, M$$

where $s_1^k(y_m) = Z$ if no free boundary is found along the line $y = y_m$. The early exercise boundary $s_1^k(y, t_n)$ is found for all $y \in [0, Z]$ by interpolating the discrete values $\{s_1^k(y_m)\}$. The exercise region $B_1^k(t_n)$ thus found is

$$B_1^k(t) = \left\{ (x, y) : s_1^k(y, t_n) \le x \le Z, \ 0 \le y \le Z \right\}.$$

To find the exercise region $B_2^k(t_n)$ we now apply the method of lines at discrete vertical lines $x = \{x_j\}$ to (7.27) with the correct source term in $B_1^k(t_n)$ and subject to the free boundary condition (7.29). We obtain the MOL solution $\{uv_j^k(y), s_2^k(x_j)\}$, $j = 0, \ldots, J$. Interpolating $\{s_2^k(x_j)\}$ yields the early exercise boundary $s_2^k(x, t_n)$ which in turn defines an updated exercise region

$$B_2^k(t_n) = \left\{ (x, y) : 0 \le x \le Z, s_2^k(x, t) \le y \le Z \right\}.$$

Thus at every time level we have an outer iteration indexed by k which updates the exercise regions, and an inner iteration which finds a new free boundary with the method of lines algorithm in the x or y direction. We note that the only communication between the x and y sweeps occurs through the source term of equation (7.27). The initial guess for the exercise regions is not critical. We usually set

$$s_2^0(x, t_n) = s_2(x, t_{n-1})$$

where $s_2(x, t_{n-1})$ is the last computed free boundary at the preceding time level. In an inner iteration, say with continuous y, we obtain the vertical solution $\{uv_j^k(y), s_2^k(x_j)\}$ from the trapezoidal rule applied to the equations of the Riccati transformation on a relatively fine grid along the lines at $\{x_j\}$. Likewise, the MOL calculation along a line for a given y_m requires a fine grid in the x-direction and yields the horizontal solution $\{uh_m^k(x), s_1^k(y_m)\}$. Since the convergence of the MOL line iteration slows down drastically (for a given time step it may even fail to converge) as the number of lines is increased we typically have far fewer lines than mesh points along a given line. Lines cross at a subset of the mesh points used for the Riccati transformation along a given line.

Numerical option values at arbitrary points in $[0, Z] \times [0, Z]$ are found by interpolating values at the nearest four grid points. All interpolations used here are linear in each variable.

Two features were incorporated into the algorithm implementing the MOL inner iteration and the determination of the solution of the outer iteration.

i) For the MOL sweep along a line at $x = x_j$ the diffusion coefficient

$$a_{22}(x, y, t) = \max \left\{ 10^{-3}, \frac{1}{2} \sigma_2^2 y^2 \right\}$$

was used. Similarly, along a line at $y = y_m$ we use

$$a_{11}(x, y, t) = \max \left\{ 10^{-3}, \frac{1}{2} \sigma_1^2 x^2 \right\}.$$

As in all previous examples this cap on the diffusion coefficients removes unbounded coefficients in the Riccati transformation. No change in the numerical results is observable when different lower bounds are chosen.

ii) The analytic solution $u(x, y, t)$ at time t_n should be

$$u(x, y, t_n) = \max(x, y) - 1$$

whenever $(x, y) \in B_1^k(t_n)$ or $B_2^k(t_n)$. However, the numerical MOL solution obtained from the inhomogeneous pricing equation (7.27) will differ from the analytic solution, particularly near the free boundary where the analytic solution has discontinuous second spatial derivatives. In all calculations the MOL solution is set to its intrinsic value in the exercise regions at the end of each converged inner iteration. This change also appears to have little influence on prices and the exercise boundaries.

The inner iteration solves a standard two-dimensional free boundary problem for an inhomogeneous Black Scholes equation. The MOL line iteration (a Gauss Seidel line iteration) converges reliably as long as Δt is sufficiently small. Δt will depend on the number of lines. Too many lines may force Δt to be too small to make this approach feasible. In the numerical examples below the inner iteration is terminated when the maximum change in the MOL solution from one inner sweep to the next sweep falls below a tolerance of

$$\epsilon = 10^{-7}.$$

The outer iteration is terminated when changes in the free boundary fall below 10^{-6}. Convergence of the outer iteration is quite rapid, decreasing from $k \sim 10$ near expiration to $k = 2$ as the solution smoothes out, because the coupling between $s_1(y, t)$ and $s_2(x, t)$ in all numerical experiments proves to be quite weak. HOWEVER, the vertical and horizontal MOL solutions solve different approximations of the Black Scholes partial differential equation and yield converged numerical values which for a given space discretization do not in general agree at the intersections of the vertical and horizontal lines. All we can expect is that both sets of solutions will converge to the analytic solution of the max call as the number of lines and the number of points along each line is increased. The difference in the two MOL solutions at the intersection of the lines is monitored, and the discretization should be fine enough that this difference has no practical significance.

Since for a fixed number of lines the convergence rate of the MOL line iteration increases with decreasing time step (for a convergence analysis for a much simpler model problem with $\rho = 0$ see [51]), and since the early outer iteration does not necessarily need a highly converged MOL inner solution, there appears to be room for fine-tuning the algorithm for increased accuracy and efficiency.

To illustrate the performance of the alternating direction MOL approach we shall look first at the American version of the European call considered in [49]. The data for this problem, after scaling by the strike price $K = 1000$, are

$$\sigma_1 = .22, \quad \sigma_2 = .15$$

$$r = .05, \quad q_1 = .02, \quad q_2 = .06$$

$$T = 1$$

$$\rho = [-.9, .9],$$

with pay-off

$$u(x, y, 0) = \max\{0, \max(x, y) - 1\}.$$

Figure 7.11 shows the early exercise boundaries at $T = 1$ for $\rho = -.9$ obtained on the computational domains $[0, 3] \times [0, 3]$ and $[0, 4] \times [0, 4]$. On the subdomain $[0, 3] \times [0, 3]$ their graphs are indistinguishable. Moreover, they change little as the number of lines and time steps are varied.

Unfortunately, it is not obvious a priori how large a computational domain should be chosen. Figure 7.12 shows results analogous to those of Fig. 7.11 when the negative correlation is changed to

$$\rho = +.9.$$

Clearly, the influence of the far boundaries at $x = y = Z$ reaches much further into the computational domain than for the negative correlation. However, in both cases the influence is no longer felt near $(x, y) = (1, 1)$.

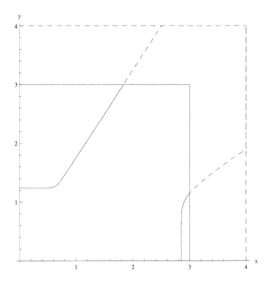

Fig. 7.11. Early exercise boundaries at $T = 1$ for $\rho = -.9$ on two computational domains.

Solid lines: right boundary $s_1(y, T)$ and upper boundary $s_2(x, T)$ computed on $[0, 3] \times [0, 3]$ with 120 lines and 6000 points per line.

Broken lines: right boundary $s_1(y, T)$ and upper boundary $s_2(x, T)$ computed on $[0, 4] \times [0, 4]$ with 160 lines and 8000 points per line.

$\Delta t = T/200$.

On the other hand, the following table shows that numerical option prices on a given computational domain are sensitive to the discretization parameters even far away from expiration.

The run on the coarsest grid takes on the order of minutes, the run on the finest grid takes on the order of hours. The numerical results suggest that the early exercise boundary can be determined very quickly with this approach, while the early exercise premium at $(x, y) = (.95, .98)$ relative to the above European price for a strike price of $K = \$1000$ (see [49]) varies between \$.30 and \$.58 and amounts to \$.37 on the finest grid. Depending on the data of the problem and on the accuracy required, the valuation of the max call with the method of lines can be a time consuming endeavor. If highly accurate American max call prices are required, and if European max calls can be accurately and quickly priced, it may be advantageous to compute the premium

$$p(x, y, t) = u(x, y, t) - u_E(x, y, t)$$

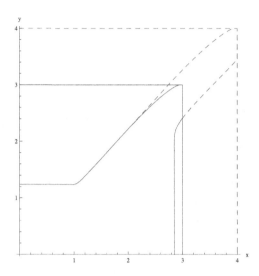

Fig. 7.12. Early exercise boundaries at $T = 1$ for $\rho = +.9$ on two computational domains.
Solid lines: right boundary $s_1(y, T)$ and upper boundary $s_2(x, T)$ computed on $[0, 3] \times [0, 3]$.
Broken lines: right boundary $s_1(y, T)$ and upper boundary $s_2(x, T)$ computed on $[0, 4] \times [0, 4]$.
Same mesh parameters as in Fig. 7.11.

Table 7.7. Option prices $u(x, y, T)$ and exercise boundaries $s_1(y, T)$, $s_2(x, T)$ at $(x, y, T) = (.95, .98, 1)$ for $\rho = +.5$.

No. of lines	time steps	uh	uv	$\|uh - uv\|$	uh_x	uv_y	s_1	s_2
75	100	.093011	.092936	5.7 −04	.40258	.25890	2.8503	1.3115
150	200	.092746	.092869	1.5 −04	.40305	.25796	2.8503	1.3098
300	400	.092796	.092801	4.4 −05	.40292	.25771	2.8503	1.3089
600	800	.092808	.092810	1.3 −04	.40289	.25765	2.8503	1.3085
European call [49]: $u_E = .0924412$					.4053	.2512		

$\|uh - uv\| = \max |uh(x_j, y_m) - uv(x_j, y_m)|$ where the maximum is taken over the intersections of all lines.

which can be expected to be much smoother than the price but which does require a more complicated contact condition on the exercise boundaries.

To give a sense of why one might want to compute the premium instead of the option directly we show in Fig. 7.13 the early exercise boundary one

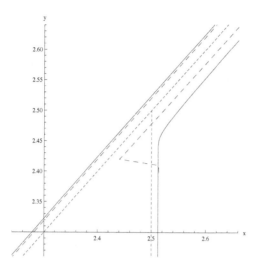

Fig. 7.13. Numerical early exercise boundaries near $(r/q_1, r/q_1) = (2.5, 2.5)$ just before expiration.
Short dashes: limit of $s_1(y, t)$ and $s_2(x, t)$ as $t \to 0$.
Long dashes: $s_1(y, t)$ and $s_2(x, t)$ found with 300 lines.
Solid curve: $s_1(y, t)$ and $s_2(x, t)$ found with 1000 lines.
$t = \Delta t = .001$. Lines evenly spaced on $[0, 3] \times [0, 3]$. 6000 evenly spaced mesh points along each line. Financial parameters as in Table 7.1 except that $\rho = .9$.

time step before expiration in a neighborhood of the point $(\max\{1, r/q_1\},$ $\max\{1, r/q_1\})$ where the curve

$$\lim_{t \to 0} s_1(y, t)$$

has a corner. For the above volatilities, interest rate and dividend rates, and for a correlation of

$$\rho = +.9$$

we find at $t = \Delta t = .001$ that the interpolated right exercise boundary $s_1(y, t)$ found with 300 horizontal lines is neither smooth nor monotone. It appears to show the numerical effects caused by finite difference formulas at nodes which bracket points of discontinuity of the analytic solution. 1000 lines yield an acceptable early exercise boundary but would be very time consuming for a long-term calculation.

For reference we list some numerical option prices associated with Fig. 7.13.

Table 7.8. Numerical option prices near expiration for $\rho = .9$.

		150 lines	1000 lines
$uh(1,1)$	$=$	.0025547	.0029003
$uv(1,1)$	$=$	.0022938	.0028636
$uh(1.5, 1.5)$	$=$	.5028772	.5019556
$uv(1.5, 1.5)$	$=$	.5026177	.5019189
$uh(2,2)$	$=$	1.0035602	1.0025916
$uv(2,2)$	$=$	1.0033100	1.0025610

The numerical early exercise boundaries will smooth as ρ decreases. For $\rho \le .4$ the boundary $s_1(y, T)$ found on 150 lines is smooth and monotone.

7.2 American calls and puts in polar coordinates

While we generally prefer to compute with (possibly non-dimensionalized) primitive variables like asset prices, volatility, interest rate, etc. and thus avoid mistakes in transforming familiar equations on intuitive domains to more economic (like constant coefficient) or elegant form, there often exist compelling numerical reasons to work in non-financial coordinate systems. Such reasons arise where early exercise boundaries are easier to describe and find in transformed variables. For example, the computation of the early exercise boundary with the method of lines tends to be particularly effective when the lines meet the exercise boundary nearly at right angles. Thus, in the scaled variables x and y of the Black Scholes equation (7.13) the early exercise boundary of the American call promises to be easier to track along rays from the origin into the computational domain $x, y > 0$ than along lines for constant x. This observation suggests formulating the call in polar coordinates (r, θ) where

$$x = r\cos\theta, \qquad y = r\sin\theta.$$

Derivatives of u in Cartesian and polar coordinates are related through the following expressions

$$u_x = \cos\theta u_r - \frac{\sin\theta}{r} u_\theta$$

$$u_y = \sin\theta u_r + \frac{\cos\theta}{r} u_\theta$$

$$u_{xx} = \cos^2 \theta u_{rr} - 2 \left(\frac{\cos \theta \sin \theta}{r} \right) u_{r\theta} + \frac{\sin^2 \theta}{r^2} u_{\theta\theta} + \frac{\sin^2 \theta}{r} u_r$$

$$+ 2 \left(\frac{\cos \theta \sin \theta}{r^2} \right) u_\theta$$

$$u_{xy} = (\sin \theta \cos \theta) u_{rr} + \left(\frac{\cos^2 \theta - \sin^2 \theta}{r} \right) u_{r\theta} - \left(\frac{\cos \theta \sin \theta}{r^2} \right) u_{\theta\theta}$$

$$- \left(\frac{\sin \theta \cos \theta}{r} \right) u_r + \left(\frac{\sin^2 \theta - \cos^2 \theta}{r^2} \right) u_\theta$$

and

$$u_{yy} = \sin^2 \theta u_{rr} + 2 \frac{\cos \theta \sin \theta}{r} u_{r\theta} + \frac{\cos^2 \theta}{r^2} u_{\theta\theta} + \frac{\cos^2 \theta}{r} u_r - 2 \frac{\cos \theta \sin \theta}{r^2} u_\theta.$$

Substitution into (7.1) leads to an equation of the form

$$\hat{a}_{11}(r, \theta) u_{\theta\theta} + \hat{a}_{12}(r, \theta) u_{r\theta} + \hat{a}_{22}(r, \theta) u_{rr}$$

$$+ \hat{b}_1(r, \theta) u_\theta + \hat{b}_2(r, \theta) u_r - \hat{c} u - \hat{d} u_t = 0 \qquad (7.31)$$

where

$$\hat{a}_{11}(r, \theta) = \left[a_{11} \frac{\sin^2 \theta}{r^2} + a_{12} \frac{\cos \theta \sin \theta}{r^2} + a_{22} \frac{\cos^2 \theta}{r^2} \right]$$

$$\hat{a}_{12}(r, \theta) = \left[a_{11} \frac{-2 \cos \theta \sin \theta}{r} + a_{12} \frac{\cos^2 \theta - \sin^2 \theta}{r} + a_{22} \frac{2 \cos \theta \sin \theta}{r} \right]$$

$$\hat{a}_{22}(r, \theta) = \left[a_{11} \cos^2 \theta + a_{12} \cos \theta \sin \theta + a_{22} \sin^2 \theta \right]$$

$$\hat{b}_1(r, \theta) = \left[a_{11} \frac{2 \cos \theta \sin \theta}{r^2} + a_{12} \frac{\sin^2 \theta - \cos^2 \theta}{r^2} + a_{22} \frac{-2 \cos \theta \sin \theta}{r^2} \right.$$

$$\left. - b_1 \frac{\sin \theta}{r} + b_2 \frac{\cos \theta}{r} \right]$$

$$\hat{b}_2(r, \theta) = \left[a_{11} \frac{\sin^2 \theta}{r} + a_{12} \frac{- \cos \theta \sin \theta}{r} + a_{22} \frac{\cos^2 \theta}{r} + b_1 \cos \theta + b_2 \sin \theta \right]$$

$$\hat{c}(r, \theta) = c(r \cos \theta, r \sin \theta), \quad \hat{d}(r, \theta) = d(r \cos \theta, r \sin \theta).$$

In this section $\hat{r}$ will denote the risk-free interest rate. The angular variable θ and the radial variable r are identified with x and y in the description of the method of lines for a rectangle.

Example 7.7. The basket call in polar coordinates.

On the rays $\theta = 0$ and $\theta = \pi/2$ the coefficients of u_θ, $u_{r\theta}$ and $u_{\theta\theta}$ vanish so that (7.31) reduces to a simple American call in the spatial variable r. Hence these rays need no special attention in the line iterative solution.

The boundary conditions for the equations along rays of constant angle θ_j are

$$u_j(0) = 0.$$

The early exercise conditions at $s_j \equiv s(\theta_j)$ are

$$u_j(s_j) = s_j(\cos\theta_j + \sin\theta_j) - 1$$
$$u_j'(s_j) = \cos\theta_j + \sin\theta_j.$$

Since the Riccati transformation method applies to first order equations with variable coefficients the numerical solution of the second order equation for $u_j(r)$ is straightforward. As in all previous examples we avoid the vanishing of $\hat{a}_{22}(r, \theta)$ as $r \to 0$ with the replacement

$$\hat{a}_{22}(r, \theta) \leftarrow \max\left\{10^{-4}, \hat{a}_{22}(r, \theta)\right\}.$$

For a numerical example we show in Fig. 7.14 the early exercise boundaries after one time step at $T = .001$ and after 300 time steps at $T = .3$ for the financial parameters of Example 7.4 except that the dividend rates are changed to

$$q_1 = .02 \quad \text{and} \quad q_2 = .09.$$

We expect from convexity arguments that in Cartesian coordinates (x, y) the early exercise boundary $s(x, t)$ for these dividend rates approaches the piecewise linear limiting curve

$$\lim_{t \to 0} s(x, t) = \max\left\{1 - x, \frac{\hat{r} - q_1 x}{q_2}\right\}.$$

The computed MOL free boundary at $T = .001$ in Fig. 7.14 has just barely moved off this limiting curve. Moreover, the graphs indicate that the speed of the exercise boundary is largest at the corner of the limiting curve.

We remark that for the data of Example 7.4 the MOL results obtained in cartesian coordinates along lines of constant x and in polar coordinates along rays of constant angle are very consistent. For 240 lines the option values and their deltas at the values of the underlying used in Tables 7.4–7.6 change by less than 1% so it makes little difference which coordinate system is used. It does appear, however, that in general fewer rays are required than lines at constant x to achieve comparable accuracy.

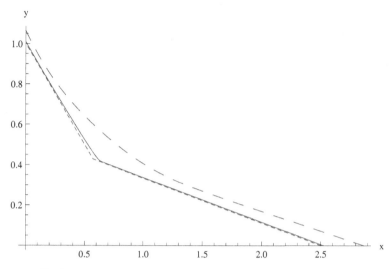

Fig. 7.14. Early exercise boundary for an American call on two assets S_1 and S_2 with risk free interest rate $\hat{r} = .05$ and dividend rates $q_1 = .02$ and $q_2 = .09$. Lower curve: $\lim_{t \to 0} s(x,t)$.
Center curve: early exercise boundary just before expiration at $t = .001$.
Upper curve: early exercise boundary at $T = .3$.
All other financial parameters are as in Example 7.4.

Example 7.8. A call on the minimum of two assets.

In contrast to a call on a sum of two assets, the American call on the minimum of two assets appears to benefit substantially from a reformulation into polar coordinates. In Cartesian coordinates the pay-off for this option is

$$u(x, y, 0) = \max\{0, \min(x, y) - 1\} \qquad (7.32)$$

and the early exercise region is bounded by curves where the solution $u(x, y, t)$ of (7.13) attaches itself smoothly to the surface defined by (7.32).

In polar coordinates equation (7.31) has to be solved on the quadrant $0 \le r \le \infty$, $0 \le \theta \le \pi/2$. For the MOL approach this unbounded domain is restricted to the the computational domain

$$0 \le r \le R, \quad 0 \le \theta \le \pi/2$$

where R is large enough so that option values are independent of it near $x = y = 1$.

The boundary conditions for (7.31) on this computational domain are

$$u(r, \theta, t) = 0 \quad \text{for } \theta = 0 \text{ and } \theta = \pi/2.$$

For points on $r = R$ belonging to the continuation region of the Black Scholes equation (7.31) we set

$$u(R, \theta, t) = u_1(x, t), \quad x = R\cos(\theta), \quad \theta \in (\pi/4, \pi/2) \qquad (7.33)$$

$$u(R, \theta, t) = u_2(y, t), \quad y = R\sin(\theta), \quad \theta \in (0, \pi/4]$$

where u_1 and u_2 are the standard one-dimensional American calls obtained from (7.13) for $y = 0$ and $x = 0$. Equation (7.33) reflects the assumption that for $x \gg y$ and $y \gg x$ the solution of (7.31) will depend essentially only on one variable.

If the early exercise boundary can be represented in the form

$$r = s(\theta, t) \qquad (7.34)$$

then $u(r, \theta, t)$ would have to satisfy the free boundary condition

$$\begin{cases} u(s(\theta, t), \theta, t) = s(\theta, t)\min(\sin\theta, \cos\theta) - 1 \\ u_r(s(\theta, t), \theta, t) = \min(\sin\theta, \cos\theta) \end{cases} \quad \theta \in [0, \pi/2]. \qquad (7.35)$$

This free boundary problem differs from the basket call only through the boundary and initial conditions and one can quickly check whether front tracking with the method of lines can find $s(\theta, t)$ and price this call.

As always, the solution near expiration will be the most difficult to find because of the lack of smoothness of the initial condition (7.32) on $x = y = 1$ and along $x = y$. For a problem with symmetry about $x = y$ with data

$$\sigma_1 = \sigma_2 = .2, \quad \rho = -.5$$

$$\hat{r} = .05$$

$$q_1 = q_2 = .02$$

we show in Fig. 7.15 the computed early exercise boundaries after one time step at $T = .001$ obtained with 101 and 1001 evenly spaced rays on $[0, \pi/2]$ and 10 000 mesh points along each ray, as well as the limiting curve

$$\lim_{t \to 0} s(\theta, t)$$

obtained with convexity arguments. Since this limiting curve contains vertical and horizontal segments it is likely that the early exercise boundary cannot easily be tracked along either vertical or horizontal lines, but that it is a graph in polar coordinates at all times.

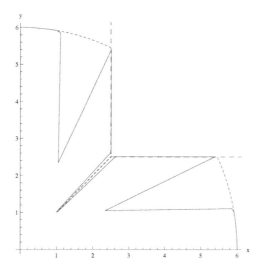

Fig. 7.15. Early exercise boundary $r = s(\theta, t)$ at $T \equiv \Delta t = .001$.
Solid curve: linearly interpolated boundary found with $\Delta\theta = \pi/200$.
Short dashes: exercise boundary found with $\Delta\theta = \pi/2000$.
Long dashes: $\lim_{t\to 0} s(\theta, t)$.

The parts of the computed early exercise boundary in Fig. 7.15 obtained with $\Delta\theta = \pi/200$ (i.e. 101 rays) coinciding roughly with $x = 1$ and $y = 1$ are numerical artifacts due to the jump in $u_{\theta\theta}$ where the ray crosses a discontinuity of $u(x, y, 0)$. They disappear when we compute with $\Delta\theta = \pi/2000$. They also disappear as the solution smoothes out with time.

The spike in the free boundary on $x = y$ might be thought to be a numerical artifact as well because of the discontinuity of (7.32) on $x = y$. However, the stability of the tip coordinates with respect to $\Delta\theta$, viz

$$x = y = 1.0046 \quad \text{for } \Delta\theta = \pi/200$$
$$x = y = 1.0016 \quad \text{for } \Delta\theta = \pi/2000$$

and the fact that the free boundary on the two rays adjacent to $\theta = \pi/4$ for $\Delta\theta = \pi/198$ (i.e. $x = y$ does not belong to the computational grid) is located at

$$(x, y) = (1.0213, 1.0055)$$
$$(x, y) = (1.0055, 1.0213)$$

and mirrors the spike at $\theta = \pi/4$ suggest otherwise. Fortuitously, the numerical free boundary obtained with the MOL only reflects what already is known from the analysis of [20] who establish that the early exercise boundary of the call-min option contains a line segment along $x = y$.

For reference we give below some numerical values for the call-min option considered in [20]. The last three columns quantify the early exercise boundary segment along $x = y$ found with the method of lines.

Table 7.9. Prices, Deltas and early exercise boundary near $x = y$ at $T = 1$.

x	y	binomial price [20]	Mol	u_x	u_y	s_{jc-1}	s_{jc}	s_{jc+1}
.9	.9	.0082	.00814	.0674	.0674	2.13	1.54	2.13
			.00811	.0672	.0673	2.11	1.54	2.11
1.4	.9	.0308	.03547	.0125	.3262			
			.03538	.0121	.3263			
1.1	1.1	.10	.10	.5	.5			
			.10	.5	.5			
1.6	1.1	.1425	.14261	.0051	.7063			
			.1425	.0049	.7067			

Parameters: $\sigma_1 = \sigma_2 = .2$, $\rho = 0$, $q_1 = q_2 = .05$, $\hat{r} = .06$, $T = 1$.
First MOL values : $\Delta t = T/100 = .010$, $\Delta\theta = \pi/200$, $jc = 51$.
Second MOL values: $\Delta t = T/200 = .005$, $\Delta\theta = \pi/400$, $jc = 101$.

To indicate that the success of the MOL approach is not tied to the symmetry of the solution implied by the above data, we show Fig. 7.16 a computed free boundary for a call-min option with a non-symmetric solution. And again, for reference, we also list some numerical values.

Table 7.10. Prices, Deltas and early exercise boundary near $x = y$ at $T = 1$.

x	y	Mol	u_x	u_y	s_{jc-1}	s_{jc}	s_{jc+1}
.9	.9	.02920	.0125	.2666	1.82	1.74	4.02
		.02900	.0122	.2662	1.77	1.72	3.98
1.1	1.1	.12316	.0580	.6118			
		.12273	.0571	.6010			

Parameters: $\sigma_1 = .4$, $\sigma_2 = .2$, $\rho = .9$, $q_1 = .02$, $q_2 = .06$, $\hat{r} = .04$.
First MOL values: $\Delta t = T/100 = .010$, $\Delta\theta = \pi/200$, $jc = 51$.
Second MOL values: $\Delta t = T/200 = .005$, $\Delta\theta = \pi/400$, $jc = 101$.

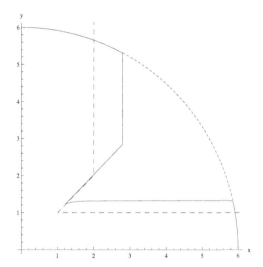

Fig. 7.16. Early exercise boundary at $T = 1$ for the parameters of Table 7.10. Solid curve: $s(\theta, T)$ found with $\Delta\theta = \pi/400$, $\Delta t = T/200$.
Long dashes: $\lim_{t\to 0} s(\theta, t)$.
Short dashes: Boundary of the computational domain.

The line segment of the exercise boundary along $x = y$ is no longer observable for the parameters of this problem, but as the next picture shows, it does become quite prominent at $T = 1$ when the volatilities are interchanged. Moreover, the almost vertical part of $s(\theta, T)$ is now distinctly convex so that its approximation by the boundary of a one-dimensional call becomes inaccurate near $y = 2$.

For the parameters of Fig. 7.17 we show in Fig. 7.18 the exercise boundary of the perpetual call-min on three nested computational domains with radii $R = 6$, 8, and 10. Shown also are the limiting curves for the one-dimensional perpetural calls at $y = 2.75859$ as $x \to \infty$ and at $x = 3.41423$ as $y \to \infty$.

Numerical values associated with Fig. 7.18 are given in Table 7.11.

One note of caution: On rare occasions the MOL iteration at a given time step can cycle and fail to converge because the boundary point $(R\cos\theta_j, R\sin\theta_j)$ on the jth ray will alternate between the continuation and the exercise region which in turn changes the value of $u(R, \theta_j)$. In all observed instances such cycling could be eliminated by decreasing the time step.

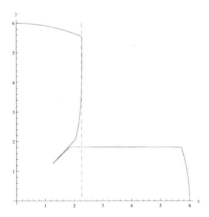

Fig. 7.17. Early exercise boundary at $T = 1$ when $\sigma_1 = .2$, $\sigma_2 = .4$.
Solid curve: Early exercise boundary of the call-min option.
Broken curve: Early exercise boundary of the embedded 1-D call with pay-off $\max\{0, x - 1\}$.
All other parameter as in Table 7.10. The influence of ρ on the early exercise boundary is small for all $\rho \in [-.9, .9]$ in this example.

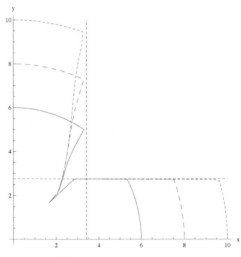

Fig. 7.18. Early exercise boundary of the perpetual call on the minimum of two assets.
Solid curve: Exercise boundary found in polar coordinates with $R = 6$.
Long dashes: Exercise boundary found in polar coordinates with $R = 8$.
Short dashes: Exercise boundary found with $R = 10$ as well as of the limiting one-dimensional perpetual calls.
All parameters as in Fig. 7.17 and $\Delta\theta = \pi/200$ (i.e. 100 rays).

Table 7.11. Price, Deltas and early exercise boundary near $x = y = 1$.

x	y	R	Mol price	u_x	u_y	s_{jc-1}	s_{jc}	s_{jc+1}
1	1	6	.23140	.22454	.22454	3.94	2.36	3.00
1	1	8	.23036	.22444	.22444	3.94	2.36	2.97
1	1	10	.23016	.22452	.22452	3.94	2.36	2.97

We expect that the vertical exercise boundary becomes convex as $R \to \infty$.

Example 7.9. A put on the minimum of two assets.

To continue our discussion of the application of polar coordinates in finance we shall apply them to find numerically the price and early exercise boundary for an American put on the minimum of two assets.

We assume the Black Scholes equation (7.12) holds for the price $P(S_1, S_2, t)$, and that the pay-off is

$$P(S_1, S_2, 0) = \max\{0, K - \min(a_1 S_1, a_2 S_2)\} \quad \text{for } a_1, a_2 > 0.$$

The early exercise boundary for the put is.expected to be the curve in the positive quadrant of the $S_1 - S_2$ plane where $P(S_1, S_2, t)$ attaches itself smoothly to the obstacle (pay-off)

$$\phi(S_1, S_2) = K - \min(a_1 S_1, a_2 S_2).$$

As $t \to 0$ the price becomes a function of S_1 above the line $a_1 S_1 = a_2 S_2$ and of S_2 below it so that we expect that the early exercise boundary approaches the vertical

$$S_1 = \min\left\{1, \frac{rk}{a_1 q_1}\right\} \quad \text{if } a_2 S_2 > a_1 S_1 \tag{7.36a}$$

and the horizontal

$$S_2 = \min\left\{1, \frac{rk}{a_2 q_2}\right\} \quad \text{if } a_2 S_2 < a_1 S_1. \tag{7.36b}$$

In general, these two lines will touch $a_1 S_1 = a_2 S_2$ at different points.

A numerical method for the put will have to contend with the lack of smoothness of the pay-off and with the unboundedness of the continuation region.

We again shall restrict ourselves to a finite computational domain over which we solve equation (7.12). Let (Z_1, Z_2) be a point on the line

$$a_1 S_1 = a_2 S_2$$

which is so far away from $(K/a_1, K/a_2)$ that the value of the put along the horizontal line $S_2 = Z_2$ can be approximated by the value of a one-dimensional put with pay-off $\max\{0, K - a_1 S_1\}$ and an up and out barrier at (or near) Z_1, and similarly, that along the vertical line $S_1 = Z_1$ it assumes the value of the one-dimensional put with pay-off $\max\{0, K - a_2 S_2\}$ and an up and out barrier near Z_2. Alternatively, one might set $\partial P(S_1, Z_2, t)/\partial S_2 = \partial P(Z_1, S_2, t)/\partial S_1 = 0$.

The computational domain will be a subset of the rectangle $[0, Z_1] \times [0, Z_2]$. It is reasonable to expect from (7.36) that the early exercise boundary will divide the rectangle into an early exercise region containing the coordinate axes, and a continuation region extending to Z_1 and Z_2. It also is reasonable to assume that each ray emanating from (Z_1, Z_2) into the rectangle $[0, Z_1] \times [0, Z_2]$ will cut the early exercise boundary at a single interior point. We are not aware of any theoretical analysis predicting the shape of the free boundary comparable to what has been discussed above for the call-min option, but if the boundary is sufficiently regular then polar coordinates centered at (Z_1, Z_2) and the method of lines can be used to track the free boundary along the rays.

We shall map the $S_1 - S_2$ plane to the $x - y$ plane so that the point (Z_1, Z_2) goes into the origin. To this end we shall set

$$Z_1 = \frac{ZK}{a_1}, \quad Z_2 = \frac{ZK}{a_2}$$

for some parameter $Z > 1$, introduce the transformation

$$S_1 = \frac{K(Z - x)}{a_1}$$

$$S_2 = \frac{K(Z - y)}{a_2}$$

and write

$$u(x, y, t) = \frac{P\left(\frac{K(Z-x)}{a_1}, \frac{K(Z-y)}{a_2}, t\right)}{K}.$$

The put expressed in terms of $u(x, y, t)$ will satisfy on $[0, Z] \times [0, Z]$ the equation

$$\alpha_{11}(x)u_{xx} + \alpha_{12}(x, y)u_{xy} + \alpha_{22}(y)u_{yy} \tag{7.37}$$
$$+ \beta_1(x)u_x + \beta_2(y)u_y - \hat{r}u - u_t = 0$$

where

$$\alpha_{11}(x) = \frac{1}{2}\sigma_1^2((Z - x))^2$$

$$\alpha_{12}(x) = \rho\sigma_1\sigma_2(Z-x)(Z-y)$$

$$\alpha_{22}(y) = \frac{1}{2}\sigma_2^2(Z-y)^2$$

$$\beta_1(x) = -(r-q_1)(Z-x)$$

$$\beta_2(x) = -(r-q_2)(Z-y).$$

The initial condition $P(S_1, S_2, 0) = \max\{0, K - \min(a_1 S_1, a_2 S_2)\}$ becomes

$$u(x,y,0) = \max\{0, 1 - \min[(Z-x), (Z-y)]\} = \max\{0, 1 - Z + \max(x,y)\}.$$

The complete boundary conditions in terms of x and y are

$$u(0,0,t) = 0$$

$$u(x,0,t) = u_1(x,t)$$

$$u(0,y,t) = u_2(y,t).$$

$u_1(x,t)$ is the solution of (7.37) when $y = Z$, subject to

$$u_1(x,0) = \max\{0, 1 - Z + x\}$$

$$u_1(0,t) = 0$$

$$u_1(s_1(t),t) = 1 - Z + s_1(t)$$

$$u_{1x}(s_1(t),t) = 1.$$

Similarly, $u_2(y,t)$ solves (7.37) when $x = Z$, subject to

$$u_2(y,0) = \max\{0, 1 - Z + y\}$$

$$u_2(0,t) = 0$$

$$u_2(s_2(t),t) = 1 - Z + s_2(t)$$

$$u_{2y}(s_2(t),t) = 1.$$

These call-like free boundary conditions correspond to one-dimensional puts along the horizontal line $S_2 = Z_2$ and along the vertical line $S_1 = Z_1$ under the above change of variable.

The early exercise boundary in the $x - y$ plane is the curve where $u(x,y,t)$ attaches itself smoothly to the surface

$$\phi(x,y) = 1 - Z + \max(x,y)$$

so that

$$u(x, y, t) = 1 - Z + x \quad \text{in the exercise region contained in } x > y$$

and

$$u(x, y, t) = 1 - Z + y \quad \text{in the exercise region contained in } x < y.$$

Hence in the (x, y) coordinate system the boundary conditions for a put on the minimum of two assets look like a call on the maximum of the assets, but the pricing equation (7.37) is not a Black Scholes equation.

We now write the problem in polar coordinates. If

$$r = s(\theta, t)$$

denotes the early exercise boundary then $u(r, \theta, t)$ can be found with the method of lines by applying it to equation (7.37), expressed in polar coordinates, and subject to

$$u(0, \theta, t) = 0$$

$$u(s(\theta, t), t) = 1 - Z + s(\theta, t)) \max(\sin \theta, \cos \theta)$$

$$u_r(s(\theta, t), t) = \max(\sin \theta, \cos \theta)$$

where $0 \leq \theta \leq \pi/2$. The rays with constant θ in the (x, y) plane correspond to rays extending from $(S_1, S_2) = (Z_1, Z_2)$ into the quadrant $\{(S_1, S_2) : -\infty < S_1 \leq Z_1, -\infty < S_2 \leq Z_2\}$.

The computational domain in the $r - \theta$ plane will be the rectangle $[r_0, R] \times [0, \pi/2]$, where $R = \sqrt{2}Z$ and where $r_0 > 0$ is introduced to avoid singular coefficients in (7.37) at $r = 0$. It defines the up and out barrier for the put. The image of the computational domain in the $S_1 - S_2$ plane belongs to the circle of radius R around (Z_1, Z_2) through $(0, 0)$. It contains negative asset values. Meaningful numerical results require that the location of the early exercise boundary correspond to non-negative values S_1 and S_2.

All numerical results found with polar coordinates in the $r - \theta$ plane are displayed below in the $S_1 - S_2$ plane. They hold for $K = a_1 = a_2 = 1$.

For the call on the minimum of two assets discussed above the exercise boundary contains a line segment along $S_1 = S_2$ jutting into the continuation region. It is not known whether the analysis of [9] for the exercise boundary of a standard call on the maximum of two assets can be extended

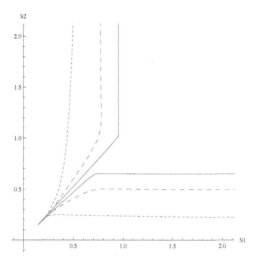

Fig. 7.19. Early exercise boundaries for a put on the minimum of two assets.
Solid line: Exercise boundary at $T = .01$, $\Delta t = T/10$, 1000 rays.
Long dashes: Exercise boundary at $T = .5$, $\Delta t = T/200$, 500 rays.
Short dashes: Exercise boundary for the perpetual put, 200 rays.
$\sigma_1 = .2$, $\sigma_2 = .4$, $\rho = -.9$, $\hat{r} = .04$, $q_1 = .02$, $q_2 = .06$, $K = a_1 = a_2 = 1$, $Z = 6$.
Computational domain: $r_0 \leq r \leq \sqrt{2}Z$, $0 \leq \theta \leq \pi/2$.
Mesh along a ray: $r_0 = .5$, $r_1 = 1$, $r_2 = Z - 1$, $r_3 = \sqrt{2}(Z - 1)$, $r_4 = \sqrt{2}Z$

> 4000 evenly spaced mesh points on $[r_0, r_1]$
> 2000 evenly spaced mesh points on $[r_1, r_2]$
> 3000 evenly spaced mesh points on $[r_2, r_3]$
> 3000 evenly spaced mesh points on $[r_3, r_4]$.

to equation (7.37) with its call-max boundary condition to prove that the entire line $S_1 = S_2$ belongs to the continuation region (see the discussion of Example 7.6).

Our numerical experiments are inconclusive. In all calculations the computed early exercise boundary crosses the line $S_1 = S_2$ at some location $S_b > 0$, but S_b depends strongly on the number of lines.

Figure 7.19 shows the early exercise boundary near $S_1 = S_2$ at $T = .01$ obtained with 1000 rays after ten time steps, at $T = .5$ found with 500 rays after 200 time steps, and the free boundary for the perpetual put found with 200 rays. Numerical values for the free boundary location $S_b(T)$ on the line $S_1 = S_2$ are given in Table 7.12.

Table 7.12. Location $S_b(T)$ of the exercise boundary on $S_1 = S_2$.

No. of lines J	T	No. of time steps N	$Z = 4$ $S_b(T)$	$Z = 6$ $S_b(T)$	$Z = 8$ $S_b(T)$
100	.001	1	.1538	.1855	.2112
100	.010	10	.1530	.1845	.2101
100	.5	200	.1465	.1765	.2009
100	inf	1	.1398	.1652	.1849
200	.001	1	.1120	.1357	.1551
200	.010	10	.1114	.1350	.1543
200	.5	200	.1070	.1294	.1478
200	inf	1	.1046	.1248	.1409
400	.001	1			.1127
400	.010	10			.1121
400	.5	200			.1077
400	inf	1			
500	.001	1	.0727	.0885	.1015
500	.010	10	.0723	.0880	
500	.5	200		.0848	
1000	.001	1	.0521	.0635	.0730
1000	.010	10	.0516	.0631	.0726

We note that doubling Z and the number of lines roughly preserves the distance between adjacent rays near $S_b(T)$ and does not change $S_b(T)$ significantly, and that for a given J and Z the location $S_b(T)$ changes little with T. The data also show that $S_b(T)$ for a given Z and T decreases noticeably as the number of lines is increased. However, the available resolution does not allow us to find

$$\lim_{\Delta\theta \to 0} S_b(T).$$

No long-term solutions with 500 and 1000 lines were computable because of excessive run times or even divergence of the line iteration.

Next we show in Fig. 7.20 the early exercise boundaries in $[0, 2] \times [0, 2]$ for the perpetual put given by the steady state solution of (7.37) for $Z = 6$ and the two correlation factors $\rho = -.9$ and $\rho = +.9$.

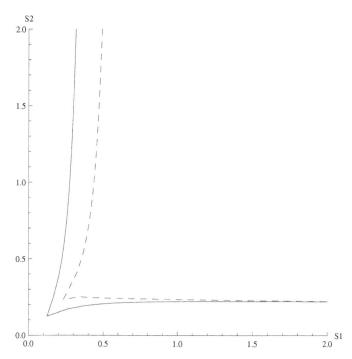

Fig. 7.20. Early exercise boundary near $S_1 = S_2$ for a a perpetual put on the minimum of two assets.
Solid line: Boundary for $\rho = -.9$.
Dashes: Boundary for $\rho = +.9$.
All other parameters as in Fig. 7.19.

Figure 7.21 shows the corresponding prices $u(r)$ of the two options along $S_1 = S_2$ as a function of the distance r from the origin. While both curves are monotonically decreasing, only the put price for $\rho = -.9$ repeatedly changes its convexity on $[0, 2]$ (and beyond) as indicated by the two plots of $\frac{\partial u(r, \pi/4)}{\partial r}$ in Fig. 7.22.

These illustrations reflect that for the above (randomly chosen) data for the put on the minimum of two assets the case of $\rho = -.9$ was consistently more difficult to price than the corresponding put with a larger correlation. In particular, the MOL line iteration for the perpetual put converged more slowly for $\rho = -.9$ than for $\rho = +.9$, but both steady state problems benefit from an overrelaxation

$$u^{k+1}(r_m, \theta_j) = u^k(r_m, \theta_j) + \omega(u(r_m, \theta_j) - u^k(r_m, \theta_j))$$
$$u_r^{k+1}(r_m, \theta_j) = u_r^k(r_m, \theta_j) + \omega(u_r(r_m, \theta_j) - u_r^k(r_m, \theta_j))$$

$$j = 2, \ldots, J$$

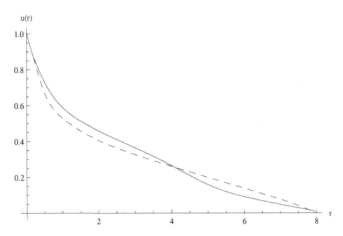

Fig. 7.21. Option price of the perpetual put along the diagonal $S_1 = S_2$ as a function of distance r from $(0,0)$.
Solid line: Price for $\rho = -.9$.
Dashes: Price for $\rho = +.9$.

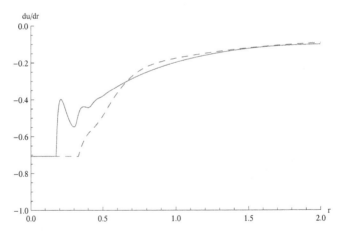

Fig. 7.22. Derivative of the option price of Fig. 7.21 as a function of r.
Solid line: $\frac{\partial u(r, \pi/4)}{\partial r}$ for $\rho = -.9$.
Dashes: $\frac{\partial u(r, \pi/4)}{\partial r}$ for $\rho = +.9$.

where k is the iteration count for the MOL line iteration, r_m denotes the radial mesh point, θ_j is the polar angle of the jth ray and $u^k(r_m, \theta_j)$ is the Riccati transformation solution. For 200 lines we choose $\omega = 1.6$ but do not claim that it is optimal. It did reduce the number of iterations required for convergence by about a factor of 3, while $\omega = 1.8$ led to divergence. But even in the benign case of $\rho = +.9$ the MOL method with overrelaxation for 200 lines took 5000 iterations to achieve a convergence tolerance for the change of prices of

$$\|u^k - u^{k-1}\| \leq 3.1\,10^{-6}.$$

The change in the derivative of du/dr and in the free boundary location between successive iterations is of the same order of magnitude after 5000 iterations.

Finally, we would like to point out that the above illustrations and Table 7.12 remain unchanged when the Dirichlet boundary conditions on $S_1 = Z$ and $S_2 = Z$ provided by the $1-D$ puts are changed to the Neumann conditions

$$u_y(x, 0, t) = 0$$

$$u_x(0, y, t) = 0,$$

which are easier to implement. In general, numerical results near the lines $S_1 = Z$ and $S_2 = Z$ appear less sensitive to the choice of Z than those obtained with Dirichlet conditions. Therefore, on the basis of our numerical experiments, the Neumann conditions are recommended over the Dirichlet conditions for the pricing of American puts on the minimum of two assets. In this case the overrelaxation is carried out also on the bounding rays $j = 0$ and $j = J + 1$.

Example 7.10. A perpetual put on the minimum of two assets with uncertain correlation.

The strong influence of ρ on the price of the perpetual put apparent from Figs. 7.21, 7.22 in the preceding example makes this free boundary problem a non-trivial test case for bounding the option price when the correlation is not given but assumed to lie between known bounds. The derivation of the equations for the bounding solutions is given in Example 1.9.

We suppose that the correlation factor $\rho(S_1, S_2)$ is a sufficiently smooth function so that the above perpetual put has a solution $P(S_1, S_2)$, and that it satisfies

$$-1 < \rho_0 \leq \rho(S_1, S_2) \leq \rho_1 < 1$$

for known bounds ρ_0 and ρ_1, which themselves may be functions of S_1 and S_2. Then it follows from Example 1.9 that P must satisfy

$$\underline{P}(S_1, S_2) \leq P(S_1, S_2) \leq \overline{P}(S_1, S_2)$$

where $\underline{P}$ and $\overline{P}$ are solutions of

$$\mathcal{L}(\overline{\rho})P = \pm F(\rho, S_1, S_2, P_{S_1 S_2}) \tag{7.38}$$

subject to the same boundary conditions which apply to the perpetual put (here with Neumann conditions on Z_1 and Z_2). $\mathcal{L}(\rho)P$ denotes the left hand side of the steady state form of equation (7.12), F is defined as

$$F(\rho, S_1, S_2, P_{S_1 S_2}) = \rho \sigma_1 \sigma_2 \rho S_1 S_2 |P_{S_1 S_2}|,$$

and $\underline{\rho}$ and $\overline{\rho}$ are the derived correlations

$$\underline{\rho} = \frac{\rho_1 - \rho_0}{2}, \quad \overline{\rho} = \frac{\rho_1 + \rho_0}{2}.$$

If (7.38) proves solvable then $\underline{P}$ is obtained with the positive source term in (7.38) and $\overline{P}$ corresponds to the negative source term.

To solve (7.38) numerically we shall work with the equations for the perpetual put in polar coordinates and simply add a source term to the equations of the Riccati transformation obtained by discretizing the right side of (7.38). To be specific, in polar coordinates we have

$$P_{S_1 S_2}(S_1, S_2) = u_{xy}(x, y) = \cos\theta \sin\theta u_{rr} + \frac{\cos^2\theta - \sin^2\theta}{r} u_{r\theta}$$

$$+ \frac{\cos\theta \sin\theta}{r^2} u_{\theta\theta} - \frac{\cos\theta - \sin\theta}{r} u_r - \frac{\cos\theta - \sin\theta}{r^2} u_\theta.$$

In iteration k along the ray θ_j we approximate the derivatives by

$$u_r = u'^{k-1}_j(r), \quad u_{rr} = u''^{k-1}_j(r)$$

and $\quad u_\theta = \dfrac{u^{k-1}_{j+1}(r) - u^k_{j-1}(r)}{2\Delta\theta}, \quad u_{\theta\theta} = \dfrac{u^{k-1}_{j+1}(r) + u^k_{j-1}(r) - 2u^{k-1}_j(r)}{\Delta\theta^2}$

$$u_{r\theta} = \frac{u'^{k-1}_{j+1}(r) - u'^k_{j-1}(r)}{2\Delta\theta}.$$

We recall that $u'_j(r)$ is furnished by the Riccati transformation and that $u''_j(r)$ is just the right hand side of the reverse sweep equation (3.6).

We do not know of a convergence proof which applies to the line Gauss-Seidel method for the non-linear equation (7.38), but our numerical simulations with the parameters of Fig. 7.19 (except ρ) show convergence for arbitrary $\rho_0, \rho_1 \in [-.9, .9]$. All numerical results given here were obtained with 5000 iterations. At that stage the maximum change in the price, the radial derivative of the price and the location of the free boundary is of the order of $5\,10^{-5}$ and decreasing very slowly. Overrelaxation had an unpredictable influence on convergence and was not implemented.

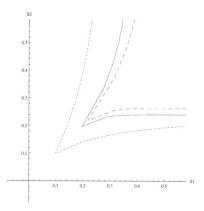

Fig. 7.23. Early exercise boundaries near $S_1 = S_2$ for a perpetual put-min with $\rho_0 = -.9 \leq \rho(S_1, S_2) \leq +.9 = \rho_1$.
Solid line: Early exercise boundary for the put with correlation function (7.39).
Long dashes: Early exercise boundary for $\underline{P}(S_1, S_2)$.
Short dashes: Early exercise boundary for $\overline{P}(S_1, S_2)$.
Parameters other than ρ as in Fig. 7.19.

Figure 7.23 shows the early exercise boundaries for $\underline{P}$ and $\overline{P}$ for $\rho_0 = -.9$ and $\rho_1 = .9$, as well as the early exercise boundary of the perpetual put for the correlation function

$$\rho(S_1, S_2) = .9 \cos\left(2\pi \frac{\sqrt{S_1^2 + S_2^2}}{\sqrt{2}Z}\right), \quad 0 \leq S_1, S_2 \leq Z, \quad (7.39)$$

which lies between the given bounds.

Figure 7.24 shows corresponding prices along the diagonal $S_1 = S_2$. Numerical values of the steady state solutions at $S_1 = S_2 = .5$ are

$$\underline{P}(5, .5) = .6716, \quad P(.5, .5) = .6799, \quad \overline{P}(.5, .5) = .7273.$$

The spread $\overline{P} - \underline{P}$ is quite large, but so is $\rho_1 - \rho_0$. Whether the spread can be decreased through static hedging as in the Black Scholes Barenblatt setting [56] is not known, but if so, the solution of an equation like (7.38) must be found. No conditions on the parameters of (7.38) are known which guarantee convergence of the line iterative Gauss-Seidel method, but the above simulation indicates that it is fairly stable. Convergence for the time dependent analog of (7.38) typically is fast for small time steps, but the discontinuity of the source term will degrade the quality of the solution near expiration.

Example 7.11. Implied correlation for a put on the sum of two assets.

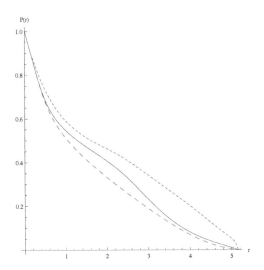

Fig. 7.24. Upper and lower bound on the price $P(S, S)$ of a perpetual put on the minimum of two assets.
Solid line: Price of the put for the correlation function (7.39).
Long dashes: lower bound $\underline{P}(S, S)$.
Short dashes: upper bound $\overline{P}(S, S)$.

Given a reliable solver for the American put on two assets, one can readily search for the correlation which is implied by the price of an option. Such a solver can be based on the time discrete method of lines.

Suppose a put $P(S_1, S_2, t)$ satisfies (7.12) and has the pay-off

$$P(S_1, S_2, 0) = \max\{K - a_1 S_1 - a_2 S_2, 0\}$$

for $a_1, a_2 > 0$. We may assume that outside a sufficiently large rectangle $[0, Z_1] \times [0, Z_2]$ the put vanishes so that

$$P(S_1, S_2, t) = 0 \quad \text{for } S_1 > Z_1, \ S_2 > Z_2,$$

and that there is an early exercise boundary of the form

$$g(S_1, S_2, t) = 0$$

linking points $g(0, S_2, t) = 0$ and $g(S_1, 0, t) = 0$. $P(S_1, S_2, t)$ attaches itself smoothly to the pay-off along the early exercise boundary.

On $S_1 = 0$ and $S_2 = 0$ the Fichera theory of Chapter 1 implies that (7.12) has to hold so that $P(S_1, 0, t)$, $P(0, S_2, t)$ and the corresponding early exercise boundaries $g(S_1, 0, t)$ and $g(0, S_2, t)$ follow from simple one-dimensional puts and may be assumed known.

As with the American call in Example 7.4, 7.7 of this section, one can attack the put in Cartesian coordinates, say with lines at constant S_1, or in polar coordinates with respect to an origin at (Z_1, Z_2) as in Example 7.9 above. Here we shall use polar coordinates again. We choose

$$Z_1 = \frac{KZ}{a_1}, \quad Z_2 = \frac{KZ}{a_2}$$

for sufficiently large Z (typically $Z \geq 3$), make the change of variable

$$S_1 = \frac{K(Z - x)}{a_1}, \quad S_2 = \frac{K(Z - y)}{a_2}$$

and define

$$u(x, y, t) = \frac{P(K(Z - x), K(Z - y), t)}{K}.$$

Then u is a solution of (7.37) subject to

$$u(x, y, 0) = \max\{1 - 2Z + x + y, 0\}$$
$$u(x, 0, t) = u(0, y, t) = 0$$
$$u(x, Z, t) = u_1(x, t)$$
$$u(Z, y, t) = u_2(y, t)$$

and the free boundary condition on the exercise boundary

$$u(x, y, t) = 1 - 2Z + x + y$$
$$u_x(x, y, t) = u_y(x, y, t) = 1.$$

u_1 is the solution of equation (7.37) for $y = Z$, and u_2 solves (7.37) when $x = Z$.

This problem is solved in polar coordinates (r, θ) in the rectangle $[r_0, \sqrt{2}Z] \times [0, \pi/2]$, where $r_0 > 0$ is chosen to avoid singular coefficients at the origin when (7.37) is written in terms of r and θ. The method of lines is used with continuous $r \in [r_0, \sqrt{2}Z]$ and discretized θ. Along the ray θ_j we determine the free boundary

$$r = s(\theta_j, t)$$

so that

$$u(r, \theta_j, t) = 1 - 2Z + s(\theta_j, t) \cdot (\cos\theta_j + \sin\theta_j)$$
$$u_r(r, \theta_j, t) = \cos\theta_j + \sin\theta_j.$$

If no free boundary is found before the ray intersects the boundary $x = Z$ (i.e. the S_1 axis) we enforce the given boundary condition

$$u(r_j, \theta_j, t) = u_2(y_j, t)$$

where $r_j = Z/\cos\theta_j$ and $y_j = \sqrt{r_j^2 - Z^2}$. Similarly, if the ray crosses $y = Z$ we enforce

$$u(r_j, \theta_j, t) = u_1(x_j, t)$$

where

$$r_j = \frac{Z}{\sin\theta_j} \quad \text{and} \quad x_j = \sqrt{r_j^2 - Z^2}.$$

In a study of a time continuous method of lines for options written on up to six assets [45], applied on a closed rectangle bounded away from the coordinate axes, the Dirichlet condition

$$P(S_1, S_2, \ldots, t) = P(S_1, S_2, \ldots, 0) \qquad (7.40)$$

is imposed on the boundary. It simplifies the formulation of the time continuous MOL, but is recognized to introduce errors near boundary points which belong to the continuation region. For the put on two assets studied here with the time discrete method of lines, the Dirichlet condition (7.40) can be imposed just as easily as the 1D put data. A comparison of results from both formulations provides some insight into the error due to (7.40).

As a first test problem we shall consider a put included in the time continuous MOL study [45]. The data for this put are

$$\sigma_1 = \sigma_2 = .2, \quad \rho = .5, \quad \hat{r} = .03 \quad \text{and} \quad q_1 = q_2 = 0,$$

and the pay-off is

$$P(S_1, S_2, 0) = 100 - \frac{(S_1 + S_2)}{2}.$$

The solution is symmetric about $S_1 = S_2$ and the early exercise boundary approaches the line

$$S_1 + S_2 = 200$$

as we near expiration.

A continuous time MOL option price reported in [45] is

$$P(100, 100, .25) = 3.13955.$$

The time discrete MOL price obtained with 100 rays and 400 time steps is

$P(100, 100, .25) = 3.139558202634591$ for 1D put data

$P(100, 100, .25) = 3.139558202634567$ for the boundary data (7.40).

Clearly, the point $(100, 100)$ is far enough from the coordinate axes so that incorrect Dirichlet data on them will do no harm. On the other hand, if

$S_1 \to 0$ and $S_2 \to 200$ then for all t according to the Fichera theory we should expect

$$P(S_1, S_2, t) \to u_2(K, t)$$

so that

$$P(S_1, S_2, .25) \to u(100, .25) = 3.6677.$$

But if (7.40) is applied then for all t

$$P(S_1, S_2, t) \to 0.$$

Hence a very unbalanced portfolio which is at the money near $(0, 200)$ will be severely mispriced with (7.40). A similar problem arises from (7.40) at the intersection of the line $S_1 + S_2 = 200$ with the computational boundary when the time continuous method of lines is applied [45]. In addition, (7.40) makes it impossible to find the early exercise boundary near these points as illustrated in Fig. 7.25.

Clearly, if uncertain or incorrect boundary data are specified then simulations with different computational domains are essential to be sure that their effect on prices is understood.

Turning to the implied correlation problem let us consider the following synthetic problem for (7.12) with non-symmetric parameters

$$\sigma_1 = .4, \quad \sigma_2 = .1, \quad \hat{r} = .04, \quad q_1 = .02, \quad q_2 = .06.$$

The pay-off is taken to be

$$P(S_1, S_2, 0) = K - \frac{(S_1 + S_2)}{2}.$$

We assume that at $T = .25$ we have $S_1 = 100$, $S_2 = 90$ and the following price quotations (obtained by randomly perturbing three Black Scholes prices computed with $\rho = .9$):

> Strike price $K_1 = 90$ option price $P_1 = .026 \cdot K_1$
>
> Strike price $K_2 = 95$ option price $P_2 = .053 \cdot K_2$
>
> Strike price $K_3 = 100$ option price $P_3 = .075 \cdot K_3$

ρ is not assumed known at this stage.

The dependence on the strike price can be scaled out of the problem by writing

$$p(s_1, s_2, t) = \frac{P(2Ks_1, 2Ks_2, t)}{K} \quad \text{for } s_1 = \frac{S_1}{2K}, \quad s_2 = \frac{S_2}{2K}.$$

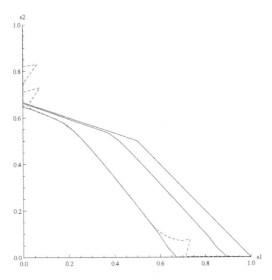

Fig. 7.25. Early exercise boundaries for a put with pay-off $p(s_1, s_2, 0) = 1 - s_1 - s_2$. Solid curves – left to right: boundary at $T = .25$, at $T = .01$ and at expiration. Dashed curve – time discrete MOL boundary at $T = .25$ obtained with (7.40). $\sigma_1 = .4$, $\sigma_2 = .1$, $\rho = .82$, $\hat{r} = .04$, $q_1 = .02$, $q_2 = .06$. MOL with $\Delta\theta = \pi/400$, $\Delta t = .001$, $Z = 3$.

Then p satisfies the Black Scholes equation (7.12) with pay-off

$$p(s_1, s_2, 0) = 1 - s_1 - s_2.$$

$p(s_1, s_2, t)$ and the early exercise boundary will be found in polar coordinates. Typical exercise boundaries in the $s_1 - s_2$ plane for the above financial parameters and a given correlation factor $\rho = .82$ are shown in Fig. 7.25 (as is a free boundary obtained with (7.40)). Quoted and computed prices relative to the s_1, s_2 coordinates are given in Table 7.13.

Table 7.13. Data and results for the implied correlation calculation.

i	(s_{1i}, s_{2i})	quoted p_i	computed price for $\rho = .82$ $p(s_{1i}, s_{2i}, .25)$
1	(100/180,90/180)	.026	.027527
2	(100/190,90/190)	.053	.049466
3	(100/200,90/200)	.075	.077405

MOL with $\Delta\theta = \pi/200$, $\Delta t = .25/200$, $Z = 3$.

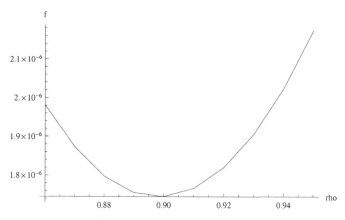

Fig. 7.26. Piecewise linear interpolant of $f(\rho_n)$ for $\rho_n = .7 + .01n$, $n = 0, \ldots, 20$.

If $p(s_1, s_2, t, \rho)$ denotes the solution of (7.12) for a correlation ρ then the implied correlation is taken here to be the value of ρ which minimizes

$$f(\rho) = \sum_{i=1}^{3} (p(s_{1i}, s_{2i}, .25, \rho) - p_i)^2$$

on the interval $[-1, 1]$. Since for a given ρ the function f can be evaluated, we shall simply search for the minimum of f.

An evaluation of $f(\rho_n)$ for $\rho_n = 1 - n/10$, $n = 0, \ldots, 20$ with 50 MOL rays and 100 time steps for each ρ_n quickly yields a convex curve with a minimum at $\rho = .8$. A refinement obtained for $\rho_n = .90 - n/100$, $n = 0, \ldots, 20$ with 100 rays and 200 time steps leads (not so quickly) to the curve shown in Fig. 7.26. We accept $\rho = .82$ as the implied correlation. The Black Scholes price for this correlation factor is given in the last column of Table 7.13.

The restriction to three strike prices and to puts with the same expiration is not essential. However, real data may not lead to graphs with a single minimum for $\rho \in (-1, 1)$. If the minimum of f occurs for $|\rho| = 1$, a more complex correlation relation may be required.

7.3 A three-dimensional problem

The time discrete method of lines is applicable in principle to free boundary problems for diffusion equations in any number of space dimensions.

Assuming that one can identify a dominant independent spatial variable y with the expectation that the free boundary can be expressed as

$$y = s(z_1, \ldots, z_M, t)$$

where $z = (z_1, \ldots, z_M)$ stands for the remaining spatial variables then it is straightforward to write down the time discrete MOL approximation

$$u''(y) = F(u, u', t) \tag{7.41}$$

where u is a vector whose dimension is the product of number of mesh points for each variable z_m in the computational domain. In practice first difficulties arise when boundary data are to be imposed on the boundary of the computational domain. As Example 7.11 illustrates, computationally convenient boundary conditions may not be consistent with the expected behavior of the solution near the boundary. Even in a simple setting like a call on the sum of three assets (z_1, z_2, y) the boundary condition on the surface $y = 0$ would require the solution of a two-dimenensional diffusion equation not involving y. For its MOL solution a new dominant variable would have to be chosen. Numerical PDE methods for such problems would appear to require considerable more programming efforts than were necessary for the above examples.

On the other hand, Venttsel type boundary conditions obtained from the full pricing equation are easy to apply since one simply zeroes out some coefficients in the pricing equation. Imposition of Dirichlet data obtained from quadratic interpolants of the line Gauss Seidel iterative solutions near the boundary are also simple to implement. Our final example illustrates the application of the method of lines to an American call with stochastic volatility and interest rate. It is a setting similar to that of Example 7.1. The earlier MOL code is readily adapted, and the numerical performance of the line Gauss-Seidel iteration reflects the behavior found in Example 7.1. However, the application also shows that our unsophisticated implementation of the time-discrete method of lines is beginning to be limited by the storage and speed capability of our desktop computer.

Example 7.12. An American call with Heston volatility and a stochastic interest rate.

For our final example we shall price an American call with Heston stochastic volatility as in Example 7.1 and a one-factor stochastic interest rate of the form

$$dr = a(b(\tau) - r)d\tau + \sigma r^\gamma dW, \quad \gamma \geq 0 \tag{7.42}$$

which is representative for the general term structure models discussed in [23, p. 132].

A European call with and without an up and out barrier and with a Hull-White interest rate ($\gamma = 0$) is priced in [32] with a time-continuous method of lines, where the numerical time integration is carried out with four competing ADI schemes. An American call with Heston volatility and a CIR interest rate ($b(\tau) \equiv b$ and $\gamma = .5$) is solved with the time discrete method of lines in [41]. A slight modification of this CIR code is applicable (in principle) to each one factor interest model of [23, p. 133] For definiteness we have chosen the above model with the mean reversion level $b(\tau)$ of [32]

$$b(\tau) = c_1 - c_2 e^{-c_3 \tau}. \tag{7.43}$$

We shall assume that the price process at real time τ

$$dS = (r - q)S d\tau + \sqrt{v} S dW_1$$
$$dv = \kappa(\theta - v) d\tau + \sigma_v \sqrt{v} dW_2$$
$$dr = a(b(\tau) - r) d\tau + \sigma_r r^\gamma dW_3$$

leads to the pricing equation

$$\frac{1}{2} vy^2 u_{yy} + \frac{1}{2} \sigma_v^2 vu_{vv} + \frac{1}{2}(\sigma_r r^\gamma)^2 u_{rr} + \rho_{12} \sigma_v yvu_{yv}$$
$$+ \rho_{13} \sigma_r y \sqrt{v} r^\gamma u_{yr} + \rho_{23} \sigma_v \sigma_r \sqrt{v} r^\gamma u_{vr}$$
$$+ (r - q) yu_y + \kappa(\theta - v) u_v$$
$$+ a(b(T - t) - r) u_r - ru - u_t = 0 \tag{7.44}$$

where $y = S/K$, $t = T - \tau$ is the time to expiry and $u(y, v, r, t) = C(S, v, r, t)/K$ for a strike price K of the American call. Equation (7.44) has to hold in the continuation region

$$0 < y < s(v, r, t)$$

for $v \in (0, \infty)$ and $r \in [0, \infty)$. The pay-off for the scaled call is

$$u(y, v, r, 0) = \max\{0, y - 1\} \tag{7.45}$$

and early exercise leads to the free boundary conditions

$$u(s(v, r, t), v, r, t) = s(v, r, t) - 1$$
$$u_y(s(v, r, t), v, r, t) = 1 \tag{7.46}$$

which in turn imply that

$$u_v = u_r = u_t = 0 \quad \text{on } y = s(v, r, t).$$

To find a numerical solution of (7.44) we need appropriate conditions on the boundary of a finite computational domain.

For pricing the European call with $\gamma = 0$ the computational domain $(0, Y) \times (0, v_{\max}) \times (-r_{\max}, r_{\max})$ is chosen in [32] which takes into account that the Hull-White model formally sustains negative interest rates. On its boundary conditions are imposed which are suggested by the behavior of the Black Scholes formula for a call as $r \to \infty$ and $v \to \infty$. They would appear to be inconsistent with the expected behavior of the American call and cannot be used here.

Here we shall work with the time independent computational domain

$$D = \{(y, v, r) : 0 < y < Y, 0 < v < v_{\max}, 0 < r < r_{\max}\}$$

and use the results of Chapter 1 to determine boundary conditions on ∂D.

The coefficient matrix $A(y, v, r, t_n)$ associated with a time discrete approximation of (7.44) at $t = t_n$ is

$$A = \frac{1}{2} \begin{pmatrix} vy^2 & \rho_{12}\sigma_v yv & \rho_{13}\sigma_r y\sqrt{v}r^\gamma \\ \rho_{12}\sigma_v yv & \sigma_v^2 v & \rho_{23}\sigma_v \sigma_r \sqrt{v}r^\gamma \\ \rho_{13}\sigma_r y\sqrt{v}r^\gamma & \rho_{23}\sigma_v \sigma_r \sqrt{v}r^\gamma & \sigma_r^2 r^{2\gamma} \end{pmatrix}.$$

We observe that the matrix A is singular for $y = 0$, $v = 0$ and for $r = 0$ whenever $\gamma > 0$. We shall assume for now that $\gamma > 0$. We observe that

$$\langle An, n \rangle = 0 \text{ for } n = (1, 0, 0) \text{ on } y = 0,$$
$$\langle An, n \rangle = 0 \text{ for } n = (0, 1, 0) \text{ on } v = 0,$$
$$\langle An, n \rangle = 0 \text{ for } n = (0, 0, 1) \text{ on } r = 0.$$

A is non-singular everywhere else if $|\rho_{12}\rho_{13}\rho_{23}| \neq 1$.

The Fichera function associated with the time discrete approximation of (7.44) is

$$h(y, v, r) = \left[(r - q)y - \frac{1}{2}(2yv + \rho_{12}\sigma_v y + \rho_{13}\sigma_r y\sqrt{v}\gamma r^{\gamma-1}) \right] n_1$$

$$+ \left[\kappa(\theta - v) - \frac{1}{2}(\rho_{12}\sigma_v v + \sigma_v^2 + \rho_{23}\sigma_v \sigma_r \sqrt{v}\gamma r^{\gamma-1}) \right] n_2$$

$$+ \left[a(b(T - t) - r) - \frac{1}{2}(\rho_{13}\sigma_r \sqrt{v}r^\gamma + \rho_{23}\sigma_v \sigma_r \frac{1}{2\sqrt{v}}r^\gamma + \sigma_r^2 2\gamma r^{2\gamma-1}) \right] n_3.$$

Hence on $y = 0$ we have $h(0, v, r) = 0$ so that the equation (7.44) has to hold. Since for the Heston model a one-time zero asset will remain zero we obtain for the call

$$u(0, v, r, t) = 0, \quad t > 0.$$

We have to insure that the remaining boundary conditions to be imposed are consistent with a vanishing solution of (7.44) on $y = 0$.

On $v = 0$ we see that

$$h(y, 0, r) = \kappa\theta - \frac{\sigma_v^2}{2}$$

so that for parameters for which $h(y, 0, r) \geq 0$ again equation (7.44) has to hold on $v = 0$. However, (7.44) for $v = 0$ reduces to the equation

$$\frac{1}{2}(\sigma_r r^\gamma)^2 u_{rr} + (r - q)yu_y + \kappa\theta u_v + a(b(T - t) - r)u_r - ru - u_t = 0 \qquad (7.47)$$

whose convective terms at fixed time t satisfy the oblique derivative condition

$$\langle ((r - q)y, \kappa\theta, a(b(T - t) - r)), n \rangle = \kappa\theta > 0.$$

It follows from Section 1.2.1 that (7.44) is an admissible Venttsel boundary condition regardless of the algebraic sign of $h(y, 0, r)$. Thus the restriction of (7.44) to $v = 0$ will always serve as a computational boundary condition on $v = 0$. We note that this boundary condition does not involve u_{yy} and does not allow us to find an early exercise boundary on $v = 0$ with the Riccati transformation method.

On $r = 0$ the Fichera function is not defined for $2\gamma - 1 < 0$. However, for the inward normal $n = (0, 0, 1)$ the convective terms of (7.44) yield the dot product

$$\langle ((r - q)y, \kappa(\theta - v), a(b(T - t))), n \rangle = ab(T - t) > 0$$

for a positive mean reversion level. It follows that equation (6.43) without the u_{yr}, u_{vr} and u_{rr} terms provides an admissible Venttsel boundary condition for all $\gamma \geq 0$. It will be imposed below on our MOL solution.

On $v = v_{\max}$ the inward unit normal is $n = (0, -1, 0)$ and the convective terms of (7.44) satisfy

$$\langle ((r - q)y, \kappa(\theta - v_{\max}), a(b(T - t) - r)), n \rangle = \kappa(v_{\max} - \theta)) > 0$$

for sufficiently large $v_{\max}$. The discussion of Section 1.2.3 suggests that the pricing equation (7.44) without the u_{vv}, u_{yv} and u_{vr} terms provides an admissible Venttsel boundary condition.

Similarly, on $r = r_{\max}$ we have $n = (0, 0, -1)$ and

$$\langle ((r - q)y, \kappa(\theta - v), a(b(T - t) - r_{\max})), n \rangle = a(r_{\max} - b(T - t) > 0,$$

for sufficiently large $r_{\max}$. Hence on $r = 0$ and $r = r_{\max}$ the pricing equation (7.44) without the u_{rr}, u_{ry} and u_{rv} terms can serve as admissible boundary condition. These tangential second order equations themselves need boundary conditions. We shall require that the solutions $u(y, v_{\max}, r, t)$, $u(y, v, 0, t)$ and $u(y, v, r_{\max}, t)$ of the Venttsel boundary equations vanish at $y = 0$ and satisfy the free boundary conditions for a call.

We again remind the reader of the caution expressed in Chapter 1 that our applications do not necessarily meet all the hypotheses for a rigorous application of the Fichera and Venttsel theory. Its conclusions are only a guide for reasonable boundary conditions for the pricing equations. As in previous examples it is mandatory that the influence of these boundary conditions on prices and early exercise be checked on varying domains and for reasonable financial parameters before they are accepted.

The MOL solution is obtained with the program of [41] by changing the interest rate dependent coefficients and zeroing out selected non-tangential second derivative terms in the boundary conditions. All difference quotients of the MOL approximation are based on central difference quotients (i.e. no upwinding is used) except on the computational boundaries where one-sided quotients are used for non-tangential convective and diffusive terms.

We remark that when the MOL code is used to price the up-and-out European call of Case A in [32], it yields a surface for $C(S, v, .025, 1)$ which "looks" identical to the surface shown in [32, Fig. 5] but no numbers are available for comparison. We also know from our simulations that the MOL line Gauss Seidel iteration for an American call will converge at the first time step $T = \Delta t = .01$ for all six data sets of Table 1 of [32], augmented with $q = .06$, when $\gamma = 0$ and $\gamma = 1.5$, so that the MOL/Riccati approach appears quite robust.

We shall conclude our discussion with some comments on the numerical challenges posed by an American call, on the performance of the method of lines for the call, and on some simulations which show the influence of the one-factor model parameter γ on the price of the call and on the early exercise boundary.

The American call would appear to be harder to solve than the put because the continuation region can become quite large for small dividend rates q. Since $u(y, v, r, 0) = \max\{0, y - 1\}$ the convexity arguments used repeatedly throughout this text yield

$$\lim_{t \to 0} s(v, r, t) = \max\{1, r/q\}.$$

The barrier Y has to satisfy $Y > s(v, r, t)$ at all times and hence must lie to the right of $r_{\max}/q$. This requirement provides an incentive to find the smallest value $r_{\max}$ which yields acceptable values for the call and its early exercise. We remark that in view of Example 1.8 it may be possible to apply put-call symmetry and thus work on the more benign bounded domain for a put when pricing the American call. Whether such approach will work remains to be seen.

All results given here hold for the mean reversion level (7.43) of "Case A" in [32]

$$b(\tau) = c_1 + c_2 e^{-c_3 \tau}$$

with

$$c_1 = .05, \quad c_2 = .01, \quad c_3 = 1.$$

The other parameters of our simulation are chosen rather arbitrarily as

$$\sigma_v = .4, \quad \sigma_r = .3, \quad \rho_{12} = -.5, \quad \rho_{13} = .5, \quad \rho_{23} = .5$$

$$\kappa = 1.5, \quad \theta = .02, \quad a = .3, \quad q = .06$$

$$T = .1, \quad K = 100, \quad \gamma \in [0, 1.5].$$

Relatively large values for σ_v and σ_r accentuate the motion of the early exercise boundary and the short time to expiration reduces the computer run times. With these data the simulations prove to be consistent and reliable, but little effort was undertaken to establish limits on the parameters beyond which the MOL approach breaks down.

We begin with an examination of the influence of the computational domain, of the space and time discretization and of the choice of boundary conditions on prices and exercise boundaries. The computational grid is

$$0 = y_0 < \cdots < y_M = Y, \quad 0 = v_0 < \cdots < v_I = v_{\max},$$

$$0 = r_0 < \cdots < r_J = r_{\max}$$

with $\Delta v = v_{\max}/I$, $\Delta r = r_{\max}/J$, while Δy may be variable. The approximation of $\{u^k(y, v_i, r_j, t_n), s^k(v_i, r_j, t_n))$ at v_i, $i = 1, \ldots, I$ and r_j, $j = 0, \ldots, J$, in Gauss Seidel iteration k at the time to expiry t_n will be denoted by $\{u^k_{ij,n}(y), s^k_{ij,n}\}$. For convenience k and n are usually suppressed. As in Example 7.1, the pricing equation is not approximated at $v_0 = 0$. Instead the quadratic extrapolant of the line Gauss Seidel solution

$$u^k_{0j}(y) = 3u^{k-1}_{1j}(y) - 3u^{k-1}_{2j}(y) + u^{k-1}_{3j}(y)$$

is used as a Dirichlet condition on $v = 0$. Similarly, the extrapolant of the deltas $u'_{ij}(y)$ is used for $u'_{0j}(y)$ in the central difference approximation

$$u_{yv}(y, v_1, r, t) = \frac{u'_{2j}(y) - u'_{0j}(y)}{2\Delta v}.$$

We recall that the Riccati transformation provides $u'_{ij}(y)$ in the backward sweep.

Selected call prices and early exercise boundaries were found for the four nested computational domains

$$\text{i) } v_{\max} = 0.2, \quad r_{\max} = 0.2$$
$$\text{ii) } v_{\max} = 0.3, \quad r_{\max} = 0.3$$
$$\text{iii) } v_{\max} = 0.4, \quad r_{\max} = 0.4$$
$$\text{iv) } v_{\max} = 0.5, \quad r_{\max} = 0.5$$

For all cases we use $\Delta v = \Delta r = .01$ and $\Delta y \leq Y/8000$ for $Y = 12$. All graphs of prices and exercise boundaries show scaled values $\{u(y, v, r, t),$ $s(v, r, t)\}$. Numerical values for the American call $C(S, v, r, t)$ and its exercise boundary listed in the tables below hold for spot prices $S = Ky$.

Numerical simulations suggest that the Hull-White model with $\gamma = 0$ leads to the most challenging pricing problem for the American call with a one-factor stochastic interest rate. Hence most of our numerical results hold for $\gamma = 0$. Two different sets of boundary conditions were checked.

Case A): Calculations with Venttsel boundary conditions:
(7.44) without u_{vv}, u_{yv} and u_{vr} terms on $v = v_{\max}$
(7.44) without u_{rr}, u_{yr} and u_{vr} terms on $r = 0$ and $r = r_{\max}$.

Case B): Calculations with modified Venttsel boundary conditions:
(7.44) without the u_{vv} term on $v = v_{\max}$.
(7.44) without the u_{rr} term on $r = r_{\max}$.
(7.44) without u_{rr}, u_{yr} and u_{vr} terms on $r = 0$.

Case B was considered because the full pricing equation is sometimes recommended on far boundaries (see [63]). Since non-tangential cross derivatives are easy to incorporate into the MOL solution method it was simple to check their influence on prices and early exercise boundaries. However, we did not retain the terms u_{vv} on $v_{\max}$ and u_{rr} on r_{rmax} in (7.44) (which could, in principle, be approximated with one-sided difference quotients as in [63]) because we would end up with an approximation of an ill-posed problem as discussed in Example 1.21.

Figure 7.27(a) contains the exercise boundaries $s(v, .04, T)$ for $v \in [0, v_{\max}]$ on the four computational domains for case A. Fig. 7.27(b) shows the corresponding boundaries for case B. All curves stop at the edge of the applicable computational domain.

Figures 7.28(a) and 7.28(b) show the free boundaries $s(.04, r, T)$ as a function of r for case A and case B on the four computational domains.

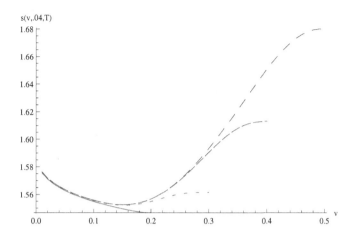

Fig. 7.27. (a) Early exercise boundaries $s(v, .04, T)$ of case A, $\gamma = 0$.
Solid line: $v_{\max} = r_{\mathrm{rmax}} = .2$.
Short dash: $v_{\max} = r_{\mathrm{rmax}} = .3$.
Long dash: $v_{\max} = r_{\mathrm{rmax}} = .4$.
Long dash: $v_{\max} = r_{\mathrm{rmax}} = .5$.
$\Delta v = \Delta r = .01$, $T = .1$, $\Delta t = T/100$.

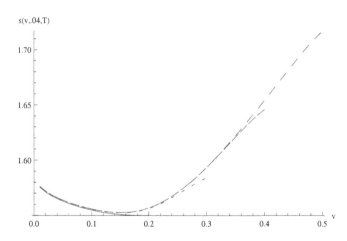

Fig. 7.27. (b) Early exercise boundaries $s(v, .04, T)$ of case B, $\gamma = 0$.
Solid line: $v_{\max} = r_{\mathrm{rmax}} = .2$.
Short dash: $v_{\max} = r_{\mathrm{rmax}} = .3$.
Long dash: $v_{\max} = r_{\mathrm{rmax}} = .4$.
Long dash: $v_{\max} = r_{\mathrm{rmax}} = .5$.

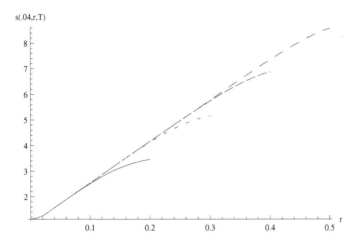

Fig. 7.28. (a) Early exercise boundaries $s(04, r, T)$ of case A, $\gamma = 0$.
solid line: $v_{max} = r_{rmax} = .2$.
short dash: $v_{max} = r_{rmax} = .3$.
long dash: $v_{max} = r_{rmax} = .4$.
long dash: $v_{max} = r_{rmax} = .5$.

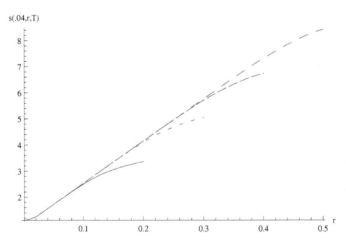

Fig. 7.28. (b) Early exercise boundaries $s(04, r, T)$ of case B, $\gamma = 0$.
Solid line: $v_{max} = r_{rmax} = .2$.
Short dash: $v_{max} = r_{rmax} = .3$.
Long dash: $v_{max} = r_{rmax} = .4$.
Long dash: $v_{max} = r_{rmax} = .5$.

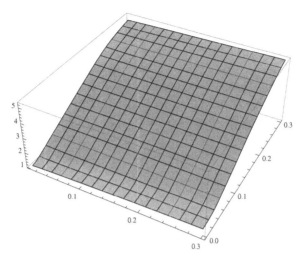

Fig. 7.29. Early exercise surface $s(v, r, T)$ over $[0, .3] \times [0, .3]$, $\gamma = 0$ for case B. $\Delta v = \Delta r = .01$, $T = .1$, $\Delta t = T/100$.

Table 7.14. Location of the early exercise boundary $S = Ks(.2, .2, T)$.

Case	v_{max}	I	time steps	$S(.2, .2, T)$
B	.2	10	50	346.68
B	.2	10	100	346.68
B	.2	10	200	346.68
A	.2	20	100	362.03
B	.2	20	100	344.80
A	.3	30	100	410.81
B	.3	30	100	407.70
A	.4	40	100	413.06
B	.4	40	100	413.04
A	.5	50	100	413.07
B	.5	50	100	413.09

All these curves are crossections of the surface $s(v, r, T)$ which is shown in Fig. 7.29 for case B over the computational domain $[0, .3] \times [0, .3]$.

The early exercise locations at $(v_{max}, .04)$ in Figs. 7.27 and at $(.04, r_{max})$ in Figs. 7.28 change about 2.2% as we switch the boundary conditions from case A to case B. Table 7.14 shows that away from the edge of the computational domain the influence of the boundary condition on the early exercise boundary becomes negligible.

We point out that on $r = 0$ only the Venttsel boundary condition was used. However, the computed early exercise boundary $s(v, 0, T)$ on the plane $r = 0$ found with this boundary condition is not consistent with the computed values $s(v, r, T)$ for $r > 0$. While not apparent in Figs. 7.27 and 7.28 for $T = .1$, the discrepancy becomes pronounced for longer term calls. Figure 7.30 shows $s(.04, r, T)$ for $T = 1$ for $v \in [\Delta v, .3]$ for $\gamma = 0, .25, .5, 1.5$ and Fig. 7.31 shows the corresponding $s(.04, r, T)$ for $r \in [0, .3]$. It is apparent from Fig. 7.31 that for $\gamma = 0$ the free boundary is discontinuous at $r = 0$ because

$$\lim_{t \to 0} s(.04, r, T) \neq s(.04, 0, T).$$

No such problem is visible at $r = r_{\max}$ where the boundary conditions of case B are enforced. Inclusion of cross derivatives on $r = 0$ leads to divergence of the MOL line Gauss-Seidel iteration for $\gamma < .4$. For $\gamma > .5$ the Fichera theory suggests that no boundary condition is required on $r = 0$, and numerical simulations seem indeed unaffected by the presence of cross derivatives in the boundary equation or by imposing a quadratic extrapolant as Dirichlet data on $r = 0$.

The different plotting scales of the above illustrations may hide or exxagerate the effect of the boundary conditions and of the computational

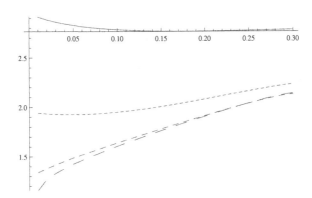

Fig. 7.30. Early exercise boundary $s(v, .04, 1)$ for different γ.
Solid curve: $\gamma = 0$.
0.01 dashes: $\gamma = .25$.
0.02 dashes: $\gamma = .5$.
0.04 dashes: $\gamma = 1.5$.
$\Delta v = \Delta r = .01$, $T = 1$, $\Delta t = T/500$.

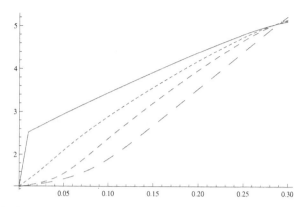

Fig. 7.31. Early exercise boundary $s(.04, r, 1)$ for different γ.
Solid curve: $\gamma = 0$.
0.01 dashes: $\gamma = .25$.
0.02 dashes: $\gamma = .5$.
0.04 dashes: $\gamma = 1.5$.
$\Delta v = \Delta r = .01$, $T = 1$, $\Delta t = T/500$.

Table 7.15. Price of the American call for the Hull-White interest rate.

					$C(S, .04, .04, T)$ at $S = K$				
					S				
Case	$v_{\max}$	I	80	90	100	110	120	time steps	run time seconds
B	.2	10	.0001	.0732	2.3996	10.2343	20.0482	50	63 sec
B	.2	10	.0001	.0732	2.4003	10.2346	20.0482	100	102 sec
B	.2	10	.0001	.0732	2.4040	10.2347	20.0496	200	157 sec
A	.2	20	.0001	.0726	2.4032	10.2347	20.0496	100	766 sec
B	.2	20	.0001	.0737	2.4038	10.2348	20.0496	100	806 sec
A	.3	30	.0001	.0738	2.4038	10.2348	20.0496	100	1892 sec
B	.3	30	.0001	.0738	2.4038	10.2348	20.0496	100	1865 sec
A	.4	40	.0001	.0738	2.4040	10.2349	20.0497	100	3511 sec
B	.4	40	.0001	.0738	2.4040	10.2349	20.0497	100	3492 sec
A	.5	50	.0001	.0738	2.4040	10.2349	20.0497	100	5638 sec
B	.5	50	.0001	.0738	2.4040	10.2349	20.0497	100	4337 sec

Notes: Execution on a 7.6 GiB desktop with four Core i5-750 2.67 GHz processors
$\Delta v = \Delta r = v_{\max}/I$. Total number of lines: $I \times (I + 1)$.

domain. To quantify their effects we list in Table 7.15 call prices corresponding to $K = 100$ and $S = Ky$ at $T = .1$. The tables and graphs show that Case B boundary conditions yield more consistent results on all meshes.

We conclude with a brief look at the influence of γ in the model (7.44) on selected prices and early exercise boundaries when all other financial and computational parameters are unchanged.

Figure 7.32 contains a plot of the scaled call u at $y = 1.1$, $v = .04$, $r = .04$, $T = 1$ as a function of the model parameter γ as we perturb the interest rate model from the Hull-White model ($\gamma = 0$) via the CIR model ($\gamma = .5$) to the limiting case $\gamma = 1.5$. The graph is the linear interpolant of the American call prices for $\gamma = j^* .125$, $j = 0, \ldots, 12$.

Figure 7.33 is a side view (along the v-axis) which shows the influence on the position of the early exercise surface at $T = 1$. Both surfaces are plotted over $[\Delta v, v_{max}] \times [0, r_{max}]$. The plotted values of $s(v_i, 0, T)$ for $\gamma = 0$ should be ignored because of the discontinuity of $s(v, r, T)$ at $r = 0$.

We conclude with the observation that in principle jump diffusion is straightforward to include in this study since it affects mainly the choice of the grid points $\{y_m\}$. We would expect convergence of the line Gauss Seidel iteration when the jump integral is evaluated at the solution of an earlier iteration. The limiting factor is the execution time so an efficient implementation of the MOL approach becomes mandatory as the complexity

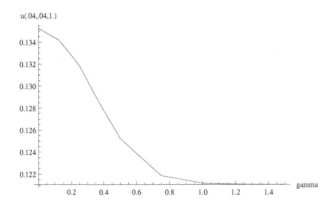

Fig. 7.32.　Dependence of $u(y, v, r, t)$ on the model parameter γ in (7.42) at $y = 1.1$, $v = .04$, $r = .04$, $T = 1$ $Y = 6$, 6000 mesh points evenly spaced over $[0, Y]$, $v_{max} = r_{max} = .3$, $\Delta v = \Delta r = .01$, $\Delta t = T/500$.

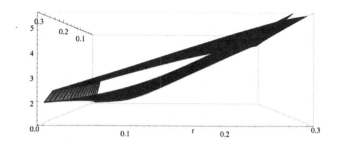

Fig. 7.33. Early exercise boundary for the Hull-White model ($\gamma = 0$) and the Constantinides-Ingersoll model ($\gamma = 1.5$) at $T = 1$. The top surface corresponds to the Hull-White model.

of the model increases. However, considering that the method yields consistent and stable prices, deltas and early exercise boundaries, it deserves consideration as an alternative to the PSOR method for benchmark calculations. The comparison of the performance of various numerical methods, including the method of lines, for options with stochastic volatilty given in [17] would seem to support this suggestion.

Bibliography

[1] Y. Achdou and O. Pironneau, Computational Methods for Option Pricing, *SIAM Frontiers in Appl. Math.*, 2005, ISBN 0-89871-573-3

[2] E. Angel and R. Bellman, *Dynamic Programming and Partial Differential Equations*, Academic Press, 1972.

[3] D. E. Apushkinskaya and A. I. Nazarov, A survey of results on nonlinear Venttsel problems, *Applications of Mathematics* **45** (2000) 69–80.

[4] J. Aquan-Assee, Boundary conditions for mean-reverting square root processes, MS thesis, U. Waterloo, Canada, 2009.

[5] U. M. Ascher, R. M. M. Mattheij, R. D. Russell, *Numerical Solution of Boundary Value Problems for Ordinary Differential Equations*, SIAM, 1995, ISBN-13 978-0-898713-54-1

[6] M. Avellaneda, A. Levy and A. Paras, Pricing and hedging derivative securities in markets with uncertain volatilities, *Appl. Math. Finance* **6** (1998) 1–18.

[7] G. Barles, J. Burdeau, M. Romano and N. Samsoen, Esxtimation de la frontiere libre des options americaines au voisinage de l'echeance, *C. R. Acad. Sci. Paris Ser. I Math.* **316** (1993) 171–174.

[8] E. Barucci, S. Polidoro and V. Vespri, Some results on partial differential equations and Asian options, *Math. Models Methods Appl. Sci* (2001) 475–497.

[9] M. Broadie and J. Detemple, The valuation of American options on multiple assets, *Math. Finance* **7** (1997) 241–286.

[10] J. R. Cannon, *The One-Dimensional Heat Equation*, Cambridge U. Press, 1984, ISBN-10 0521302439

[11] X. Chen, H. Cheng and J. Chadam, Nonconvexity of the optimal exercise boundary for an American put option on a dividend-paying asset, *Mathematical Finance,* **23** (2013) 169–185.

[12] Yang Chengrong, Jiang Lishang and Bian Baojun, Free boundary and American options in a jump-diffusion model, *European Journal of Applied Mathematics,* **17** (2006) 95–127.

[13] C. Chiarella and A. Ziogas, Evaluation of American strangles, *J. Economic Dynamics and Control* **29** (2005) 31–62.

[14] C. Chiarella, B. Kang, G. H. Meyer and A. Ziogas, The evaluation of American option prices under stochastic volatility and jump-diffusion dynamics using the method of lines, *Int. J. Theoretical Appl. Finance* **12** (2009) 393–425.

[15] C. Chiarella and A. Ziogas, American call options under jump-diffusion processes, *Applied Math. Finance* **16** (2009) 37–79.

[16] C. Chiarella and J. Ziveyi, Pricing American options written on two underlying assets, *Quantitative Finance* **14** (2014) 409–426.

[17] C. Chiarella, B. Kang and G. H. Meyer, *The Numerical Solution of the American Option Pricing Problem*, World Scientific Publishing, 2014.

[18] N. Clarke and K. Parrott, Multigrid for American option pricing with stochastic volatility, *Applied Math. Finance* **6** (1999) 177–195.

[19] L. Clewlow and C. Strickland, Implementing Derivative Models, Wiley, 1998, ISBN 0-471-96651-7

[20] J. Detemple, S. Feng and W. Tian, The valuation of American call options on the minimum of two dividend-paying assets, *Ann. Probab.* **13** (2003) 953–983.

[21] Y. d'Halluin, P. A. Forsyth, K. R. Vetzal and G. Labahan, A numerical PDE approach for pricing callable bonds, *Applied Math. Finance* **8** (2001) 49–77.

[22] J. C. Dias and M. B. Shackleton, Hysteresis effects under CIR interest rates, *Europ. Journal Operational Research* **211** (2011) 594–600.

[23] D. Duffie, *Dynamic Asset Pricing Theory*, Princeton U. Press, 1996, ISBN 0-691-02125-2

[24] J. B. Durham, Jump-diffusion processes and affine term structure models, Federal Reserve Board, FEDs Working Paper No. 2005-53, 2005, 59 pages.

[25] E. Ekstrom, P. Lotstedt and J. Tysk, Boundary values and finite difference methods for the single factor term structure equation, *Applied Math. Finance* **16**, (2009) 253–259.

[26] E. Ekstrom and J. Tysk, Boundary conditions for the single-factor term structure equation, *Annals of Applied Probability* **21** (2011) 332–350.

[27] C. M. Elliott and J. R. Ockendon, Weak and Variational Methods for Moving Boundary Problems, *Research Notes in Mathematics* No. 59, Pitman, 1982, ISBN 0-273-08503-4

[28] L. C. Evans, *Partial Differential Equations*, American Math. Soc., 1998, ISBN 0-8218-0772-2

[29] G. Fichera, On a unified theory of boundary value problems for elliptic-parabolic equations of second order, in *Boundary Problems in Differential Equations*, R. E. Langer, edt., U. Wisconsin Press, 1960.

[30] A. Friedman, *Variational Principles and Free-Boundary Problems*, J. Wiley, 1982, ISBN 0-471-86849-3

[31] D. Gilbarg and N. Trudinger, *Elliptic Partial Differential Equations of Second Order*, Springer, 2001, ISBN 3-540-41160-7

[32] T. Haentjens and K. J. in't Hout, Alternating direction implicit finite schemes for the Heston-Hull-White partial differential equation, *J. of Comp. Finance* **16** (2012) 83–110.

[33] E. G. Haug, *The Complete Guide to Option Pricing Formulas*, McGraw-Hill, 1998, ISBN 0-7863-1240-8

[34] S. L. Heston, A closed-form solution for options with stochastic volatility with applications to bond and currency options, *Review Financial Studies* **6** (1993) 327–343.

[35] S. L. Heston, M. Loewenstein and G Willard, Options and bubbles, *Review of Financial Studies* **20** (2007) 359–390.

[36] Yang Hongtao, American put options on zero-coupon bonds and a parabolic free boundary problem, *Int. J. Numerical Analysis and Modeling* **1** (2004) 203–215.

[37] S. D. Howison, C. Reisinger and J. H. Witte, The effect of nonsmooth payoffs on the penalty approximation of American options, *SIAM J. Financial Math.* **4** (2013) 539–574.

[38] J. C. Hull, *Options, Futures, and Other Derivative Securities*, Prentice-Hall, 1993, ISBN 0-13-639014-51

[39] S. Ikonen and J. Toivanen, Pricing American options using LU decomposition, *Applied Mathematical Sciences* **1** (2007) 2529–2551.

[40] F. Jamshidian, An exact bond option formula, *J. of Finance* **44** (1989) 205–209.

[41] B. Kang and G. H. Meyer, Pricing an American call under stochastic volatility and interest rates, in *Nonlinear Economic Dynamics and Financial Modelling*, R. Dieci et al., edts., Springer, 2014, ISBN 987-3-319-07469-6.

[42] A. G. Z. Kemna and A. Vorst, A pricing method for options based on average asset values, *J. Banking Finance* **14** (1990) 113–129.

[43] T. Kimura, American fractional lookback options: Valuation and premium decomposition, *SIAM J. Appl. Math.* **71** (2011) 517–539.

[44] D. Kinderlehrer and G. Stampacchia, *An Introduction to Variational Inequalities and their Applications*, Academic Press, 1980, ISBN 0-12-407350-6

[45] P. Kovalov, V. Linetsky and M. Marcozzi, Pricing multi-asset options: A finite element method-of-lines with smooth penalty, *J. Sci. Comput.* **33** (2007) 209–237.

[46] Y. K. Kwok, *Mathematical Models of Financial Derivatives*, Springer, 1998, ISBN 981-3083-255

[47] O. A. Ladyzenskaja, V. A. Solonnikov, N. N. Uralceva, Linear and Quasilinear Equations of Parabolic Type, American Math. Soc., 1968.

[48] G. M. Lieberman, *Second Order Parabolic Differential Equations*, World Scientific, 1996, ISBN 981-02-2883-X

[49] Matlab Financial Instruments Toolbox, www.mathworks.com/help/fininst/maxassetbystulz.html

[50] G. H. Meyer, *Initial Value Methods for Boundary Value Problems*, Academic Press, 1973.

[51] G. H. Meyer, An analysis of the method of lines for the Reynolds equation in hydrodynamic lubrication, *SIAM J. Num. Anal.* **18** (1981) 165–177.

[52] G. H. Meyer, On computing free boundaries which are not level sets, *Pitman Research Notes in Mathematics* No. 185, 1990.

[53] The numerical valuation of options with underlying jumps, *Acta Math. Univ. Comenianae* **67** (1998) 69–82.

[54] G. H. Meyer, On pricing American and Asian options with PDE methods, *Acta Math. Univ. Comenianae* (2001) 153–165.

[55] G. H. Meyer, Numerical investigation of early exercise in American puts with discrete dividends, *J. Comp. Finance* **5** (2001) 37–53.

[56] G. H. Meyer, The Black Scholes Barenblatt equation for options with uncertain volatility and its application to static hedging, *Int. J. Theoretical Applied Finance* **9** (2006) 673–703.

[57] G. H. Meyer, On the derivation and numerical solution of the Black Scholes Barenblatt equation for jump diffusion, *Advances in Mathematical Sciences and Applications* **29** (2008) 279–304.

[58] K. Nishioka, The degenerate Neumann problem and degenerate diffusions with Venttsel's boundary conditions, *Ann. Probability* **9** (1981) 103–118.

[59] O. A. Oleinik and E. V. Radkevich, Second Order Equations with Non-Negative Characteristic Form, American Math. Soc., 1973.

[60] N. J. Sharp, Advances in Mortgage Valuation: An Option-Theoretic Approach, PhD Thesis, School of Mathematics, University of Manchester, 2006.

[61] W. E. Schiesser, *The Numerical Method of Lines: Integration of Partial Differential Equations*, Academic Press, 1991, ISBN 0-12-624130-9

[62] W. E. Schiesser and G. W. Griffiths, *A Compendium of Partial Differential Equation Models, Method of Lines Analysis with Matlab*, Cambridge U. Press, 2009, ISBN 978-0-521-51986-1

[63] D. Tavella and C. Randall, *Pricing Financial Instruments*, J. Wiley, 2000, ISBN 0-471-19760-2

[64] P. Wilmott, *Derivatives*, J. Wiley, 1998, ISBN 0-471-98389-6

[65] C. Yang, L. Jiang, B. Bian, Free boundary and American options in a jump-diffusion model, *Euro. J. Applied Math.*, **117** (2006) 95–127.

[66] Yi Zeng and Yousong Luo, Linear parabolic equations with Venttsel initial boundary conditions, *Bull. Austral. Math. Soc.* **51** (1995) 465–479.

[67] Y-I. Zhu, X. Wu and I-L. Chern, *Derivative Securities and Difference Methods*, Springer, 2010, ISBN 978-1-4419-1925-0

[68] R. Zvan, P. A. Forsyth, and K. R. Vetzal, Robust numerical methods for PDE models of Asian options, *J. Comp. Finance* **1** (1997) 39–78.

Index

About the Author

Gunter Meyer is Professor Emeritus of Mathematics at the Georgia Institute of Technology in Atlanta, where he helped develop and taught in the MS program in quantitative and computational finance. His research interests focus on numerical methods for partial differential equations and free boundary problems in finance.

Printed in the United States
By Bookmasters